Religion and the Human Future

Blackwell Manifestos

In this new series major critics make timely interventions to address important concepts and subjects, including topics as diverse as, for example: Culture, Race, Religion, History, Society, Geography, Literature, Literary Theory, Shakespeare, Cinema, and Modernism. Written accessibly and with verve and spirit, these books follow no uniform prescription but set out to engage and challenge the broadest range of readers, from undergraduates to postgraduates, university teachers and general readers – all those, in short, interested in ongoing debates and controversies in the humanities and social sciences.

Already Published

Forthcoming

Religion and the Human Future

An Essay on Theological Humanism

David E. Klemm and William Schweiker

Blackwell
Publishing

This edition first published 2008
© 2008 David E. Klemm and William Schweiker

Blackwell Publishing was acquired by John Wiley & Sons in February 2007. Blackwell's publishing program has been merged with Wiley's global Scientific, Technical, and Medical business to form Wiley-Blackwell.

Registered Office
John Wiley & Sons Ltd, The Atrium, Southern Gate, Chichester, West Sussex, PO19 8SQ, United Kingdom

Editorial Offices
350 Main Street, Malden, MA 02148-5020, USA
9600 Garsington Road, Oxford, OX4 2DQ, UK
The Atrium, Southern Gate, Chichester, West Sussex, PO19 8SQ, UK

For details of our global editorial offices, for customer services, and for information about how to apply for permission to reuse the copyright material in this book please see our website at www.wiley.com/wiley-blackwell.

The right of David E. Klemm and William Schweiker to be identified as the authors of this work has been asserted in accordance with the Copyright, Designs and Patents Act 1988.

Library of Congress Cataloging-in-Publication Data

Klemm, David E., 1947–
Religion and the human future : an essay on theological humanism / David E. Klemm and William Schweiker.
    p. cm.—(Blackwell manifestos)
Includes bibliographical references and index.
ISBN 978-1-4051-5526-7 (hardcover : alk. paper)—ISBN 978-1-4051-5527-4 (pbk. : alk. paper)
1. Religion and civilization—Forecasting. 2. Religion—Forecasting. 3. Civilization—Forecasting.
4. Humanism—Forecasting. 5. Ethics—Forecasting. I. Schweiker, William. II. Title.

BL55.K59 2008
211'.6—dc22

2007048318

A catalogue record for this book is available from the British Library.

Set in 10.5/12.5pt Bembo by SPi Publisher Services, Pondicherry, India
Printed in Singapore by C.O.S. Printers Pte Ltd

1   2008

Contents

Acknowledgments

This book is the fruit of years of friendship and conversation on matters religious, moral, and personal. The friendship has deepened through times of success, but also in periods of grief, loss, and travail. The fires of experience have melded kindred spirits dedicated to understanding and orienting our lives in these global times.

Collaboration implies differences, and we should acknowledge ours. This book represents conclusions that the authors have reached from different vantage points and legacies of thought, different fields of expertise (philosophical theology and theological ethics), and even different heritages within the Christian tradition, in our cases Roman Catholic and Protestant Christianity. We even express theological humanism with different sensibilities. These differences are reflected in the writing that follows, although we have reworked together the whole book. Our differences are important in order to show that there are various ways of being a theological humanist. Of course, we know that some readers will find our work insufficiently Christian or dogmatic or orthodox or religious. Others will reject the philosophical and hermeneutical stance we adopt and try to advance. We can only remain true to the journey which has led us to this point. Our hope is that others will join us from within their own distinctive traditions and convictions.

We have many people to acknowledge. The initial conversations about this book were supported by an Interdisciplinary Research Grant awarded to the authors during the summer of 2001 at the Obermann Center for Advanced Studies, University of Iowa. David Klemm was supported during 2006–7 by a Career Developmental Assignment also spent at the Obermann Center. William Schweiker wishes to thank the University of Chicago Divinity School, the Martin Marty Center, and the Internationale

Acknowledgments

Wissenschaftsforum in Heidelberg, Germany for support in the writing of this book. We express profound gratitude to Maria Antonaccio, Kelton Cobb, Kristine Culp, Catherine Deming, W. David Hall, Phillip Jackson, David Jasper, Hannah Klemm, Matthew Klemm, Stephen Klemm, William H. Klink, Terence Martin, Paul Schweiker, Jay Semel, Michael Welker, Glenn Whitehouse, and Dale Wright, as well as Dan Boscaljon, Nathan Dickman, Verna Ehret, Sage Elwell, Michael Johnson, Kevin Jung, Bruce Rittenhouse, Elizabeth Sweeny, and Chris Wiley. We also warmly thank Rebecca Harkin of Blackwell Publishing for her insight and commitment to scholarly work.

David E. Klemm, *University of Iowa*
William Schweiker, *University of Chicago*

Introduction

Debates about religion and the human future rage around the world. From the highest seats of government to local mosques, churches, synagogues, and temples, the power of religion to shape, invigorate, but also destroy human social life is recognized. Belief in the triumph of the modern secular age, a world free of the passions of religion, has proved wrong and wrongheaded. At "the dawn of the twenty-first century, religion is strutting onto the world stage as a powerful though volatile actor, playing in an ever-changing range of roles – a development that was inconceivable to most Westerners a generation ago."[1] The question is not whether there will be a future for religion. The question is what *kind* of future is to come. Will the resurgence of religious practice contribute to a humane future or will it condemn societies to unending violence, ignorance, and want? If history is any indication, the religions will play both roles, forging and also forsaking the human future. Religion, like secularity, is a many-sided thing.[2]

Simple answers to complex challenges never suffice. It is no use to insist that the religions are only forces of evil, as some ardent secularists hold, nor that, in fact, they are really good and only fanatics have hijacked them for destructive purposes. The religions bring insight, care, and redemption but often they breed ignorance, foster conflict, and satisfy the base longings of the human spirit. The religions as practiced around the world are *essentially* ambiguous social and cultural forces. Given that fact, the challenge is to decide how they can and ought to be *interpreted* and *lived* thereby to contribute to a viable future for human and non-human life on this planet. This book takes up the interpretive and practical challenge by outlining a novel vision of the religious and moral life. We call it *theological humanism*.

Changing the Debate

In our global times there is a sense about deep flaws in religious heritages and also in the core of modern Western civilization. Modernity and its beliefs about freedom, human equality, science, and democracy are challenged. There seems to be little confidence that inherited cultural values and practices can support a livable global future. Those who sense these problems in our civilization usually adopt one of three outlooks that are treated throughout this book. They have set the terms of the current debate about religion and the human future.

Secular humanists see in religion nothing but tyranny, ignorance, violence, and the hatred of finite life. They embrace scientistic or naturalistic values in order to escape the excesses of religion. *True believers* return to inherited religion. Around the world people are reclaiming established religious authorities and the belief that religion offers redemption from the world. Humanistic values of freedom, reasonableness, tolerance, and human dignity are judged to be vacuous, mere remnants of the failed modern project, or, worse, the veiled rhetoric of secular cultural imperialism. Finally, people who are *open but uncommitted* fall between the extremes. They bemoan the ambiguity of the situation in which ultimate religious values are both collapsing and proliferating, and they await the future with alternating impulses of anxiety and hope, apathy and interest. They would like to commit themselves to a vision of a future worth living, but they are wary of both secular humanism and traditional religion. The question of religion and its place in the human future is debated among those who demand conformity to the divine will, those who march under the banner of the creative assertion of human power, and still other people who anxiously wait for some cause for commitment.

Can we learn to *inhabit* religious and non-religious visions of life in ways that sustain a humane future? This book makes a case for theological humanism beyond well-known frameworks. In order to do so, we reclaim the insights and principles of legacies that sustain social existence, advance a genuinely religious and yet humanistic outlook, and meet challenges that arise on the global scene. Of course, the very notion of theological humanism will seem implausible for many. Does not humanism deny in principle a theological outlook? How can a theological orientation in life be defined as humanistic? Is it not the case that both theological and humanistic outlooks are naïve and dangerous in a time when religion and human power endanger life on the planet? Our insistence on being both "theological" and "humanist" seems to be excluded by the terms of customary debate. We intend to change the terms of the debate.

At the core of this book is a claim about freedom *within* religion. Of course, we also endorse the freedom *of* religion, that is, the idea that everyone should have the right to practice openly and without coercion her or his religion. In addition, we endorse freedom *from* religion, namely, the right not to participate in any institutionalized religion. The relation between religion and freedom is one of the most basic issues being debated in our time. We hear calls for Christian or Islamic or Hindu nations. Others want to eschew religion completely within the secular state. But those forms of authoritarianism – religious and secular – threaten the integrity of social life.

Our argument is different. We advocate freedom *within* religion. That is to say, we provide a way of being religious in which religious and other authorities are submitted to criticism and tested in light of actions and relations that respect and enhance the integrity of life. Theological humanism is dedicated to human freedom and responsibility, since human life can be lived fully nowhere else than in the rough and tumble of personal and social existence. Coercion, tyranny, unthinking obedience to authority, and apathy rob human beings of the dignity of being agents in their world. Without freedom human life becomes subhuman, even if religious officials make grand claims about the dignity of subservience to the divine. By the same token, theological humanism advocates freedom within *religion*. Genuine human freedom is not mere license, the strange notion that we are most free if our lives lack any direction, are devoid of ideals, or happen outside the bonds of responsibility. True freedom, we show, is dedication to what respects and enhances the integrity of life.

The challenge theological humanism addresses, then, is the increasing denial of human freedom among many of the world's religions and so reversion to kinds of authoritarianism. (Later, we call this *hypertheism* and explore it in detail.) Conversely, theological humanists must also confront ideas about freedom unmoored from the demands and joys of responsibility for the integrity of life. (We name this *overhumanization* and explore it, too.) In our time, people need a conception of freedom and also religious authority that places both freedom and authority within a robust dedication to the integrity of life. Providing that kind of conception of freedom *within* religion is one purpose of theological humanism. It has deep resonance with a host of thinkers working with other traditions and religions.

Essays and Manifestos

We have entitled the book *Religion and the Human Future: An Essay on Theological Humanism*, and it appears, happily, in the Blackwell Manifesto series. The connection between an essay and a manifesto requires a few words in terms of the style and intention of the book, since we aim to change the terms of debate about humanism and theology.

A manifesto seeks to awaken, inform, challenge, and move its readers to action. Throughout history, manifestos have been used as battle cries to incite judgment and promote social causes. An essay is different. Coined by Michel de Montaigne, an *essai*, means, in its original sense, a trial or testing of oneself in response to various topics, subjects, and situations. An essay aims at understanding self and others; a manifesto is a declaration of policy. The two ideas, and the styles in which they are presented, seem utterly opposed. How, then, can we write an essay as part of a manifesto series?

This book does seek to awaken, inform, challenge, and also move people in response to the current global urgency. Yet by calling it an essay we signal that our interest is the *quest for truth* rather than the novelty of the position or policy of action. The quest for truth requires a rhetorical form suited to self-critical inquiry and which invites discussion and argumentation beyond strife between hardened convictions. Rather than denouncing other positions or proclaiming the radical character of one's own discourse, an essay is an adventure in reflection. In a time when too many intellectuals apparently hanker after the new and the strange, it is appropriate, we believe, to focus sustained attention on how to understand and orient life realistically and responsibly. Because this is an essay, we have also not engaged in the scholarly duty (and joy!) of providing endless footnotes or extended analysis of texts and thinkers. The notes provided, the concepts coined and analyzed, and the theories we engage are well considered and certainly defensible even if we provide, coin, analyze, and engage with greater brevity than found in a typical academic treatise.

Nowadays many people cast a skeptical eye on books that use ideas like "truth" or "goodness" or "humanity," let alone "the integrity of life." The diversity of cultures, human fallibility, and the sad reality of failure or fanaticism fuels skepticism about big questions and big ideas. This skepticism, so understandable in its origins, too easily leads to a relativism wherein nothing is claimed and defended as true, good, and just. In that way, such skepticism endangers the human future insofar as it threatens the belief that there are valid limits and measures to human existence and social life. The seduction

4

of skepticism dictated that we write an essay. As a kind of trial, one does not accept reigning ideas and beliefs but puts them to test, mindful of the limits of human understanding. Granting proper skepticism about getting hold of "The Truth," the demand to understand and to orient human existence nevertheless remains. The smallness of human intelligence and the fallibility of judgments ought not to dissuade one from asking about and trying to use big ideas. Through reflection human life is understood, enriched, and enlarged.

The Journey Ahead

How then will we write this *essay*? The argument of this book is complex. It might help our readers if we briefly outline it at the outset of this journey of thought.

Part I presents the "shape" of theological humanism along several lines of reflection. After clarifying the basic challenges and some leading ideas (chapter 1), Part I moves in three steps. We turn initially to engage the legacies of humanism (chapter 2) and theology (chapter 3). These chapters are not meant to be extensive accounts of the history of thought, although some history is involved. More importantly, we mean to isolate the flaws in humanism and Western theism which appear on the global scene and in fact endanger the human future. If religion is to contribute to the human future these flaws must be addressed. In order to respond to those flaws, the chapters also explore what we judge to be some of the main metaphors of the human and of the divine deep within the legacies of humanism and theism. These metaphors are the imaginative and conceptual tools needed to understand the flaws and criticisms of humanism and theistic belief, but also, as the reader finds, to develop our case for theological humanism.

Chapter 4 turns to a specific form of religious humanism, that is, Christian humanism. We do so for the obvious reason that our own thought is rooted in the Christian tradition and also Western sources. Our interest and expertise is not in providing a history of thought or thinkers. The aim is to articulate what we believe to be the inner logic of Christian humanism, even if historians might quibble with aspects of our account. Christian humanists always sought to surmount the clash between religion and humanistic commitments; that is also our agenda. In our case, theological humanism is an extension of but also a revolution in the legacy of Christian humanism for the sake of our global age. The revolution comes from making the *integrity of life* the centerpiece of theological and humanistic thinking. We hope that representatives of other traditions will undertake an analogous adventure of thought in their own communities.

Part I of the book ends in chapter 5 by drawing together the findings of the previous chapters to clarify the shape and import of theological humanism. Using metaphors from humanism and theology, the chapter develops an account of the range of goods important for the flourishing of human existence within the wider compass of life on this planet. Extending the "logic" of Christian humanism, the chapter also clarifies an imperative of responsibility needed to guide actions and relations for the sake of a humane and yet religious future. Finally, we also present an account of "conscience" important for understanding the religious and moral task now set before persons and communities. All of this culminates in the idea of the integrity of life which is the heart of theological humanism.

Part II sets forth the "task" of theological humanism by putting the position "on trial" with respect to current debates raging in the academy and around the world. These are obviously exemplary debates; it is not possible to address every controversy surrounding the theme of religion and the human future. The topics we have chosen to address swirl around the levels of goods isolated in Part I through the use of the various metaphors of the humanistic imagination. These are crucial points in which the flaws of humanism and theism are manifesting themselves most dangerously in our global age. We take up these challenges to the integrity of life with respect to theological insights gleaned in earlier chapters, as well as our account of responsibility and conscience. Addressing endangerments to natural life (chapter 6), the clash between religion and politics (chapter 7), debates about consciousness and art (chapter 8) and religion as a cultural form (chapter 9), we want to show the contribution of theological humanism to current thought and life. Throughout these chapters we pick up and address criticisms of religion and humanism heard around the world. Again, our treatment of topics cannot be exhaustive, and there are obviously many other challenges which must be addressed. We leave those treatments to future work, our own and (hopefully) that of others.

The book ends with the reasons for adopting theological humanism (chapter 10). By that point in the essay the humanistic and theological images explored throughout the book will have been gathered together beyond the lines of criticism by means of a specific logic of thinking around the idea of the integrity of life. The last chapter is then really the transition from argument to life and therefore the shift from an essay to a manifesto. Living theological humanism requires persons and communities to respect and enhance the human future within its integral relations to other forms of life, natural and divine. That is the challenge and possibility of religion and the human future.

Struggle for the Future

It is often said that people now live during a clash of civilizations. Consider the fact that there is no shared cultural or religious framework within which to interpret, understand, and evaluate what might seem to be rather obvious facts. What appears like an act of terrorism to some is hailed as martyrdom in obedience to God by others. Basic human rights for many are perceived by others to be foreign values wrongly imposed on their culture. Beliefs about women's dignity and freedom in some nations and cultures are bemoaned elsewhere as an affront to traditional values. The clash between economic development and ecological sustainability plays itself out around the world. While some people place hope in the promise of technology to rid human life of disease and deformity, others fear that the promise conceals an inhuman future and violates the limits on human existence by trying to play God. These conflicts are well known and deeply felt. They fill newspapers and the global media. Little wonder there is anxiety and dispute about the meaning and purpose of being human and the shape a human future should take.[3]

In fact, the idea of a global "clash" is too simple and it is also too optimistic. The idea is too simple because "civilizations" are not block-like entities that somehow can "clash" with each other. The global sphere is a complex reality of interacting dynamics, only a few of which we explore in Part II. The idea of a clash of civilizations is also too optimistic. It fails to grasp the struggle *within* cultures and *within* religions, a struggle, we insist, that is at root *within* the human heart and mind. The clash that is now raging around the world originates and spreads within people's souls. It is a clash between, on the one side, the desire for unconstrained freedom and power, and, on the other side, the longing for some ultimate, spiritual authority to save one from the burden of freedom. People are indeed in the midst of a global religious, moral, and spiritual struggle in which individuals and communities must decide whether or not to orient our lives freely by the demands of responsibility for the integrity of life.

The idea of spiritual struggle is not a strange one for a humanist. Whether religious or not, humanists have always understood that the real "war" of human existence is the constant and unending battle to live by our greatest ideals and our own dignity rather that to follow the seduction of powers, desires, and "gods" that demean the soul. There are many "techniques of degradation," as Gabriel Marcel once called them, which lurk throughout societies and in our minds and hearts.[4] The spiritual battle is to counter those forces of degradation and thereby to respect and enhance the integrity of human and non-human life. The purpose of this *essay*, this trial, is, at its deepest, to enter into this religious struggle for the sake of the human future.

Part I

The Shape of Theological Humanism

1

Ideas and Challenges

This book outlines theological humanism as a way to think about the human project that circumvents usual options rooted in political, religious, economic, or technological powers. What is needed, we contend, is a way beyond a constricted anthropocentrism where "man" is the measure of everything the various "theisms," the rule of the gods, which struggle for human faith and obedience. We also need a way beyond the rejection of humanism in any form in terms of what is called anti-humanism as well as the rejection of religion by ardent secularists. Those options are no longer capable of sustaining and directing human existence. A different vision is needed. The terms of the debate need to be changed.

This chapter orients the argument of the book by introducing basic ideas and challenges for theological humanism. The initial treatment of these matters will be developed and deepened in later chapters. We also note our pathway of reflection, our method, what we call "third-way thinking." In these various ways the chapter provides orientation for the rest of our essay.

Religion, Theism, and Humanism

The world's religions have insisted that God, the sacred, the deities, or The Real constitute ultimate reality in relation to which human life derives value and purpose.[1] They contend that the purpose of human existence is to live in *conformity* to "God" and "God's will." Even non-theistic religions, using the term "religion" in a capacious way, hold that one ought to live in conformity to what is ultimately true, ultimately real, however conceived. Of course, there are many ways to define religion. Religion is belief in a god. Religion is the "cult of the invisible." Religion has also been defined as a psychological illusion. And so on. There are also endless disputes about what actually counts as a religion. For the purposes of this essay, we say that what makes a myth, ritual, practice, community, or set of beliefs "religious" is that it provides ways for human beings to orient existence in relation to what is deemed to have unsurpassable importance *and* reality amid intractable problems of life.

On this account, *theism* is a specific kind of religion found in many societies that conceives of the sacred, or ultimate, or what is unsurpassably important and real as a "God" (*theos*). A god, a deity, is a being who acts in and on the world and is unsurpassably important – most perfect, most holy. There are types of theism. Traditional monotheism conceives of God as the one unconditioned agent upon whom all reality is dependent. In polytheism there are many gods, often ordered in some pantheon, like the Greek gods. Pantheism conceives of the world itself as divine, as a deity.

The rise of the modern Western world, we are told, was in many ways the death of a theistic conception of reality and purpose for human life. For many modern thinkers, truth or goodness or beauty were no longer found in the *conformity* of mind or action or art to what was "real" or "divine."[2] The meaning of truth, goodness, and beauty shifted humanward. With this shift religion and "theism" seemed to wane. As popularly understood, Italian Renaissance "humanists" of various stripes proclaimed that human beings, and humans alone, are ends-in-themselves, possessing intrinsic worth or supreme importance.[3] All other forms of life (natural or divine) are appraised in relation to human well-being. Further, while the natural world might function by its own "laws," human beings, not God, are agents, the makers of history. As Tzvetan Todorov notes, humanism "refers to the doctrines according to which man is the point of departure and the point of reference for human action. These doctrines are 'anthropocentric' doctrines, just as others are theocentric, and still others put nature or tradition in this central place."[4] The end or good of human life for traditional humanism is the free, productive, and creative exercise of human capacities for the sake of human flourishing. "The distinctive feature of modernity," Todorov continues, "is constitutive of humanism: man *alone* (and not only nature or God) decides his fate. In addition, it implies that the ultimate end of these acts is a human being, not suprahuman entities (God, goodness, justice) or infrahuman ones (pleasures, money, power)."[5]

There are basic contrasts between a theistic and a humanistic standpoint. Theism holds that the right orientation of human life is to *conform* to the will of God(s). The divine, whether one or many, is conceived as an unsurpassably important and real causal force, an agent. Theism is an orientation in life in which reality is defined by the interaction of human and non-human agents. Humanism, by contrast, holds that the right orientation of human life is the *creative* exercise of power to shape one's existence and to seek flourishing. As an outlook this means that the reality is constituted by non-agential forces (e.g., laws of nature or social systems) amid which human agents act and live.

Humanism, like theism, has taken different forms, depending on how the idea of "man" or "humanity" was conceived. Humanism in its various types (scientific, secular, religious) presents different outlooks and orientations on life.[6] What every humanist agrees upon is that human beings possess intrinsic worth. The most basic difference among humanists, as Tony Davies notes, is whether " 'Man' denotes an essential *starting point* ... or ... a *destination*, less a given set of intrinsic qualities than the goal of an epochal and never-to-be-completed process."[7] "Man" as *origin* and "man" as *end* provide related but starkly different orientations in life and also outlooks on existence. Does one live out from one's humanity or does one struggle to bring one's humanity into being?

The next two chapters will explore humanism and theism in more detail. Now, we can introduce some other basic ideas to this book. They are, perhaps, awkward terms, but they are coined in order to identify flaws in traditional humanism and classical theism and therefore to name the challenges now posed to the human future.

Overhumanization and Hypertheism

To be human is to be engaged constantly in the task of world-making, culture creation. We are profoundly social creatures and also beings that must, come what may, make sense of our lives. Outside of the bonds of society, existence would be meaningless and wretched. Human beings imagine the struggles and vulnerabilities of existence within meaningful forms in order to buttress, console, and inspire their lives. We unavoidably seek to "humanize" reality, make it our own, in order to share it with others.

There is a downside to the work of culture creation. In the current age, human power more and more intervenes to direct the dynamics of life on this planet. Régis Debray writes that increasingly people in advanced nations live within "transistorized, fiber-optically cabled, air-conditioned, video-surveilled surroundings." Night and day are awash in man-made light. Little seems outside the human realm in which spirit can live and

13

move. There is a loss of a sense of what transcends human meanings. The advancement of human power and purposes has ironically meant the loss of the human dimension of life. Debray rightly observes that "humans still crave, in order to breathe, non-human spaces."[8]

The triumph of human power in shaping reality is what we call "over-humanization." The idea designates a social condition in which what possesses real worth, what should orient actions and social relations, is the extension of the human power to shape and create realities. To be sure, the inscribing of forms of life within cultural projects, symbolic forms, and power is meant to further human flourishing. This project has brought advances in knowledge, the lessening of disease and want, and the formation of freer and more open democratic societies. Yet it has also led to the profaning of life through wars, ecological endangerment, and cultural banality. Part of overhumanization is also the unjust distribution of its goods – say, medicine, clean water, stable social orders – and the unfair distribution of destructive features of modern societies: pollution, environmental damage, lack of access to hi-tech resources, astonishing poverty. Overhumanization is a term for the inner distortion or flaw of humanism. It is a now a challenge to the human future.

The worldwide resurgence of the religions over the last century has exposed a contradiction within theism analogous to that found in the legacies of humanism. Often reacting to a virulent secularism and legacies of power and injustice associated with the "modern West," the religions have become global political, social, and cultural forces. On this vision, to be human is to be responsive to the divine will as it reveals itself in culture and history. Many anthropologists and historians of religion hold that cultures of the past have been religious. Human beings can be construed as *homo religiosus*.[9] Outside of religious communities with their sacred traditions and their communions with deity, life would be empty and senseless. Human beings belong not to themselves and their puny designs, but to God alone. Theists take joy and hope in their ultimate purpose of pleasing God. Presently, we see the resurgence of theism after its waning in the modern age, often in the most secular parts of the world.[10] Theistic religions have relieved suffering, furthered human dignity and self-determination, and advanced understanding among the world's peoples. These religions in certain forms and at certain times are also forces of destruction, obscurantism, and opponents to knowledge and science. The appeal to conform to God's will has too often and too readily been used to destructive ends.

The distortion in religion works much like the flaw in humanization. It is the attempt to enfold life within a specific understanding of "God"

14

when "God" is only rightly known and loved within the confines of *one special community*. In truth, God is not a Christian God or a Muslim God or a Jewish God or a Hindu God or a Buddhist God. As Rabbi Jonathan Sacks has rightly noted, "God is the God of all humanity, but between Babel and the end of days no single faith is the faith of all humanity."[11] The diversity of human faiths does not necessarily imply a diversity of gods. Yet insofar as members of any religion claim ultimate truth for their all-too-human conception of the divine, it is not clear what status other communities can and ought to have in orienting society.

"Hypertheism" is the term we use for the conviction of a community or tradition that its faith and interpretation of God are one and the same with the divine, obviously true and ultimately real. Hypertheism claims that one's vision of God and it alone is sufficient to speak of the mystery, power, and truth of the divine. Accordingly, human life must become enfolded within that community's vision and faith and every aspect of existence made to conform to its convictions about God. Hypertheism is a term for the flaw of theistic religion that endangers the meaning and purpose of diverse forms of human life.

Hypertheism and overhumanization are concepts for internal distortions of theism and humanism and which also necessarily pit religion against humanism. Ironically, they are both forms of over-reach on the part of human beings, either in terms of the radical extension of human power beyond bounds or in terms of claims to know without failure or distortion the will of God. It is not surprising, then, that there are thinkers and movements who reject any form of humanism, secular or religious. Humanism is false on this account not only because it focuses on the worth of actual human beings to the seeming exclusion of other living beings, but because it tries to explain the working of complex systems solely with reference to the lives and actions of individual human agents. The rejection of the priority of human agency is one defining feature of contemporary forms of secular *anti-humanism*. Likewise, it is understandable that other thinkers and movements disclaim all forms of theism and especially the idea of one supreme divine agent. Theism is wrong in this view both because it denies other religious communities and because it believes in a supernatural divine agent somehow operating within a universe otherwise functioning according to natural laws. These claims fuel the fires of religious and secular *post-theism*.

Anti-humanism is not somehow anti-human. It means, rather, an outlook that rejects humanistic assumptions about the forces that define the world. To be human is to be part of some larger whole, and it is this whole, variously defined, that must be explored in order to understand the proper measure of human social life. Similarly, post-theism does not signify atheism, a stance that rejects all theology or discourse about God. Post-theism tries to affirm and reformulate religious sensibilities within contemporary structures of thought and experience. It displays a humility of thinking which backs off the triumphalism of much theistic religion. As seen later in this essay, both anti-humanism and post-theism grasp insights that are important for theological humanism.

In order to change the terms of debate we need to step back and ask, what do we mean by the "human"?

Defining the Human

It is important to remember the richness of the English word "humanity." "The root-word is, quite literally, humble (*humilis*), from the Latin *humus*, earth or ground; hence *homo*, earth-being, and *humanus*, earthly, human."[12] Whatever else human beings are, we are earthly creatures. Many of the world's great religions speak of the creation of human beings from the dust of the earth; myths and stories tell that the deepest failure of human beings is the prideful assertion of power beyond our capacities. As Paul Ricoeur notes:

> The ancients called man a "mortal." This "remembrance of death" indicated in the very *name* of man introduces the reference to a limit at the very heart of the affirmation of man himself. When faced with the pretense of absolute knowledge, humanism is therefore the indication of an "only:" we are *only* men.[13]

Awareness of mortality and bonds to the earth should foster humility among mortals. Too often it does not. The clashes and collisions played out on the world scene, the distortions we call overhumanization and hypertheism, are testimony to human pride and presumption rather than a humble acknowledgment of our shared plight and spiritual longing for the integrity of life.

While we are earth creatures limited by mortality, "humanus" is also defined by aspiration, the drive and desire to become otherwise than our present state of life. Thinkers in the West have used a range of metaphors to make this point about human beings. As Laszlo Versényi puts it in his study of Socratic humanism:

> Metaphorically speaking, [man] is only a symbol, a fragment, something fundamentally incomplete and unwhole which, aware of its incompleteness, is moved towards self-completion, strives for what would make it into that

16

which it by nature must be in order to fulfill itself ... [Man] is a movement, a transcendence, a "thing in between" (*metaxu*).[14]

The human is a "bridge" (to speak metaphorically) between realms of life, at once animal and yet exceeding our animality. Human beings, in more biblical terms, are dust that breathes, made of the earth and yet an image of God. The decisive question, noted above, is whether "humanity" is an *origin* or a *destination* or, we now add, lived in the *tension* of both. Is being "a thing in between" a condition that human beings must, tragically and joyously, live out and yet never fully overcome, or does it mark out "humanity" as a destination that goes beyond, transcends, its mixed, fragmented nature? Or is the real challenge, as we believe, to live with integrity amid the tensions of everyday existence, the turmoil and vitality of the human heart?

Often when thinkers make forays into the "study of man" there is the impulse, just like in any careful inquiry, to provide a definition and theory of the subject matter. But who can define "man"? This problem of definition has led some thinkers to note that the question of human "nature" is really a theological one. They reason that since human beings cannot get out of their skins to see themselves objectively and thus provide a real definition of "man," only God, a superhuman but knowing reality, could provide the perspective for rightly defining human nature. All that the philosopher or anthropologist or historian can do is to explore what Hannah Arendt called the "human condition" and thus intentionally avoid any attempt to define human "nature." It is hardly surprising that when philosophers lost interest in the question of human nature, theologians continued to speak of the "nature and destiny of man" in relation to God.[15]

Other philosophers have insisted that one cannot dodge the question of definition of the human, but that it is important to shift from a substantive one to a functional definition, an examination of what human beings *do*. As Ernst Cassirer put it:

Man's outstanding characteristic, his distinguishing mark, is not his metaphysical or physical nature – but his work. It is this work, it is the system of human activities, which defines and determines the circle of humanity.[16]

Of course, the problem then becomes what are distinctly "human" activities or capabilities and how ought one to study them. Tzvetan Todorov, cited earlier, isolates three basic humanistic convictions rooted in capacities, what he calls "the autonomy of the I, the finality of the you, and the universality of the they." In and through freedom, moral respect for others, and human

17

social well-being, Todorov structures his account around longstanding humanistic themes, like individuality, love, a humane morality. Humanism is for him the wager that while human happiness is always in doubt, that suspense enables one the chance to live in truth.

Other examples could be cited. The point is that any account for rightly orienting human life involves a vision of human existence, a definition of the "human." We acknowledge the difficulty and appeal to the idea of human being as "beings in between," the unfinished animal constantly striving to disclose and to become what it truly is. How, then, does this vision of the human enter into a theological reflection? This brings us to the last set of ideas we want to introduce in this chapter, ideas that build on what has already been noted.

Religious Humanism and Theological Humanism

"Theological humanism" is a paradoxical name for a stance and orientation in life that combines humanistic aspirations with a genuine theological outlook. We need, then, to distinguish how theological humanism relates to religious humanism.[17] There are two basic forms of *religious humanism* – two ways of combining humanism with religion. Members of both forms believe that genuine human flourishing comes from learning, cultivating, and enacting basic human qualities. They are different, however, in the way they relate to the historical religions.

The first form is the *humanism of organized religions*. There have always been those people who hold that human dignity and happiness are foremost among the benefits of right conviction and practice within their own religion. Under this conception, religious humanism appears only in the specific guise of Jewish humanism, Christian humanism, Islamic humanism, Buddhist humanism, and so on; there is no generic version of religious humanism. The convictions of one's religion are viewed as the necessary and sufficient conditions for being truly humanistic. For these folks, the aim of religion is to bring people close to God or the divine – to know or love what is unsurpassably important and real – *so that* humans may flourish in their own lives. Pleasing the gods at the expense of human happiness, or seeking redemption from this worldly vale of tears in an other-worldly heaven, nirvana, or place of eternal bliss are not the primary goals of religion for this kind of religious humanist.

For example, one finds this form of religious humanism within Eastern and Western Christianity when theologians speak of the "humanity of

God." The purpose of Christian humanism, as we explore in chapter 4, is to show how beliefs about God's incarnation as a human being in Jesus Christ provide the backing and the aim of an authentically humanistic outlook. Because God became human in Jesus Christ, Christian faith, the believer holds, is then the truest expression of a humanistic view of the world. As Thomas Merton once wrote, "True Christian humanism is the full flowering of the theology of the Incarnation."[18] The grounds of this outlook, and every similar kind of religious humanism, remain within the confines of a specific religion.[19]

The second form of religious humanism can be called *spiritual or speculative humanism*.[20] In this form, the humanistic impulse focuses on common spiritual qualities (or supposedly universal structures of human existence), abstracted from the particularities of religious traditions. This form of religious humanism comprises a family or spectrum of approaches with a shared conviction that whereas religions are many (as are languages or other dimensions of culture), the human spirit is one and universal. They all seek the common spiritual unity that underlies the diversity of human religions and cultures. Spiritual or speculative humanists tend to believe people can become too attached to their inherited religions and fail to see what is common in the human spiritual quest. The future of humanity, they would say, depends on plumbing the depths of the human spirit and articulating its shared principles, practices, and common longings. In contrast to the humanists of organized religions, the spiritual-speculative humanists find the necessary and sufficient conditions for being truly humanistic in analyzing and interpreting human being as such and never solely in the convictions of one specific religion.

Humanists of this kind may have either a spiritualistic or speculative bent. The spiritualist takes the religions of the world as repositories of profound insights and experiences. In spite of differences, each religion in its core comprehends the heart of human being in relation to the divine.[21] Their aim is to identify the common structures and universal forms underlying every religion. The spiritualist sees that the modern person is privileged to behold the big picture of religious diversity within a globalized world and is no longer confined within the boundaries of one religion. They define the spiritual task of modernity as the effort to distill into systematic form the human wisdom that abides in different degrees within all religions.[22]

Speculative-leaning religious humanists look for universal truths about human being in relation to what is of ultimate importance and reality in the great philosophical systems, and not so much among the historical religions. For example, Platonism or Hegelianism can be interpreted in humanistic terms to show how an understanding of the Form of the Good or the Absolute Idea may be intrinsic to the human spirit. These and other philosophies have religious roots on close examination, but they purport to rise above them into rarified, speculative heights. Recently constructed philosophies related to existentialism, phenomenology, hermeneutics, and even postmodernism are used to articulate the meaning of human being as open to and receptive of the divine in the fabric of human life.

Too readily, we judge, humanists within organized religions (Christian humanists, etc.) undervalue important efforts outside their own traditions to understand the common shape of the human drive for meaning, value, and truth. They prefer to remain within the interpretive circles of particular narratives, symbols, and theological formulae; they do not seek to expand their traditions to a more cosmopolitan point of view. Likewise, spiritual-speculative humanists tend to underestimate the degree to which their thinking, which aspires to universality, is nonetheless embedded within historical traditions of language, culture, and religion. No one is religious or even a human being in general. Human thought, precisely as human and thus limited, is situated within particular social and cultural legacies, like the legacies of distinctive religions. The writings of any speculative humanist concerning universal human meanings can be localized within particular cultural trajectories. Even humanistic philosophers live within (loosely) organized historical communities.

Theological humanism changes the terms of the debate raging about the meaning of religious humanism. It entails living *through* a religious tradition; it denotes a way of freely inhabiting a religious outlook. Nevertheless, theological humanism also entails a *critical* relation to one's religious community and its beliefs and practices. It tests the truth of religious convictions, and, conjointly, the meaning of humanistic commitments must be probed to their theological depths. While a theological humanist always inhabits some religious tradition, he or she does so in ways different than someone who believes his or her tradition's convictions are the necessary and sufficient condition of humanistic and theological commitments. A theological humanist believes that the resources of his or her religious community are *distinctive* among the many ways of being religious and human on this planet. Those resources are nevertheless not utterly *unique*. One's religious tradition can be compared with other religious outlooks, criticized, revised, even rejected in the light of interactions with others who also seek integral existence.

A theological humanist also insists that there is no ahistorical access to a universal structure of the human spirit, such that the influence of historical life marked by diversity somehow drops away. Humans live within historical traditions; each of us is shaped by a host of cultural and religious symbols, narratives, rituals, and the stream of their interpretations that exert powerful influence on thinking. Theological humanism, then, is mindful of the human entanglement in all dimensions of historical religion and culture. It intends to fathom these influences, rather than to become stuck in or to flee from them. In the following chapters we show that the central ideas of theological humanism, especially the integrity of life, resonate with profound spiritual longings. The integrity of life is not revealed from on high but is an idea and norm for theological humanism that arises from dogged reflection on human individual and social existence in its diversity within the wider compass of life on this planet.

One way we are changing the terms of debate is by showing how theological humanism is related to and yet different from other forms of religious humanism. Theological humanism as presented in this essay is drawn from Christian and Western sources even if its outlook is global and cosmopolitan. That should not be surprising. We can only use, and use critically, the resources of the traditions of which we are a part. We agree with Kwame Anthony Appiah, who writes about "rooted cosmopolitans."[23] One adopts a vision of the human adventure, an inclusive concern for human and non-human life, but rooted in some distinctive cultural, social, and religious resources.

Here too our position is different. Part of the novelty of this argument is that we insist on "third-way" thinking which acknowledges the internal complexity of the very tradition in which our thought is rooted. One is rooted not in a block-like "tradition," because, as Christian humanists have long understood, a tradition is multiple and internally complex and contested. Christianity, for instance, arises in the dynamics and explosive intersection of ancient Semitic, Greek, and Roman forces, among others. What then is Christian "identity?" This means one must think beyond the conflict between (say) biblical sources, theological reflection, and Western philosophy because these helped to constitute the tradition itself. Unlike some churchly theologies, as explored later, we do not seek to isolate Christian beliefs from other speculative and critical resources for thought and life. Ours is not an argument for Christian particularism. However, we also reject the wholesale deconstruction and denial of particular religious claims too often found among forms of contemporary theology and ethics. By probing particular religious and cultural resources we aim to discover

21

something about the aim and orientation of religious and moral existence. One keeps a humanist outlook truly only when it is given theological articulation, and, conjointly, the theological dimension of existence must always also be given humanistic expression.

Conclusion

Theological humanism as an outlook and orientation in life uses the distinctive claims and speculative and spiritual resources of a specific tradition in order to find points of contact with other people who share similar aspirations and convictions. While we happen to draw from the Christian tradition, we do not write only for Christians and we also hope and expect to find theological humanists in other traditions. Our aim is to clarify how the religions can enable people to live freely into a humane future once the internal complexity of any religious identity is acknowledged and open to interpretation. Some Christians will find this a betrayal of what is distinctively Christian. Many humanists will hardly see the relevance of theological claims within our approach. Part of the argument of this book is to stave off charges of betrayal and irrelevance while holding fast to our main concern to present the aim and task of theological humanism.

Current debate about religion and the human future tends to devolve into a clash among religious particularists, secularists, those who hold their religious convictions humanely but still insist on being unique, and still others who seek some more speculative or spiritual idea of religious humanism. The debate is leading nowhere, and, in fact, it contributes to the endangerment of life in the failure to provide an alternative perspective on the forces, religious and otherwise, that are now rampant around the world. In order to change the debate, this essay presents theological humanism in a succinct and hopefully compelling form.

We turn next to the legacy of the Western humanistic imagination.

2

The Humanist Imagination

One common feature between much Western humanistic and theological thought has been the belief that what is morally good and right is bound to the flourishing of human persons and human communities. As Immanuel Kant put it, humanity is an end in itself; this insight is the foundation for a universal categorical imperative to orient freedom. Similarly, the *Westminster Shorter Catechism* (1647), hardly a humanistic manifesto, insisted "man's chief end is to glorify God and enjoy him forever." God is the highest good; God is the end of human flourishing. In the Middle Ages Thomas Aquinas argued that the highest human good is to know God in and through God's own being, a perfection of love that is also the perfection of human being. Today, thinkers like the Jewish philosopher Emmanuel Levinas have championed a "humanism of the other man."[1] Most Western thought, religious and otherwise, has had a decidedly anthropocentric and so humanistic flavor, even if conceptions of the human and of the human good have differed. After all, what Kant or Protestant divines or Aquinas or Levinas meant by the human good differs in substance and grounding. Yet human well-being and cultivation seems intrinsic to what is morally good and right.[2]

The affirmation of human dignity and worth has not always been taken as obvious. The pitch of violence by human beings against human beings is as old as civilization itself. The twentieth century was distinctly horrific and a weary chronicle of wars, gas chambers, killing fields, and rape camps. The horror continues in the twenty-first century.[3] The brutality of human beings gives rise to kinds of anti-humanism. In the nineteenth century Friedrich Nietzsche had bluntly stated, "the world is beautiful, but has a disease called Man." Twentieth-century thinkers were more ambiguous in their criticism of "man" than Nietzsche, if no less strident. These and other critiques of humanism center on conceptions of human capacities and aspirations as well as the distinctive value Western religious and cultural traditions have assigned to human beings within the scheme of things. It is important to see that anti-humanism was never lacking "moral passion." Even Nietzsche sought to overcome man in the name of a higher type of human being.[4] There is a passion for the dignity of life that drives much of the anti-humanist attack on humanism.

The purpose of this chapter is thereby twofold. It is, first, to isolate features of classical humanism and also to unfold some main metaphors of human freedom created by its representatives. Later in the book we will put those metaphors to work in formulating theological humanism. The second task is to clarify criticisms of humanism, what is called "anti-humanism," and also the current revision in humanism dubbed "neohumanism." In brief, anti-humanism challenges the distinctive worth given to human beings by humanists and also sets human life within a wider, non-human context. Neohumanists, conversely, revise humanism in response to anti-humanist criticisms; their central revision, we will see, is to shift from a classical humanistic focus on self-realization and cultivation to a principled concern for the other, for the "finality of the you," as Todorov puts it. Theological humanism joins this neohumanist revision but takes it even further insofar as the integrity of life, and not just the other human being, is the primary focus.

We begin, then, with basic features of humanism.

The Human Focus

The contrast between assessments of human life noted above is not a modern phenomenon. Some ancient philosophers cursed the day they were born. Seneca, the Roman Stoic, writer, and man of affairs, committed suicide, as did others. In his last words, Socrates asks that a cock be sacrificed to the gods in thanks for healing him from the disease called life. Centuries later, in 1198 before he became pope, Innocent III wrote on the misery of man. He begins the treatise with scripture: "Why did I come forth from the womb to see toil and sorrow, and spend my days in shame?" (Jeremiah 20:18). Innocent III then reflects on human misery from the cradle to the grave sustained only by the hope of heaven.

There have always been counter-voices. Four centuries after Innocent III and during the flowering of the Italian Renaissance, Giannozzo Manetti countered the pope's charges of the frailty and baseness of human life in order to celebrate the dignity of humans. Scripture itself is insistent on the distinctive status of human beings created in the image of God.[5] The Psalmist sings to God:

> When I look at your heavens, the work of your fingers,
> the moon and the stars that you have established;
> what are human beings that you are mindful of them,
> mortals that you care for them?
> Yet you have made them a little lower than God
> and crowned them with glory and honor.
>
> (Psalm 8:3–5)

"What are human beings that you are mindful of them?"

Throughout much of its history in the West, humanism has meant a celebration of human freedom, creativity, and autonomy. Behind these values were a set of images of what it means to be human and how human life ought to be freely lived in order to manifest and achieve the human good. Those images or pictures of existence are the products of the humanist imagination. Below, we will explore some of these metaphors about human freedom and flourishing.[6]

Yet what does one mean by "humanism"? The term is notoriously difficult to define. Typically, scholars trace the lineage of humanism to the Renaissance and the origins of the study of the "humanities." More important for our inquiry than the historical question of the roots of humanism is the debate about its main types. Corliss Lamont, an advocate of naturalistic or secular humanism, writes that for the "humanist," the "chief end of human life is to work for the happiness of man upon this earth and within the confines of Nature that is his home."[7] In a recent "humanist manifesto," one reads, "Humans are responsible for what we are or will become. No deity will save us; we must save ourselves."[8] Lamont is even more adamant. "Passing to the New Testament," he contends, "we see plainly that its theology, taken literally, is totally alien to the Humanist viewpoint … New Testament ethics is based on the assumption that the most meaningful and worthwhile part of man's life lies in the realm of immortality."[9] Religious humanists, conversely, challenge the idea that the human good is limited to the "confines of Nature." The scope of human transcendence and human destiny reaches beyond the domain of natural life. As previously noted, religious humanists make their case from within a specific historical religion or in spiritual and speculative forms. None of them accept that human beings by their own power can "save" humanity.

25

Despite profound differences in history and also contemporary thought, every humanist aims to respect and enhance human existence within and not against other realms of life on this planet. This commitment to human well-being or flourishing carries with it other commitments: the authority of evidence and argument against dogmatic authoritarianism; the importance of intelligence and reason in guiding human life; the truth and goodness of freedom; tolerance and education; and the social nature of human life and the human good so that all human beings – not just me or my kin – are due respect and esteem. Tzvetan Todorov has recently streamlined the list of humanistic convictions and noted that humanists hold that "freedom exists and that it is precious, but at the same time they appreciate the benefit of shared values, life with others, and a self that is held responsible for its actions."[10]

Humanists have always been interested in the study of language, culture, and history insofar as these are media in which human distinctiveness is manifest, freedom exercised, and happiness won or lost. Rather than seeking the principles of human action or the definition of human "nature" in some metaphysical realm of pure essence, humanists typically explore the messiness of human interactions, modes of expression, and also the historical careers of persons and people in order to discern what contributes to human flourishing and what thwarts aspiration. This also means that humanism admits the fallibility of human beings and so insists on humility about the certainty of one's ideas, beliefs, and values. Humility about human foibles brings with it a deep and abiding commitment to the criticism of things human, including self-criticism. "Humanism," Edward Said writes, "is not about withdrawal and exclusion. Quite the inverse: its purpose is to make more things available to critical scrutiny as the product of human labor, human energies for emancipation and enlightenment, and, just as importantly, human misreadings and misinterpretations of the collective past and present."[11]

Beyond freedom, shared life, responsible action, and intelligent criticism, there is a deeper claim about human existence important to classical humanistic thinkers. Recall from the previous chapter Laszlo Versényi's summation of Socratic humanism, "[Man] is a movement, a transcendence, a 'thing in between' (*metaxu*)."[12] What does that mean? The experiences behind the belief that we are mixed beings are obvious enough; we have all had them. Human beings seek happiness but hardly ever completely achieve it. We are fallible creatures duped by our own illusions, but also truth-seeking beings. Mortal beings are condemned to die and also strive for more and more life. As incomplete beings, humans struggle for some wholeness to existence no

26

matter how fleeting that might prove to be. If one's life is to be anything more than fancy and sorrow, one must undertake a process of self-transcendence whose end is integrity with and for others on earth. One does so aware, tragically or comically, that perfect integrity is never attained in time. That is the lot of being a "thing in between."

Granting broad lines of agreement on these ideals, debates begin among thinkers. A Christian or religious humanist of some stripe will insist that what defines the integrity of human existence and thus the distinctive good of human life is a unique capacity on the part of human beings for a free, responsive relationship to God. Human transcendence is already and always in part a movement towards and in response to the divine. The heart is restless until it rests in God, as St. Augustine famously put it. Conversely, a non-religious humanist denies this claim and argues, in the words of Todorov, that humanism "marks out the space in which the agents of these [human] acts evolve: the space of all human beings, and of them alone."[13] The debate among humanists is over the range of human transcendence, the extent of the moral space of life, conjoined to an affirmation of the preciousness of freedom. Classical humanists explored "self-transcendence" whereas current neohumanists focus on relations to the other, intrasubjective or lateral transcendence. Theological humanism charts its own course. But the debate at root is about the spiritual dimension of human life, the reach of human transcendence.[14]

Anti-Humanism

The debate among humanists will concern us later. At this juncture it is necessary to note positions that reject humanism root and branch. There is a lineage of anti-humanism in Western thought that challenges any focus on human well-being as the point of thinking and action. Consider briefly four S's that span the history of Western thought from the ancient world to the contemporary United States: Stoics, Spinoza, Schopenhauer, Singer.

The Greek and Roman Stoics thought that human life takes place in a determined universe and accordingly the only happiness a human being can attain is *apatheia*, a state of unconcern and tranquility about things that happen outside of one's control. What is within one's control is the tranquility of one's own emotion, and nothing else. For the true Stoic, the loss of child, spouse, fame, honor, or one's own life ought not to disturb the tranquility of the soul. Human attachments are transcended by consent to the "god within," that is, the divine spark of the power determining reality. The Stoic maxim, accordingly, is to live according to nature, meaning by that demand

27

the norm for attaining rational tranquility in doing one's duties. The emperor Marcus Aurelius and the slave Epictetus, both Stoics, agreed on that maxim.[15]

In a similar way, the radical Jew, excommunicated Christian, and chastised philosopher Benedictus Spinoza railed against the inability of persons to grasp a purely rational and disinterested vision of life and the working of reality. God alone is "substance," and so real. Everything else is actually a mode of God's being. Human beings, as modes of God, can know this truth and by rational insight increase their power of being, their *conatus*, in which is to be found human well-being. "The world was not created with a view toward human well-being."[16] Human beings, as rational creatures, should adjust themselves to reality and thereby find some measure of rational happiness.

In a way opposite to Spinoza's or Stoic criticisms of a humanistic attitude, Arthur Schopenhauer looks not to *apatheia* or rationality but to will. Drawing inspiration from ancient India, he argued that a non-conceptual and non-perceptual awareness of the dynamics of living and growing means that will is basic. Will as the unsurpassable metaphysical reality can become operative in human beings even while will follows the laws of nature. Reality from a human perspective seems divided against itself: the will to live always struggles against the will to live. Existence is conflict and evil and suffering. We cannot escape this reality. Pessimism is a realistic and truthful outlook on life. What little joy there is comes from the contemplation of ideas in the form of beauty even if there is no escape from the blind will to exist. One must extinguish the will to live in oneself and thereby escape bondage to the will to live. "Finally, with the destruction of experience and thought and self-consciousness, the Will to Live, also, deprived of its expressions, would be laid to rest."[17]

Stoics, Spinoza, and Schopenhauer reject the basic ideals of humanism. They set the human adventure within a cosmic reality whose purpose, order, or goodness do not aim at human flourishing. In an odd way, they can be seen as proposing hypertheistic criticisms of humanism insofar as Nature or Substance or Will is the supreme causal "agent" in reality and supremely important as well, a "god." Another criticism of humanism root and branch is hardly metaphysical or broadly theistic in nature. It is hostile to speculative thought and aims merely to relieve the suffering of sentient beings. Associated with the animal rights movement, its leading advocate is Peter Singer, the widely read philosopher.

Singer holds that Western religious and philosophical thought teaches that human life ought to be the object of reverence. For him, we must "unsanctify human life" in order to escape conceptual ambiguity and entrenched forms of anthropocentricism.[18] "Reverence for life" and the "sanctity of life" are mystifications that impede the march of science and rational consistency necessary to meet the moral imperative to relieve suffering. Assisted suicide to aid those in chronic pain, unrestricted genetic research to help future generations, and the escape from entrenched ideas about human dignity in order to stop the exploitation of animals, require attention to morally valid ways in which to relieve suffering. Singer also utterly rejects longstanding religious and moral beliefs that certain virtues (courage, patience, compassion) only arise in response to suffering, loss, and death.[19] Any religious claim within ethics warrants a false and dangerous view of human transcendence, a search for some other-worldly good. Singer uses a utilitarian calculation to determine what policies and courses of action best advance preferences and reduce suffering. The rejection of humanism is in terms of the special value Western cultures and especially religions have granted human beings, a type of specism which does not hold once we focus on sentient life and its interests.

The four positions we have briefly noted have found different expression in thought and society. They exemplify the range of anti-humanist arguments, including theistic rejections of humanism. After all, one could argue that God alone governs all that is for the sake of his glory, God alone is worthy of supreme devotion because God alone is good, or that God's Will or Substance is ultimate reality and everything else an illusion or mere figment of God's being. In each case, classic humanism would be rejected as atheistic but in ways similar to the position we have briefly explored. Humanism is plainly not without its detractors.

As the next step in the argument we turn from criticisms of humanism *in toto* and explore images and metaphors classical humanists developed to speak about human beings as "things in between." This will also allow us to isolate further criticisms of humanism especially important for the more recent forms of neohumanism found throughout the academy and around the world.

Masks in the World's Theatre

"All the world's a stage," Shakespeare wrote. The idea that the place of human existence is a "stage" and that human beings are actors is widespread among humanistic thinkers.[20] Juan Luis Vives, the Renaissance Spanish author, wrote in his *Fabula de homine*, that "man himself is a fable and a play." The distinctiveness of a human being is the power to transform herself or himself, to appear under various "masks" and even be the archmime of the gods. "Verily, man, peering oft through the mask which hides him, almost ready to burst

29

forth and reveal himself distinctly in many things, is divine and Jupiter-like."[21] Indebted to Pico della Mirandola and Cicero, Vives locates human dignity in the power that free action has to define human existence. Humans have complete power to fashion their lives unencumbered by natural or super-natural limits. Moreover, what it means to be a human being is revealed precisely in those things and realities shaped by human power. Culture and society are the artifacts that reveal the Jupiter-like power that is human nature.

Delivered in 1486 in Rome when he was 24, Pico's *Oration on the Dignity of Man*, as it is now known, is a powerful expression of the Renaissance mind and also a basic text of classical humanism. He begins the oration with the image of the stage:

> Most esteemed Fathers, I have read in the ancient writings of the Arabians that Abdala the Saracen on being asked what, on his stage, so to say, of the world, seemed to him most evocative of wonder, replied that there was nothing to be seen more marvelous than man.[22]

The struggle of human life, accordingly, is to rise and not fall, to move towards the divine rather than fall to the level of the brutes. Pico has God say that "We have made you (man) a creature neither of heaven nor of earth, neither mortal nor immortal, in order that you may ... fashion yourself in the form you prefer."[23] Pico denies that human beings have a "nature." We are chameleons, infinitely changeable and plastic; like Vives, the idea is that the human appears in different masks. By God-given free will, human beings can define their own nature. In other words, human beings are "things in between," whose existence is not defined by the nature of mortality or immortality or the laws of heaven or the laws of earth. Russell Kirk notes the link between humanism and religion in the *Oration*:

> Yet all this dignity of human nature was the gift of God: the spiritual and rational powers neglected – and through free will Man is all too able to neglect them – Man sinks to the level of the brutes. The humanist does not seek to dethrone God: instead through the moral disciplines of *humanitas*, he aspires to struggle upward toward the Godhead.[24]

Human beings are created good, but *changeable*. Human beings can freely seek the highest good, seek God, but they can also fall below their dignity and become brutes. This basic instability, lack of constancy, and changeability characterizes the moral and spiritual struggle of life.

One can see a forerunner of radical existentialism in this account of human freedom. Existence precedes essence, as Jean-Paul Sartre wrote much later.[25] This conception of radical freedom is the principal object of criticism in one strand of current neohumanism. The idea of unencumbered freedom implies an effacement of other realms of being as well as a reduction of other forms of life solely to instrumental purposes for human beings. The project of radical freedom backs the "overhumanization" of the world, that is, the enfolding and encoding of all existence within the kingdom of human power. Not surprisingly, many twentieth-century thinkers challenged the idea that human power shapes all realms of being. Martin Heidegger in his response to Sartre argued that "humanism" too easily reduces Being to "standing reserve" for human purposes. Heidegger saw in humanism the roots of the modern technological domination of being.[26] Humanism must be revised because the idea of the human as mime, the image of Jupiter, isolates human existence from the rest of life and warrants the human domination of Being. The human must be conceived, Heidegger argued, as the "Shepard of being." Our task is to protect and preserve being.

Many thinkers have followed Heidegger's criticism. Some ecological philosophers see the drive to domination rooted in ideas about radical freedom and in the biblical tradition's sanction of human sovereignty over nature due to the unique dignity of the human being as the *imago dei*, the mime of God who dominates the world.[27] The idea is not to be "anti-human." Once human life is rightly seen within larger patterns of life, then it might be properly oriented to some greater good than mere human flourishing. What has finality in this kind of neohumanism is not human self-realization but care for the earth, or tending Being.

Theological humanism strikes a different if related path to this kind of neohumanism. The metaphor of the world as theatre is not a claim about the human power of self-invention, a staging of the masks under which human being appears. But the focus is also not on "Being" or ecosystems. The theatre of the world has reference to the integrity of life and not just human creativity. Freedom is not the power of self-creation but a distinctive way of being in a world saturated with value and in response to others. We return to this insight throughout the remainder of this book.

Self in the Garden

The metaphors of the garden and the school are also prevalent in classical humanistic discourse about human freedom in the world. The accent in these metaphors is not on self-invention but self-cultivation and moral formation. "'I also know,' said Candide, 'that we must cultivate our own garden.'

31

'You're right,' said Pangloss, 'for when man was placed in the garden of Eden, he was placed there *ut operaretur eum* – that he might work – which proves that man was not born to rest …' 'That is well put,' replied Candide, 'but we must cultivate our own garden.'"[28] Voltaire retrieves a longstanding image of human life in the world in order to complete the story of Candide.

The image of life in the garden is found in the Book of Genesis and the commentaries it has spawned, but also among the ancient Epicureans and, later, Michel de Montaigne. The aim of life on this account is self-cultivation. One must have an honest, if not always appreciative, awareness of the limits placed on human existence. Within those limits, the human task is to cultivate a character befitting one's own judgment and one's relations with others. Valuing friendship and sociality, the garden image has nonetheless given rise to the praise of solitude. As Montaigne would put it, "As much as I can, I employ myself entirely upon myself." Again, in the *Essays*, "You have quite enough to do at home, don't go away."[29] True freedom is self-labor removed from the tangle of social cares that too easily and too often preoccupy us with matters of penultimate importance. We must cultivate our gardens, that is, our personal lives.

The image of the garden, and metaphors of growth and cultivation that surround it, obviously entail a different conception of human freedom and the orientation of life than the theatre. Self-cultivation means that within the limits of mortal existence, the bonds of affection, love, and desire, a good human life must be nurtured and developed. Humanists of this type focus on the development of virtues and the refinement of taste and sentiment. Civility and friendship are important to a measured good life. The "humanizing of human nature consists in the gradual organization of instincts or impulses or original tendencies in harmony with the growing conception of individual and social worth, i.e., in harmony with a community of interests."[30] There are natural impulses and desires in human life that must be oriented toward their proper ends. The work of cultivation is soul-work; it is the formation of the personal and social virtues.

In this light we can understand other criticisms of classical humanism that have led to other forms of current neohumanism. These criticisms come in two forms. In one, the idea that the purpose of life is to "cultivate self" has fallen to the critique of totality famously made by Emmanuel Levinas. Any system of thought that begins with the "I" enfolds the "other" into "totality," into the same.[31] Totality is similar to what we have called overhumanization: the project of enfolding and encoding of the other in the realm of the self. Despite this criticism, Levinas is a kind of neohumanist; he writes of a humanism of the other, and, as we will see later, his thought harkens towards theological humanism.[32]

32

The second line of critique of the image of the garden has taken a decidedly anti-humanist form. This position challenges the idea that we have natural propensies that can be "cultivated" to their perfection. "Perfection" requires some notion of distinctive human "nature" that is hard to sustain in light of what we know of other species.[33] Unlike humanists such as Vives and Pico, who see human dignity in the power to define self, or those, like Montaigne, who want to cultivate life, some anti-humanists deny any difference between the human and the non-human. They speak of the "post-human," cyborg existence, or the "end of nature."[34] Human beings have no "nature" and therefore the idea of forming or cultivating life is wide of the mark. The power of human beings is to remake themselves, to morphe and fashion cyborg existence. The very idea of nature as the defining essence or feature is denied by these critics. Insofar as humanism persists in believing in human "nature," it is a quaint philosophy hardly capable of providing orientation to human power in a technological age.

Some contemporary neohumanists have responded to these criticisms. Todorov, for instance, retrieves and revises the image of the human as the "imperfect garden" in order to speak of the humanist project. His point is that the "I" is not an origin, but an end, a goal to be valued and achieved. To be a human being is to be an incomplete project. But the goal of action is not only one's own life, but to respond to other actual persons as well. To be human is to be on the way to an identity that is bound to others, but only human others. Indeed, "human being takes the place of the divine. But not just any human being, only one who is embodied in individuals other than myself."[35] In theological humanism the reach of human transcendence is not limited to the encounter with the human other alone. Yet the image of the garden will remain important.

Discipline and the School

One other metaphor of human freedom has been especially important among classical humanists: the school. Humanists of various kinds have always been interested in education; importantly, they often thought that life itself is a *school of virtue*. Self-cultivation is not simply a matter of autonomous judgments aimed at cultivating one's own garden, as Montaigne and Voltaire believed. It is also a form of learning and habituation, *paideia*, through patterns of spiritual discipline.[36] The image of the school articulates the place of freedom in the moral space of life in a way decidedly different than the theatre. Formation is not invention. Yet the metaphor of the school also stresses the social character of human existence rather than the solitude of the garden.[37] Discipline and practice are the means of self-overcoming on the way to the integration of life in community and tradition.

The importance of education runs deep among humanists. Classical Renaissance treatises were written on how best to educate a proper gentleman. Rabelais, the great Christian humanist and satirist, organizes much of his famous *Gargantua and Pantegruel* around the education of Gargantua, the giant. Through serious play, *serio ludere*, Rabelais sought to communicate, just as others of his age, truths about human existence and also, like Erasmus, Christian faith.[38] Later humanists too, like the Humboldt brothers in Berlin, were committed to education. In the American context, pragmatism was linked not only to humanism but also to a philosophy of education. "Life is," John Dewey writes, "a self-renewing process through action upon the environment." With respect to social life, "Education, in its broadest sense, is the means of this social continuity of life."[39]

The image of the school underscores the importance of formation and excellence, and also the transmission of social and even religious ideals and values. While the garden pictured human life as a process of cultivation, the school is a more social, less organic image of life. Erasmus, in his *Enchiridion Militis Christiani* (1503), saw the Christian life as spiritual warfare. Much later, Søren Kierkegaard imagined the Christian life as training or a drilling in Christian love. His famous *Training (Indøvelse) in Christianity* is edifying discourse meant to build up Christian existence through following the "pattern" of Christ who is the truth. Living in truth is a process of transmission and reduplication in oneself which demands training oneself.[40] Jews and Muslims have also written about discipline, practice, and spiritual struggle.

The image of the school with its educational discipline means that the proper aim of human existence is not the acquisition of knowledge for knowledge's sake, but, more deeply, to embody a moral or spiritual truth in one's life and community. One could also look at the metaphors of athletic training or spiritual warfare and how they help to complete the picture of life in the school. The image of the school links several basic humanistic values (character formation, ideals of excellence, cultural transmission, discipline of life through the use of reason) in order to grasp the meaning and purpose of human beings as "things in between." One is "in between" failure and excellence, discontinuity and transmission or heritage, chaos and the disciplined life in truth.

Around the image of the school one also confronts neohumanist rhetoric. The revision of humanism in this form centers not on "Being" (Heidegger) or the finality of the other (Todorov, Levinas), but on social forces beyond the self that fashion the self. Michel Foucault, while profoundly interested in self-fashioning, would see the metaphor of the school as a discourse for mechanisms of power, discipline, and punishment. Foucault's central focus in his early work was the way human beings are made "subjects," are subjugated, within the hidden workings of power that are the real forces in the world.[41] Some thinkers want to explore the idea of spiritual disciplines in the fashioning of the self, like Pierre Hadot does in his famous *Philosophy as a Way of Life*, but nevertheless a specific conception of freedom remains basic. The enterprise for these neohumanists is one of *self-fashioning* through the rigor of spiritual discipline, a school. Here, too, theological humanism will chart a related but different course. We will speak later of the formation of the cosmopolitical conscience in order to address forces working on the global scene.

Towards Theological Humanism

We have explored the basic convictions of classical humanism and also various images of human existence found among Western thinkers. Insofar as freedom names the distinctive human form of causality, and so our power, what is the nature and extent of our freedom? How does freedom relate to the incompleteness of human life and the struggle for integrity? Does freedom situate us within the wider compass of life on this planet or it is the very power to create worlds, as Vives and Pico seem to suggest? In light of the incredible extension of human power in a technological age and the threat of overhumanization in its various forms, what realm of value might limit the endless expansion of human power and so help us protect the fragile integrity of life on this little planet?

To imagine human beings as "things in between" in our age requires attention to the place, the locality, of human freedom in relation to other realms of life on this planet. Mary Midgley writes that,

> human freedom centres on being a creature able, in some degree, to act as a whole in dealing with its conflicting desires … Though it is only an endeavour, though the wholeness is certainly not given ready-made and can never be fully achieved, yet the integrative struggle to heal conflicts and to reach towards this wholeness is surely the core of what we mean by human freedom.[42]

The human struggle for wholeness, for integrity, situates us in the wider complex of life as well as amid conflicts among our desires.

Accounts of situated freedom have allowed for the emergence of what is now called neohumanism, intimations of which we have noted above. Neohumanist thinkers like Todorov, no less than Levinas, show that, ontologically considered, the "I" that is the goal of action includes the other human being, the finality of the "you." Autonomy is important, but the self is always situated with respect to the moral claim of the other and also the finality of the human community. Human beings exceed, overcome, or transcend their given existence in response to the human other, *and the human other alone*. The proper aim of life is the well-being of human beings within the bonds of existence on this earth. This is called lateral or inner-worldly transcendence. Here, too, there are differences among neohumanists important for theological humanism. Levinas, for instance, finds a trace of the divine in the encounter with the face of the other; Todorov denies the reality of the divine and insists on intrahuman goods and these goods alone.

In order to avoid overhumanization, must we think beyond "lateral transcendence," beyond intrahuman ends? Must we see that our inner-worldly relations are the prisms or traces for a relation to the divine? Does responsibility for the other human reveal what exceeds, transgresses, the kingdom of human power? The claim of the other person is thus an opening to a realm of value more extensive and intensive than intrahuman goods. The challenge is then to fashion a form of thought and way of life that respects and enhances the integrity of human existence within but not against other forms of life. In a word, can we show why inner-worldly neohumanism and the legacies of anti-humanism are finally inadequate as visions of the moral vocation of our lives? These positions, we hold, lead to a flattening of the world that misses the depth and reach of human existence. Theological humanism intensifies and widens the account of human transcendence in relation to the reality of the integrity of life. The space of the integrity of life as the fullness of being includes but also exceeds lateral transcendence. To make our case for that account is the challenge of the rest of this book.[43]

It is at this juncture that the symbolic and conceptual resources of a religious tradition function to articulate and respond to the plight that befalls human beings in a flattened world.[44] The religions have diagnostic and illuminative power to decode the complexity of human action and the space of life. Yet it must also be said that a theological humanist is suspicious of deploying any one master metaphor as sufficient to articulate the aim and purpose of life. A religious tradition as well as every human life is more complex than one root metaphor, say, a garden or school or theatre. Many metaphors are necessary and actually exist in a moral lexicon, while none alone exhausts the meaning of life and its worth. Theological humanism articulates a multidimensional perspective on human life through the use of a range of metaphors about freedom's place in the world.

The images we have traced in this chapter open reflection on the range of goods that taken together help to form the integrity of life. Like the image of the garden, human life is primordially situated in the realms of life manifest in terms of basic and natural goods (chapter 6). Yet with the metaphor of the school, human life and our struggle for the wholeness that is genuine freedom are profoundly social (chapter 7). There are social goods available to us only insofar as we engage in those practices necessary to form character and sustain communities. The metaphor of the theatre shows that human beings are not only participants in the realms of sentient life and profoundly social beings; we are also reflexive creatures whose self-understanding does in some fundamental way shape our existence (chapter 8). Through the metaphors charted, one can see that responsible freedom aims to respect and enhance a complex interaction of basic, natural, social, and reflexive goods in the struggle for integrity.

Of course, other metaphors are needed as well. Especially needed are metaphors of human transcendence (chapter 9). With contemporary neo-humanists, like Todorov or Levinas, the central revision theological humanism makes to traditional thought is to understand freedom in terms of responsibility with and for others. A theological humanist must show that insisting on radical transcendence does not and cannot detract from the pressing inner-worldly challenges people around the world now face. Only in that way do we avoid the abyss of hypertheism. True speaking about the divine aims to articulate realms of value beyond human preference and power; it seeks also to evoke a love of life rooted in the integrity of life. A theological humanist can only imagine that reach of value by drawing on the many ways of naming God, as well as images of the whole host of human responses to divine action found in a religious tradition.[45] A careful examination of the meaning of the ways of naming God is part and parcel of the enterprise of providing a complex vision of human transcendence within and not against the wider realms of life.

In this light, it is vital in the next chapter to chart the criticism of theism and its resources for thinking about the divine and human transcendence. In chapter 4 we will engage the logic of Christian humanism. Those inquiries will enable us to develop the idea of the integrity of life and its relation to the range of goods that orient freedom.

37

3

Thinking of God

This chapter is about theology – the ancient and constantly revised traditions which inquire about the meaning, truth, and goodness of religious beliefs and spiritual longings. Theology means "God-talk," speaking and reasoning (*logos*) about divine things (*theos*). The legacy of theology is mixed: the once-proud queen of the sciences now dwells at the margins of the academy and public life. Scholars in other fields rarely cite the writings of theologians in academic work. It was not always so. What has happened?

This chapter explores theism and theology in a way similar to the previous account of the humanistic imagination. We will do so by exploring some basic metaphors used to think about God in the history of Western thought. These metaphors not only clarify main options in theology but also hold some potential, when critically used, for the work of theological humanism about human transcendence and the claim, reality, and presence of the integrity of life. Yet we also want to isolate flaws and criticisms of theology and theism. The chapter thus has critical and constructive purposes.

The Plight of Theology

Contemporary theology is torn between two contending impulses. On one hand, we witness the proliferation in the Christian community of *churchly theologies*, in which theologians defend beliefs or practices handed down through their confessional communities. They take the creeds, dogmas, symbols, narratives, or practices of their church traditions as self-evident, authoritative, and exclusive points of contact with the divine. Churchly theologies easily reduce God to "my" or "our" God. They reject the modern demand to make general claims of meaning and truth. They do so not only on conservative, religious grounds, but sometimes also on highly sophisticated postmodern grounds.[1] Churchly theologies are content to remain within "neo-tribal" communities, affirming a "fideism of the faithful, the committed ones, in a world of possibilities."[2]

On the other hand, we see a profusion of radical *post-theistic theologies* (or *a/theologies*).[3] These theologians deconstruct supernatural and mythological beliefs or ritual practices of religious communities for the sake of liberating people from unjust prejudices and institutional power structures. Suspicious of unifying metanarratives which tyrannize human differences, these theologians embrace the autonomous power of critical interpretation. There are no unmediated points of contact with the divine. Nothing – neither the self's presence to itself in so-called immediate self-consciousness, nor God in some kind of religious or spiritual consciousness – can assume real presence. Religion, for them, is a social production, the effect of heterogeneous systems of discursive, technological, and institutional relations.[4]

The plight of theology trivializes it and renders it mute. The marginalization of the theologians in culture has consequences, however. The wider public is losing the ability to speak meaningfully about what is "divine" or of utmost importance and reality within a situation of endangerment to the entire life-system. Theological humanism proposes another way, and for two reasons. First, when churchly theologies and popes make openly exclusive claims ("There is no salvation outside the church," or "The only way to God is by accepting Jesus as your personal Savior"), they become forms of *hypertheism*: my faith and the divine are one and the same. They demand conformance of thought, belief, and action to the divine will as their own special community discerns it. Yet if every group, or individual, retreats into a "fideism of the faithful," an infinite regress opens up, dividing humanity into smaller units, each claiming to be the one true religion and selling its wares of salvation in the global marketplace. Truth is reduced to being truthful to one's sacred story, practice, or community (whether real or virtual), but with no possibility of understanding why *this* lifestyle (*this* religion) is true among others.

Second, when post-theistic a/theologies substitute unending critique for genuine theological thinking, they become forms of *overhumanization*. They celebrate the creative capacities of autonomous human beings by deconstructing what is considered sacred. Amid the wreckage, they testify to a negative presence – the presence of difference that instantiates ultimate undecidability. Undecidability reduces signs *of the sacred* to signs of systemic linguistic, political, technological, or social oppression. Divine nothingness

39

fails to make a normative claim on human life. It is a short step from the principle of undecidability to overt nihilism. The world is seen and experienced as enclosed and constantly reshaped by the shifting power alignments of human will, in which the highest values devalue themselves.

We need a way to articulate the claim of transcendence on human beings that reduces it neither to undecidability nor to "my" community. Most importantly, we need a way to understand the positive, substantive, and normative meaning of transcendence as it makes a claim on human lives within historical existence. Can we combine the insights of a religious community with the felt demand for universal justice and individual autonomy? "The integrity of life" provides the norm and ideal for so doing. That is the case we want to make.

We turn now to understand the dynamics of theological thinking in the Western Christian tradition in order to show both how the present dilemma arose and how theological humanism responds to it. This requires that we isolate metaphorical clusters of images used to speak and think about the divine, to practice theology.

Religion, Critique, and Beyond

Paul Ricoeur notes that it is "not regret for the sunken Atlantides that animates us, but hope for a re-creation of language. Beyond the desert of criticism, we wish to be called again."[5] Modern, critically minded human beings are aware of an original – that is, a structurally basic – religious consciousness ("the sunken Atlantides") as something that is meaningful and yet lost to them. People are aware of religious consciousness through myths, rituals, and traditions, through their memories of childhood wonder, and through fleeting moments of being caught up in the magical mentality of religion. People want the security of answers; religion seems to give them answers from a place far away from this one. Oddly, religious fundamentalism and much current churchly theology seems motivated by this longing for the sunken Atlantides.

The aim of theology is not to recover this lost mode of being in the world. To become a child again would mean to abandon the capacity to think and to make one's own judgments on the basis of critical principles. That is why many contemporary people are disgusted at the upsurge of fundamentalist religion. Theological thinking wishes to feel and experience the "call" of sacred powers "beyond the desert of criticism," but by interpreting, and thereby re-creating, the meaning and power of religious language in a post-critical or "second" naïveté that is reflective as well as responsive.[6] Genuine theology has always felt the twofold claim of *religion* and *critique* and has sought some way of reconciling, balancing, or even uniting them. Theology arises and undergoes changes in history precisely because of the dynamic interaction between religious consciousness and critical consciousness in human life.

Consider two poles of interaction. On some accounts, the fundamental characteristic of religious consciousness is the human capacity for immediate openness and receptivity to the real presence of sacred powers. Through a hierophany, as Mircea Eliade called it, the god or gods reveal how, *in illo tempore*, they brought forth a world. Reciting the stories of the gods and performing rituals re-creates the original time when the god or gods created the world and fixed proper human purposes like stars in the sky. Conversely, the basic trait of critical consciousness is the power of the human mind to suspend or interrupt the immediate receptivity to whatever appears as given and self-evident – including the sacred. Whereas religion takes its place within a given symbolic world, critique has the capacity to break direct, immediate participation in the given world.

The critical attitude asks, "How do I know that what appears to be divine truly is the divine?" Critique severs the connection between appearance and reality, the meaning expressed and the signified referent. Critique need not destroy religious consciousness. It can be held in check and assigned a subordinate role of organizing, prioritizing, and interpreting the meanings of religion without calling the sacred into question. However, when critique does unfold its full powers, as it does with the rise of modernity in the West, it challenges the idea of a supernatural agent (God) and ultimately makes it vanish. The price of critical reflection, when taken to its extreme forms, is the desacralization of the world. The sacred cosmos as a human dwelling place is lost; one is left with the "desert of criticism."

Religion and critique, taken in full, are incompatible when directed toward the appearing, sacred power. If I believe in the appearing god or sacred power, then I am religious, not critical, in my fundamental relation to reality. If, by contrast, I question whether the sacred power of religious belief is in fact what it purports to be and I answer "no," then I am being critical, not religious, in my stance toward existence. The conflict between religion and critique seems to force a choice between them, just as we see it in the opposition between churchly theology and post-theistic a/theology. Each is a form of theology. That is, each is a form of *second-order reflection* on religious belief and practice. However, the key word is "reflection." If "reflection" means "faithful mirroring" of divine appearances, then theology sides with religion and becomes its advocate, as in *churchly theology*. If, however, "reflection" means "truthful explaining" of divine appearances, then theology sides with critique and becomes the prosecutor of religion as many *a/theologies* contend. Theology today is largely divided between these two incompatible poles on a spectrum of possibilities.

Theological humanism proposes a way of thinking beyond the current impasse, one that is appropriate to our context of endangerment to life. One conceives God in and through the idea and norm of "the integrity of life." On the way to that proposal we want to review three metaphorical clusters which organize much theological thinking in the Western Christian tradition: God as heavenly deity, God as light of the world, and God as not God. These metaphors function in theology much like the images of human existence isolated before in the legacy of humanism (garden, school, theatre). The first two metaphors are expressions of Christian theism. The third cluster is the form of post-theistic theology. We can find oscillating combinations of religious and critical consciousness within these clusters.[7] Beyond the criticism of these metaphors, we seek to reclaim insights about the presence, claim, and transcendence of the integrity of life in human existence.

God as Heavenly Deity

With the metaphorical cluster of God as heavenly deity, theology takes the form of biblical interpretation. It came to be known as revealed theology. The metaphor that God is a heavenly deity, a divine person above and beyond the world he created and in whose image human beings were made, derives directly from the biblical narrative. Within this cluster, theology begins with religious consciousness, but responding to the divine as a supernatural agent, a God. In its reception over time this form of theology incorporates increasing amounts of critical consciousness.

One of the early examples of Christian theology – the Apostles' Creed – exhibits picture-thinking (*Vorstellungensdenken*, as Hegel called it) in narrative form:

> I believe in God, the Father almighty, creator of the heavens and earth; and in Jesus Christ, his only Son, our Lord; who was conceived by the Holy Spirit and born of the Virgin Mary; suffered under Pontius Pilate, was crucified, died and was buried; he descended to hell. On the third day he was raised into heaven, and sits at the right hand of God the Father almighty; from where he will come to judge the living and the dead. I believe in the Holy Spirit; in the

42

holy catholic church; the communion of saints; the forgiveness of sins; the resurrection of the flesh and eternal life.[8]

In this creedal expression, critical thinking is at the service of religion. Critique extracts the articles of faith from the New Testament story in the form of a synopsis. Critical thought prioritizes the episodes of the larger story and orders them into a new creedal unity. Jump ahead now to the late Middle Ages.

Martin Luther, the great reformer, clearly belongs in the metaphorical cluster of biblical personalism. Luther's theology arose within a context of anxiety and guilt caused in part by the breakdown of the "protective unity of the religiously guided medieval culture" and the rise of an educated middle class in the larger cities.[9] Luther was not alone among religiously serious people who could no longer assume that confessions at Mass in reciting the Lord's Prayer ("Forgive us our trespasses, as we forgive those who trespass against us"), or any other religious observance, would suffice for forgiveness from a righteous God. For Luther, the thought of the righteousness of God was terrifying and brought him to despair.[10] He knew that the just law of God ("Be perfect, as the Lord your God is perfect!") could not be fulfilled by any human, for anything we do is tainted with sin. He was haunted and hunted by the fear of facing God as both just lawgiver and judge, with eternal life hanging in the balance.[11] Luther's readings of Paul's Letter to the Romans 1:17 – "the righteous shall live by faith" – saved him from the despair of guilt and made him feel as though he had been born again. He placed the dynamics of justification, which comes by faith through the unmerited grace of God, at the heart of theology.

Luther's followers expressed the doctrine of justification through faith by grace alone by imagining a divine–human courtroom drama.[12] The accused is rightfully judged guilty and condemned to hell. To the astonishment of the condemned, he or she then hears God the judge add, "yet forgiven" – not on account of one's good works, but in recognition of faith in Christ, who stands by the sinner as substitute. Luther's theology is by no means devoid of critique. He brought criticism against the abuses of the Church and its "Babylonian captivity" to the papacy in Rome and the selling of indulgences. He railed against the dependence of scholastic theology on Greek philosophy and insisted on a return to biblical sources (*sola scriptura*). Luther, of course, never questioned the authority of the Bible as God's Word. With the modern period, however, criticism arrived with full power, thanks in no small part to Johann Semler (1725–91).

Johann Semler was an early proponent of historical criticism of the Bible. He attacked the possibility of using biblical revelation to provide a solid basis for theology and so endangered the vision of God as heavenly deity. In his *Treatise on the Free Investigation of the Canon* (1771), Semler read the Bible as a collection of documents in the history of religions, not as straightforward divine revelation.[13] By analyzing the meanings, significations, and references of words within reconstructed historical contexts, Semler identified authors of the biblical books and showed how different books belonged to different social contexts and periods of history.[14] The result of his historical criticism was the breakdown of any literal identification of biblical texts with the word of God. Once the distinction is rigorously drawn between the author and God, no historical reasons can re-identify the biblical text and the word of God. In what sense, then, could the Bible be considered as "revelation"?

Semler, in the style of critique, made revelation dependent on the free judgment of the human mind. The human mind possesses an original, universal revelation, which consists in the ability to determine whether something purporting to be the word of God is in fact what it claims to be. For Semler, the criteria are these: (1) whether the material content of the purported revelation corresponds to the rational, moral idea of God, and (2) whether the language of revelation has the capacity to transform ethically the one who receives it.[15] True revelation, he reasoned, elevates its hearer to a higher level of ethical existence than he or she would otherwise have achieved. Semler retained an openness to a religious presence – an original revelation of goodness – which both respects historical differences among presentations of possible revelation and provides a critical norm for free judgment. This universal revelation of goodness, however, trumps any particular religious revelation to which it must submit as its norm.

Following Semler, radical critical thought exploded. Ludwig Feuerbach and later Sigmund Freud, among others, developed the notion that the idea/image of God as heavenly deity is a projection of human consciousness. They argued that because theological thinking cannot refer to supernatural things, since such things exceed human knowing, theology must be a coded language that is really about something else. For Feuerbach, religious consciousness is normal self-consciousness alienated from itself and projected in objective form onto the infinite background of human reason, will, and affection. "*Theology is anthropology*: in other words, the object of religion, which in Greek we call *theos* and in our language God, expresses nothing other than the essence of man; man's God is nothing other than the deified essence of man."[16] What religion views as divine is actually human nature. Religion can be reduced to "the dream of the human mind." To awaken from the dream of religion is to "cease to be the victim, the plaything, of all those hostile powers which from time immemorial have employed and are still employing the darkness of religion for the oppression of mankind."[17]

Freud's critique focused on the harshness of human life, given the "majestic, cruel and inexorable" forces of nature, which rise up against us and expose our weakness and helplessness.[18] According to Freud, the mental assets of civilization, such as art, cultural ideals, and economic wealth, offer some meager but real psychological satisfactions to compensate for instinctual renunciations. By contrast, the idea/image of God and the practice of religion offer nothing that is psychologically beneficial. Freud purported to unmask biblical personalism as the result of a cunning psychological strategy designed to gain consolation and protection in face of the hostile powers of nature. On the basis of an infantile prototype, we humanize the forces of nature into a father-image, in hopes that we can appease the deity as we appeased our own fathers when we were children. Theism constitutes an *illusion*, in that it expresses a neurotic wish-fulfillment as one of "the oldest, strongest and most urgent wishes of mankind."[19] People believe in God because they *want* it to be true in order to make life tolerable for them in their suffering and weakness.

In the upsurge of critique in such figures as Semler, Feuerbach, and Freud, theism turns into humanism. The destructive work of critique, in negating theism, serves the positive purpose of setting free an authentic human life that forms its own goals in self-determination. The last word was not yet spoken, however. Biblical personalism does not simply vanish under the withering eye of criticism. It finds new ways of asserting its fundamental religious vision.

In the twentieth century, Karl Barth's theology is the most spectacular example of a post-critical form of biblical personalism. The metaphor of God as heavenly deity is denied in the form of a divine person, yet nonetheless affirmed in the form of the "wholly other" deity. He was a leading figure in the post-World War I critique of the "liberal theology" of the nineteenth century, which intended to accommodate critique by reinterpreting Christian beliefs in culturally acceptable idioms. For Barth's generation, a historical epoch had ended: "a bourgeois age, which had united faith in technical progress with the confident expectation of a secured freedom and a civilizing perfectionism."[20] Barth saw liberal theology as an idolatry of the human writ very large.

Can a non-idolatrous theology survive the full force of critique? Barth answered the question with his dialectical theology.[21] Having appropriated the historical criticism of the Bible, he could not turn to the Bible as proof text. Instead, he accepted the idolatry of every theology and religion, saying, "Only God himself can speak of God." God's word is always a "No" to human words that purport to speak of God. When the congregation gathers to hear God's word, what the theologian can do is to recognize that he or she cannot speak for God, while holding open the possibility that human words might nonetheless, impossibly, be heard and received as God's own word. The theologian keeps theological questions alive, while giving God the glory for overturning God's own "No" to theology in the event of hearing God speak.

Dialectical theology has a problem in this so-called solution. It is one shared by many postmodern forms of thought. In saying "No" to theology and religion, in negating their pretensions to say anything about God, dialectical theology says "No" to itself. To be consistent, Barth must deny that even his own denial of a non-idolatrous theology can instantiate a non-idolatrous theology. He does not provide a criterion for determining whether or not God speaks in distinction from human words. His claim that to hear God speak is an "impossible possibility" must issue from some basis, which he never makes clear. That basis can only be a new biblical personalism, in which God as heavenly deity, now pictured as "wholly other" to any human image or idea, nonetheless chooses to speak and to be heard. Barth's biblical personalism is evident in his preserving the language of the Bible as the one place where God might be heard in God's own voice.[22] It asserts the claim of God on human existence.

Following Barth, theology grounded in the metaphorical cluster of God as heavenly deity tends to retreat into *churchly theology* in which the hand of God sanctifies some religious phenomenon, such as the Bible, the community, church practice, etc. Neo-tribalism is the result, even when churchly theology embraces postmodern theories in order to avoid the critical demands of modernity.

God as Light of the World

A second metaphorical cluster in Western Christian theology has been important: God as light of the world. This cluster focuses on the metaphysical forms of theology, which prospered in the Roman Catholic Church, and, whether in Catholic or in purely philosophical forms, became known as "natural theology." The metaphor of God as light of the world captures the immediate, religious openness to a universal religious symbol of divine light.

In *The Republic*, Plato's Socrates distinguishes between changing, mutable *things* that exist, and the eternal, immutable *forms* of those things. How is it possible for us to know these things *as* the kind of things they are (which we do – we can identify this thing as a chair or a dog)? We can do so because the thing appears to us as an instance of its form; the eternal form is the condition of the intelligibility of a thing. The form makes it possible to say, "this is a chair." The form is the light in which the mind's eye conceives what the physical eyes perceive *as* the kind of thing it is. The eternal world of forms inhabits and also grounds the changing world of appearances.

Since forms imply a standard of goodness as perfect correspondence ("participation" or "imitation") between appearance and reality, the form of the good is the highest form and the "ultimate object of knowledge": "the end of all endeavour, the object on which every heart is set."[23] When called on to give an account of the good, Socrates says, "I'm afraid it's beyond me, and if I try I shall only make a fool of myself and be laughed at."[24] Indeed, the form of the good, as first principle, cannot be defined, although we use it in making judgments of value and worth. Accordingly, Socrates fashions similes and analogies to show what the good might be like. He begins with the simile of the sun. Just as the experience of seeing something requires not only eyes endowed with the power to see and something to be seen, but also a "third element," the light of the sun, so the experience of understanding something requires a mind endowed with intelligence, something to be understood, and a third thing – the form of the good.[25] Here we have the classical reference point for metaphysical theology and its metaphorical cluster of God as light of the world.

Consider Augustine, one of the most important theologians in Christian history. In *Soliloquies*, the basic form of thinking is Platonic (or neo-Platonic).[26] Augustine wants to know God and the soul, and reason (*logos*) addresses him as the interface between the two. In knowledge something transcends us, so the goal of knowledge is somehow already present at the start; it needs to be brought into clarity. There is, he admits, no necessity in sensory experience, so he negates that form of experience in terms of providing knowledge of how God and the soul necessarily are. Only through intellectual knowledge can one know how things necessarily have to be; we know the flux only in light of eternal realities, which are in the mind of God. Human thinking has an intrinsic obligation to the highest standards – truth and goodness – and so the human thinker stands in the presence of God as he or she reflects these standards in thinking and doing.

By the time of Thomas Aquinas in the thirteenth century, the metaphor of God as light began to shift its emphasis from the pervasive sense of the "one in the many" (the being of all entities, which is truth or goodness) to a more determinate sense of the "one above all else" (the highest and supreme being).[27] In his "five ways" of proving the existence of God, Thomas adopts Aristotle to argue for God as "uncaused cause" or "first mover" of the created world.[28] He understands the world, and everything in it, as an effect of its ultimate cause or ground. Thomas argues backwards from the effect to its ultimate cause in demonstrating that God exists. The "first" way begins with the self-evident experience of our senses that things are moving or changing.[29] He defines motion with Aristotle as the reduction of something from potentiality to act. Since something cannot arise from nothing, the change from potency to act can only come about through something that already possesses that actuality as a mode of being. "Thus a fire, which is actually hot, makes wood, which is potentially hot, to be actually hot, thus changing and altering it." An infinite regress of movers is inconceivable, else nothing could have started anything moving and there would consequently be no motion. We must think the necessity of a prime or first mover that is not itself moved by anything and is the source of all movement, to avoid denying the evidence of our senses that things are in fact moving. The final step of the argument is to identify the first mover with God: "everyone understands that this is God."

This kind of formal, metaphysical reasoning from empirical experience to the ultimate principle entails a critique of Platonism. With the infusion of Aristotle, thinking moves toward the autonomous investigation of the natural world. Philosophy and science will follow this path toward independence from theology. So, the metaphysics of Thomas appears to have a tenuous connection to religious consciousness. This is not true. Just as the created world points to God as the effect of an uncaused cause, so does the rational mind of human beings and its functions. The *mind* (as principle of all mental activity), *knowing* (involving speaking and thinking), and *love* (as the act of volition which unites mind and knowing) are structural vestiges of the Trinity: God the Father, the Son, and the Holy Spirit, respectively.[30] The capacity to do metaphysics is given by God as a sacred trust and a sign of God's being.

Immanuel Kant brought critical thinking in the eighteenth century to a new level in his *Critique of Pure Reason* (1781), which is a rigorous measurement of the scope and limits of reason by reason itself. This critique delivered the death blow to metaphysical theology. It gave a major push to move from a world whose structure and laws were preexisting and immutable givens for members of society, to a world wherein one could discover its nature and define its norms. The key fault in metaphysical thinking is that it substitutes a necessity of thinking (we must think an unmoved mover) for the necessity of experience in knowing.

According to Kant's critique, knowledge cannot dispense with the element of experience. Knowledge is the synthesis of an experienced element (the concretely given "intuition," or perceived particular within time and space) with an intellectual element (the abstractly conceived thought or "concept").[31] Human minds can and do have knowledge of empirical objects, when our intuitions of them are subsumed under the correct concepts. It is even possible to have knowledge of the pure (*a priori*) categories of the understanding, such as substance and causality, because they in turn refer to forms of intuitions of time and space, which fall under them. The idea of God, however, is neither an empirical concept nor a pure category of the understanding; it is a regulative *ideal* of pure reason. God as supreme being (the "sum-total of all possibility" and the "supreme and complete material condition of the possibility of all that exists") is a necessary thought – the ultimate condition of the possibility of knowledge. "God" supplies reason with an indispensable standard of perfection, intrinsic to thinking itself, thereby enabling reason to measure both quality and defect. Its necessary, regulative use is to direct the understanding towards the goal of the systematic unity and completeness of knowledge. "This unity is *the criterion of the truth* of its (reason's) rules."[32] However, knowledge of whether God exists or not is quite impossible for human beings. "Its objective reality cannot indeed be proved, but also cannot be disproved."[33] Metaphysics tries to dodge the lack of any possible experienced element in connection with the idea of God through its appeal to logical necessity.

G. W. F. Hegel attempted to revise metaphysics beyond the Kantian critique in the new garb of absolute idealism. To do so, Hegel reconceived the infinite as the negation of the fundamental opposition within finitude, the opposition between finite subject and finite object.[34] In knowing or experiencing of being, a finite self relates herself *to* something in the finite world, while distinguishing herself *from* it. The subject is defined as *not* an object. According to Hegel, the absolute is the negation of this negation, or the absolute ground or ultimate identity of the identity and difference between subject and object. Cultural and religious history could be explained on the basis of the dialectical logic of the absolute's self-actualization in time. And "God's" self-embodiment in history is also the elevation of human consciousness to "absolute knowledge." However, Hegel's project of modern theology did not quiet the critical question. It had problems of its own.

Ernst Troeltsch pinpointed one problem. Human thinking is historically conditioned in a thorough-going way. Thinking has no position from which

49

to grasp the absolute. Hegel understood the historical dimension of spirit; he did not grasp the temporality of his own thinking. From a different direction, Søren Kierkegaard exposed a weakness in Hegel's system, asking: even if we could think the absolute, is God the absolute? Or is God different from the absolute? Hegel failed to understand the infinite qualitative difference between God and being (the absolute). These problems shattered Hegel's idealist and speculative answer to the problem of how to think God beyond the collapse of Platonic-Aristotelian metaphysics. What was left but nihilism? – the condition exposed by Nietzsche in which "the highest values devaluate themselves. The aim is lacking: 'why' finds no answer."[35] "Truth" breaks down into "values," posited as our own. As Nietzsche's madman says, "God is dead, and we have killed him."

The horrors of the twentieth century – gas chambers, rape camps, systematic tyranny – were the end of most forms of theism as the right way to think of the divine. What kind of God could allow this world? The breakdown of metaphysical theology into nihilism leads to theologies which accept the loss, the death of God in critical thought. Theologians like Thomas J. J. Altizer and Mark C. Taylor affirm the death of God as the fulfillment and completion of theology itself. The death of God is God's own act which nonetheless, according to Altizer, makes authentic faith possible in the form of faith in a God who is wholly immanent in the profane, secular world.[36] The light of the world has become the world; the visible has engulfed the invisible. The presence of God is known as divine absence.

God as Not God

We have traced how the tension between religion and critical thought has divided theology. These tensions mirror in theism the flaws and tensions in humanism that drive towards overhumanization. The internal dynamics of biblical personalism have tended toward neo-tribalism, whereas the metaphysical theologies have tended toward nihilism in a/theologies. In order to avoid these extremes many attempts have been made to articulate a "postcritical equivalent of the precritical hierophany."[37] They cluster around a third and paradoxical metaphor: God as not God.[38]

Theologies within this metaphorical cluster accept the results of both historical and rational critique; they appeal neither to biblical nor to metaphysical proofs for the existence of God. However, the name "God" can still resound with precritical associations through the metaphors of heavenly deity and of light of the world. In order to do so, theologians point to a dimension of human experience which satisfies the expectations aroused by the name God. Theologies in this metaphorical cluster attempt to unite while distinguishing extreme forms of religious consciousness, on one hand, and critical consciousness, on the other.

One twentieth-century theologian in this last metaphorical cluster is Paul Tillich. He labored to transcend the opposition between the personal God of Christian theism and the nothing of nihilism in his idea of the "God beyond the God of theism." Theology for him is the systematic *correlations* between two independent and distinct approaches to ultimate meaning and reality. On one hand, Tillich identifies existential questions – such as "what is the meaning of being?" – which are based on the shock of possible non-being. These existential questions are analyzed in order to show how they are rooted in the "structure of being," which is the "self-world ontological structure." Existential questions manifest the self-transcending nature of human experience as both aware of a potential infinity in its striving toward ultimate truth and goodness and yet at the same time aware of its finitude, death. In asking the question of the meaning of being, humans ask about the ultimate ground of the self-world structure, but they find the question to be unanswerable. "Reason looks into its own abyss … Only revelation can answer this question."[39]

On the other hand, Tillich describes religious symbols, such as the symbols of God as heavenly deity or as light of the world, as having been coined in response to a revelation of the holy and preserved within the religious communities. Religious symbols "participate" in their referents when they evoke ultimate concern. The symbol "God" participates in its referent – the same referent which is asked about in the existential question – namely "being-itself," the ground of being and non-being, the depth and abyss of the self-world ontological structure. As Tillich says, "The being of God is Being-Itself," i.e., the meaning of being.[40] The symbol "God" answers the existential question "what is the meaning of being?" when it empowers the questioner with the courage to be in spite of the threats of non-being. Faith is the state of being grasped by "God" as a matter of ultimate concern.[41]

Theology finds then a way beyond the "desert of criticism" without a regression to the "sunken Atlantides." The criterion for truth in religious symbols is whether or not the symbol expresses the ultimate (by enabling faith) and expresses its own lack of ultimacy (by recognizing that as a finite entity, it is *not* God). For Tillich, the Christian symbol of the cross is objectively as well as subjectively true. Jesus is the Christ only through the cross, as the "defeated Messiah." This reflexive symbol successfully unites religion and critique when it empowers the courage to be in the face of the threat of non-being, nothingness. In those events, Tillich was even willing to speak of "ecstatic humanism," a humanism in which the self is grasped by a power beyond itself and enabled to endure in life.

Other thinkers have sought to think beyond the opposition between religion and critique. Feminist and womanist theologians, black and Latin American liberation theologians, as well as particularized theologies from Africa and Asia, have used various and different critical methods to combat the sexism, classism, and racism of traditional theistic belief and theology.[42] The name "God" is connected with some mediated experience that is literally not God – that "not God" is the metaphorical predication of God. So, the God who liberates the poor or empowers women is not poverty or "womanhood" itself but is manifest in the experience of liberation from oppression. Similarly, the Jewish philosopher Emmanuel Levinas has undertaken a similar project within his tradition. The God of ontology, the God of traditional theism, is not God. God is only disclosed as a "trace" within the encounter with the face of another human being. But God is also not the face. God is a trace. This conception of lateral transcendence, as we called it before, pushes Levinas's "humanism of the other" in the direction of theological humanism. The finality of the other, the demand to care for the other, opens a trace of the divine. In all these cases, the reality of God requires, paradoxically, that one negate traditional theism in light of what respects, enhances, and liberates human life.

God and the Integrity of Life

Theological humanism is mindful of the past. Yet the present situation is different from previous generations. The pressing concerns are different ones. Overriding other concerns is the fact that human and non-human life stand under extreme endangerment in myriad forms. People are too often reacting to the seriousness of the threat in dangerous ways, which we have called hypertheism and overhumanization. Theological humanism resists both of these tendencies, while understanding the force of their appeal. Our intention is to incorporate some of the deepest positive meanings and intentions from both theology and humanism into a new dynamic vision. We are changing the terms of the debate.

Theology must now begin with a paradoxical recognition: critique is an expression of human freedom, yet, when pursued to its end, critique destroys the order of highest values (enshrined in the idea and images of God) that give meaning and substance to freedom. Critique thus deprives freedom of its proper motivation toward noble and true ends, even as it actualizes freedom. Conversely, theistic claims about "God" too easily thwart human freedom when they deny the challenge of critique. Religious authority and rational critique seem in conflict. Can one engage in unrestrained critique while preserving conviction and commitment to God? Consider a possibility.

St. Anselm of Canterbury said in his *Proslogion* that theology is "faith seeking understanding."[43] In understanding something, I comprehend what or who something is by relating it to appropriate concepts. In believing someone, I am open to and receive an image and feeling of who someone is when I hear her or his words. Understanding is the mind's act of grasping an object as it is — understanding aims at *truth* (although we can often get it wrong!). Believing is the act of responding to another subject as she or he addresses me — believing aims at *trust* (although we can often be deceived!). In much traditional theology, "being" is the ultimate object which I understand in understanding anything at all: when I understand this tree or that place, I understand the meaning of "being" in particular existence. Similarly, in traditional Christian thought, "God" is the ultimate subject to which I respond (i.e., am open, believe) in being open to anyone at all: when I respond to this voice or to that presence, I am ultimately believing in "God."[44] The question then becomes for traditional theology: What is the relation between "God" and "being"?

One possibility is to say that in some important sense "God *is* being." God, considered objectively, is the power of being; being, considered subjectively, is the expression or act of God. This position collapses into the metaphor of God as light of the world. The other possibility is to say that God is *not* being. There is always a gap, an infinite qualitative distinction, between them. God is a heavenly deity or God is thought through claims about the gift of love that exceeds being.[45] Dividing these two lines of theology is disagreement about whether God or being is the superior term. The dispute is intelligible: understanding and believing are two different forms through which humans relate to surrounding environments. It *is* possible to understand something without believing it, and it *is* possible to believe something without understanding it, although these forms are never completely independent of each other. The discourse of theology, past and present, spins around these matters.

For theological humanism, what is important is that human all-too-human capacities for understanding and believing are always and intrinsically connected in spite of their differences. Human understanding begins with a gift to the creative imagination: someone feels a sense of wonder

53

and believes that there is something there to understand. Understanding also has an inner tendency to grow toward believing, as we come to trust to what we understand. Likewise, believing begins with someone or something announcing itself to me. Believing similarly has an inner tendency to increase in understanding, as we grow in understanding of the one to whom we respond.

Precisely because of this interconnectedness, theological humanism does *not* want to abstract the ultimate objects of understanding and believing ("Being" and "God"), nor does it want to get caught up in the debate about how the symbol "God" relates to the concept "Being." The focus is on the human dimension of these interconnected activities of understanding and believing. The metaphoric clusters explored above have it wrong either because they presuppose this distinction of God and being or try to surmount it and thereby unwittingly endorse it. The debates concerning God and being lead us away from the pressing issue that defines our time: the endangerment to life, both human and non-human. Focus and concern should be on the integral relation of understanding and believing, as denoting both the elemental capacities of a living, experiencing creature, and the forms of the human organism's relations to the social and natural environments around it. For theological humanism, to think theologically is to relate both the form of thinking and the object we are thinking about to the integrity of life. This insight unites in a new way religious consciousness and critical consciousness into "third-way thinking." We seek to reclaim the claim, the presence and reality of the divine found in the various metaphorical clusters, but now through the idea and norm of the integrity of life. How so?

The integrity of life is an idea and norm that guides and measures thinking and doing in the context of endangerment to life. It gathers together the metaphorical clusters, again recognizing them *as metaphors*. First, the integrity of life has the status of a *critical ideal* that is an ingredient in thinking and doing itself, that guides them, and that imposes a freely accepted *claim* on them. In this regard, the integrity of life participates in the metaphorical cluster of God as light of the world. We see the ideal as the *light* that makes judgments of value and worth possible and that directs our thinking toward a truth that can never be possessed. The integrity of life gathers together the sense that the form of the good (Plato), divine truth (Augustine), or uncaused cause (Thomas) assumes for us when submitted to critique. For us, the ideal is an indispensable standard, regulative in use and not, as Kant saw, an object of knowledge, even as, we insist against Kant, it points to reality and how we can and ought to inhabit the world.

At the same time, we are not tempted to convert the *ideal* of the integrity of life into an infinite substance or a highest being, a "god," nor to reduce this ideal to nothingness under conditions of nihilism. The integrity of life evokes and invites unlimited critique, setting into play permanent questions. What does the integrity of life mean here and now? How do we know what counts as "integrity" in life? In the nature of the case, this open debate and argumentation directs itself to local appearances of the integrity of life. The ideal dimension of the claim naturally seeks actualization in the concrete situations of existence.

Second, the ideal or norm has the status of a sacred power or *religious* presence. Human beings find themselves confronted and claimed by sacred powers precisely in the specific contexts of the struggles and joys of their lives. What counts as a sacred power today? It is the appearance – the incarnation – of the integrity of life in stories of courageous or creative individuals or communities, in the sight of an integral ecosystem, in the experience of truthfulness in a loved one's death, or in the wholeness of a perfect symphony or novel. The visible can bear the invisible, we might say, without reduction or separation. In principle, anything whatsoever can strike us with the claim of the integrity of life as a concrete and local event, even when we see the opposite in injustice or falsehood that affronts us and demands that life *should not* be this way. This religious arousal of a sense of ultimate significance in this time and place also carries with it an absolute claim to the integrity of life universally speaking. Just as a river seeks the sea, the local, religious claim in one person's life expands to encompass a commitment to the integrity of life as such. Yet the claim of integrity, the call of conscience, arises in and through our actual encounters with and presence before others.

The demand of the integrity of life is formulated in the imperative of responsibility: *in all actions and relations respect and enhance the integrity of life before God.*[46] That claim, explored in more detail later, is an absolute one on our lives which engages freedom and summons critical thinking. In saying so, we critically reclaim the tradition of biblical personalism in theology, running from the early creeds to Luther and Barth. God as heavenly deity demands perfection, as the Lord God is perfect; and he grants forgiveness, recognizing purity of heart and constancy of faith. God's word is the negation of our word. From this tradition, we learn that the claim of the integrity of life is sovereign over other things and ideas.[47] Mindful of the history of theology, however, we are not tempted to take any one image of God as somehow exclusive and authoritative.

Theological humanism holds together the dimensions of the claim of the integrity of life. By doing so, we unite religion and critique in third-way thinking. This mode of thought allows us to gather together the metaphoric clusters explored above and to use them constructively, critically, and yet also beyond the desert of criticism. All domains of life, in different scales and scopes, can play the role of religion, if and when something strikes the imagination, will, and mind with the experience of the holy, the absolutely good. The *reality* of the integrity of life is ubiquitous and ever present. It can appear anywhere, at any time, to anyone. In this way, we avoid tendencies toward neo-tribalism, while encouraging communities to flourish by submitting their religious beliefs and practices to the norm of the integrity of life.

In the next two chapters, we will explore more deeply what we mean by the integrity of life and how it appears in different dimensions of life, beginning with a tradition dear to our hearts, namely, the legacy of Christian humanism.

4

The Logic of Christian Humanism

The 'Third Man'

The present chapter is a bridge in two important senses. First, it connects the two preceding chapters on humanism and theology and gathers together the metaphors we have been exploring mindful of the legacy of criticism. The chapter does so with respect to the historical roots of theological humanism in Christian thought and life, which is admittedly the tradition we know best and which we inhabit. Drawing together a set of thinkers, not all of whom would call themselves humanists, we want to show that "Christian humanism" articulates a form of human existence which bridges different ways of thought and life. That bridge was forged throughout the ages among Christian thinkers who linked biblical faith and philosophy, theology and humanism, religion and critique, into a living synthesis. The Christian humanist is a kind of "third man," at once a "cultivated Christian" and a "believing Greek." The "third man," we submit, is "ourselves."[1]

Second, this chapter points forward toward the fuller elaboration of theological humanism and its focus on the integrity of life. "Third-way thinking," as we call it, carries us beyond Christian humanism, without abandoning it, into a new option, namely, theological humanism. Christian humanism limits itself to Christian resources in combination with the Greco-Roman traditions; theological humanism is another step of humanistic and religious transformation in and through religious resources, but with respect to the integrity of life.

Most Christian humanists agree with the ideals and images of humanism we have explored so far in this book, but they also transform them in accord with Christian faith and learning. Christ is the incarnate heavenly deity and also the light of the world who has come into the world (cf. John 1:1ff.). The Church as the body of Christ in the world is the *school* in which Christian existence is to be trained and disciplined. The *garden* is the human soul that must be cultivated to flower in the love of God. The *theatre* of the world is much more the theatre of God's glory wherein God's goodness as the light of the world, not just human beings, appears under many "masks," hidden, as it were, on the world's stage. In a similar way the basic humanistic aim and ideal of human flourishing is transformed in the hands of Christian humanists, often in paradoxical ways.

If our concern was purely historical, we would explore specific Christian humanists and the relations among them. Our aim is constructive and not just historical. Under what ideas or rules or norms could Christians use and yet transform the humanistic legacy, thus connecting religion with critique? Our tactic will be to specify what we judge to be the necessary inner *logic* of Christian humanism and to illustrate it with reference to important historical figures.[2] This tactic is especially helpful because it will enable us to show in the following chapter how the idea of the integrity of life is an appropriate bridge concept in the move from Christian humanism in an exclusive sense to theological humanism and our contemporary situation threatened by overhumanism and hypertheism.

This logic of Christian humanism on our understanding has three parts: a claim about the intimate relation between human existence and the divine; a standard for correct thinking about the divine; and, finally, an understanding of how the divine-human relation sustains the highest good. These are, as we will see, closely bound together in the thought of most Christian humanists; they will be held together in theological humanism around the idea of the *integrity of life*. Even the whole constellation of ideas, as shown below, forms its own distinctive perspective on human life. Granting that claim for now, it will help if we consider the elements in turn.

A Capacity for the Divine

In the classical Christian formulation, the human capacity for a relation to the divine is conceived in terms of a connection between true self-knowledge and the love of God. The idea finds its philosophical roots in Plato, but continues through history. St. Augustine, in his *Confessions* but also in *On the Trinity*, found a trace of the Trinity, the distinctly Christian conception of God, in the self. Further, he insisted that, "When I recognize myself, I recognize you!" In his treatise *On True Religion*, he wrote, "Go not outside of yourself, but return within yourself, for truth resides in the inner part of man." God is the inner illumination of the mind, which propels the self beyond itself into the divine. God is the light of the world reflected in the human soul.

This idea can be easily misunderstood. It has rightly been criticized by theologians when it is taken to mean that there is an easy link between "me and my God." God is not a projection of the self and its wants. Many criticisms of humanism have rightly attacked this point, claiming that humanism reduces the divine good to the human good, as Feuerbach advocated. Humanism, even Christian humanism, thereby becomes a form of anthropocentrism because everything, including God, is valued in relation to human flourishing.[3] This makes God into an image of the self or at least a servant of human desires for happiness. That was not Augustine's point. His idea was that by "an ascetic discipline, one ascends in the scale of reason, receiving illumination not from that Platonic anticipation, the Form of the Good, but from God. The illuminated mind is enabled to choose rightly between the various objects of desire which confront it."[4]

This idea of a human capacity for relation to God was made by other classical Christian thinkers as well. Erasmus, for instance, claims in his *Enchiridion Militis Christiani* (1503), that God simply is the life of the human soul. Calvin opens *The Institutes of the Christian Religion* (1535), easily the most comprehensive statement of Protestant faith in the Reformation era, with the claim that true and sound wisdom consists of knowledge of God and knowledge of self. He went on to claim that these two are bound together so closely that it is difficult to say which brings forth the other. Does knowledge of God lead to right self-understanding? Is the inverse the case? God is always nearer to us than we are to ourselves. Calvin insisted that "it is beyond dispute that the human spirit possesses through natural instinct a sense of the Deity."[5] He called this the *sensus divinitatis* and related it to conscience.

However, Calvin was aware that this sense of the divine was vague as well as "fleeting and vain." The human imagination is a factory of idols, driven by fear, guilt, and anxiety into fabricating and worshipping idolatrous images rather than the true God. The sense of the divine can be the engine of idolatry just as much as it testifies to a bond between the human spirit and the divine spirit. The doubleness or ambiguity of the "sense of the divine," that it testifies to the human capacity for a relation to God and yet is also fleeting, vain, and even distorted, is important in Christian humanism.

This claim about the relation of God and self continued into the modern Western world among theologians who would not call themselves Christian humanists in a precise sense. John Wesley, who insisted on vital, living faith, proclaimed that "true religion, or a heart right towards God and man, implies happiness as well as holiness ... [T]he Spirit of God bearing witness with the spirit of a Christian, that he is 'a child of God.'"[6] Friedrich Schleiermacher, reformed theologian and the great translator of Plato, claimed that the immediate self-consciousness is a testimony to one's relation to the divine. Despite the dangers of "subjectivism," later theologians made virtually the same point. The American theologian H. Richard Niebuhr argued that "God" is the center of value around which the self in its relation to others comes to be as a self.[7] Granting the fault and fallibility that riddles human life, God is not without witness in the rough and tumble of personal and social life. At the core of human existence is some testimony, some desire, for what can only be the divine. To love God is to know one's self truly, and, conversely, to have a true apprehension of one's self is to grasp the ultimate object of one's desiring. This relation to the divine in the depth of the self defines the distinctiveness of human existence.

However, these and other theologians were not always clear about the causal *relation* between the human heart and the living God. What it means to be a self, an actual living individual, cannot mean that somehow one comes to self-awareness and then in a subsequent act decides to love God! Knowledge of self does not *cause* the knowledge of God. The knowledge of self and love of God arise simultaneously or they do not arise at all. One does not peer inside of oneself somehow to find God. If one does, the sense of the divine remains vague, fleeting, and too often vain. While a good deal of contemporary "spirituality," especially in late-modern Western societies, is a longing for something sacred, Christian humanism rightly understood is not a version of religious narcissism or bland natural theology. A distorted relation to God means that the self, despite its illusion of existence, is not really alive. Outside of a right love of God we do not and cannot truthfully know ourselves. That is the condition of sin, a denial of God. There is living death in which the self, while biologically alive, is spiritually dead.

On this construal of the human self, one can diagnose various moods or states that manifest the right or distorted relations between self, God, and others: moods like anxiety, holy sadness, human folly, the terrified and free conscience, or real joy in a life of love. Christian humanists examine these "moods" that disclose the condition of human existence within the defining relation to the living God. However, the state of the "soul" and its signifying moods (guilt, joy, sadness, hope) does not *cause* a relation to the divine. The human plight from this perspective is that people are not rightly aware of themselves precisely because they do not properly love God. Human beings exist in a haze, a profound sleep or spiritual death, unmindful of their condition or the actual depths of their existence. As the Protestant reformers put it, one must be shocked into self-awareness through the convicting power of the "law" to expose our misdirected loves. God as the heavenly deity is the operative metaphor for the divine life. And one must look to where God and human existence are disclosed in proper relation; one looks to Christ and the witness of scripture to the living Christ.[8] As St. Augustine put it, "Unless you will have believed, you will not understand" (*nisi credideritis non intelligetis*). Given the fallen and sinful state of human existence, a Christian humanist believes that one must look to the revelation of God in Christ, the faith of the Church, *and these alone*, in order rightly to understand human existence in God.

Typically, Christian humanists have differed on this point about belief-full understanding in ways similar to how humanists differ in their account of "man." Some theologians look to the incarnation of God in Christ as the *origin* of the Christian message, while others look to the cross and resurrection of Christ, the *end* or purpose of the Christian story. In either case, what makes Christian humanism distinctly *Christian* is the focus on Christ as uniquely revealing and restoring the right relation of God and humanity. True selfhood is received from God in grace and achieved through the cultivation of Christian character in following Christ. There is a double transcendence of the self: one always and already exists in relation to the other who is God, and, what is more, genuine life is a constant struggle to have right relations of love to God, others, and oneself. Causal language is inadequate: human beings are not just "clay pots" in the hands of an otherworldly divine craftsman (that would be hypertheism) and the living God is not the product of human wants or feelings or thoughts (as forms of overhumanism would claim).

To be a human self, on this distinctly Christian humanist account, is to find oneself in another, in God, and always to surpass self in the free struggle for the cultivation of character marked by love of others. On the one hand, this outlook continues some of the classical "Hellenistic" focus on *eudaimonia*, that is, well-being or happiness. What is meant by happiness has been radically changed through reference to the demands of holiness, a right relation to the living God. In a moment we will see that this connection between happiness and holiness is the third element in the bundle of ideas. The proper relation of happiness and holiness is what on our account Christian humanists mean by the highest good, the *summum bonum*, the true aim and end of responsible existence.

With respect to the human capacity for a relation to God, Christian humanists differ from other versions of Christian faith. Knowledge of self and knowledge of God arise simultaneously, and they do so in such a way as to affirm, rather than deny, distinct human capacities for action and free relations to others. Unlike strident forms of Christian faith, including significant portions of Augustine and Calvin, that verge on determinism in order to preserve God's sovereignty, this argument protects and promotes the distinctiveness of human beings as moral agents with freedom and purpose. The fear that human freedom might usurp the priority of God's action has driven some theologians into forms of hypertheism in which God and God alone is the only "agent." The long legacy of Christian humanism has always denied that claim and insisted, in the words of St. Athanasius, an ancient Church Father, that "God does not save us, without us."[9] The possibility and the reality of this creative interpretation of biblical and non-biblical thought is the insight that the human capacity for a relation to the divine is found in the fact that we are beings defined by self-knowledge and the freedom to act with and for others.

God and the Logic of Perfection

A second element in the constellation of ideas that characterizes the logic of Christian humanism is a complex idea insofar as it has to do with how to think rightly about the human relation to the living God. It is a demand of critique *within* the religious relation to God. One must formulate a rule or norm for proper thinking about God so that one does not imagine that God is just a projection of human needs and desires. In order to understand how Christian humanists solved the problem of critique one needs first to grasp an important distinction found within the legacy of the Christian tradition. It takes us back to the definition of religion offered in chapter 1: religions, with their myths, rituals, and community life, are about what is unsurpassably important *and* real. The grounds of critique also continue the two basic forms of classic Christian belief explained in the previous chapter, namely, God as heavenly deity and God as light of the world.

In Christian thought, and other traditions too, the human relation to the divine has often been conceived in distinct ways. One typical way God is approached is through an encounter with an Other, a stranger. God is totally different and other than human existence and any relation to God is an unexpected, even accidental, encounter. Here we find God as heavenly deity. God thunders the Law to Moses on Sinai; Christ appears to the disciples walking on the water; St. Paul is struck blind by the resurrected Christ on the road to Damascus. God is essentially different, other, and non-reducible to human thought and desire. There is no necessary relation of God to

62

humanity rooted in human knowing or freedom or love. God is free to encounter or to abandon human beings. The human relation to the divine, accordingly, is marked by a range of emotions from fear to love, and, additionally, the demand for obedience to God's law. The norm for right thinking about God must be nothing else than God's free encounter with human beings. Valid theological reflection begins with God's revelation and moves humanward: it follows the story of God's self-disclosure and the human encounters with this divine Other.

A different way to God is through a journey of discovery in which the self is found or lost in God (as mystics might say). God is the light of the world; God is the One in whom all are found. In this way "man discovers *himself* when he discovers God; he discovers something that is identical with himself although it transcends him infinitely, something from which he is estranged, but from which he never has been and never can be separated."[10] The religious struggle is to examine and penetrate the self in order to discover that "we live, move, and have our being in God," as St. Paul says at Mars Hill.

Paul's speech is in some respects paradigmatic of this outlook. He proclaims to the Greeks in Athens in front of the Areopagus about the God whom they worship but do not know. Paul continues:

> From one ancestor he made all nations to inhabit the whole earth, and he allotted the times of their existence and the boundaries of the places where they would live, so that they would search for God and perhaps grope for him and find him – though indeed he is not far from each one of us. For 'In him we live and move and have our being,' as even some of our own poets have said. (Acts 17:26–28)

In this respect, God is the presupposition of any valid knowledge of God precisely because God is the presupposition of the self, not far from each one of us. One does not try to reason towards a God who is a stranger and must be encountered to be known, as in biblical personalism. Theology articulates the insight that God is the first and foremost truth of all reality, including the depth of the self. How the self is conceived to exist in God differs among theologians who hold this outlook, ranging from mystical darkness where the soul is lost in God to highly rational and metaphysical systems in which reality is conceived as modes of God's being. Still, the journey is towards the insight or thought that God is in all things and all things are in God. The test or norm for properly theological claims is accordingly that God is only validly conceived when grasped as the presupposition and condition of every truth, including true self-knowledge.

These two outlooks, what we can call the revelatory-prophetic model of encounter and the metaphysical-mystical vision of discovery, have dominated and continue to dominate most Christian thought.[11] Importantly, Christian humanism and also theological humanism drawn from Christian sources do not fit either model. These represent third-way thinking, with their own impulses, norms, and aims. While closely associated with the way of discovery, because Christian humanists insist that human beings have a natural capacity for a relation to the divine, there is on our account an important difference. Christian humanists from Erasmus to Thomas Merton and now John de Gruchy and others insist that without the proclamation of the Christian message, human beings would not know that God is "not far from each one of us." The stories, images, and metaphors of the Christian community are necessary in order to articulate the human capacity for God and in this respect "revelation" is the means for discovery. One engages scripture in order to discover the truth of God. Like Christian humanists, theological humanists claim that in principle we only know ourselves in God through resources given to us in the history of particular communities. That which is given has the force of an encounter with what is, initially at least, other and different. Unlike Christian humanists, theological humanists do not restrict the received words and stories that trigger the natural, human capacity for a relationship to God only to biblical words or stories.

If this is the case, then the norm or test of valid theological claims cannot be just God's act of revelation or God as the presupposition of all truth. Garnering insights from the whole of the Christian tradition, seeking a third way beyond propheticism and mysticism, a different norm is required. This norm is the second element in the logic of Christian humanism. We call it the *logic of perfection*; as noted before, it was first enunciated by the medieval monk Anselm of Canterbury.

In his famous *Proslogion*, Anselm stated that "God is that than which nothing greater can be conceived." He thought he could prove the existence of God from this formula, since there is something greater that can be conceived than God's non-existence, namely, God's necessary existence. The logic of the idea of God as unsurpassable drives Anselm to believe that one can prove its reality. The idea of God unites what is unsurpassably important and its reality. Anselm offered different versions of the formula in terms of both the necessity of God's existence and also the idea of perfection. Centuries of debate surround the "ontological proof" of God, ranging from those like Kant who reject it outright since it seems to confuse language and existence, to those who have sought to show its validity. It is not the purpose of this book to enter those debates and certainly not to try to resolve them.

We call attention to Anselm's formula not as a proof of God's existence, but, rather, as a test for theological thinking and speaking.[12] The God who is "not far from each one of us" is only rightly conceived when any thought about God can withstand the test of perfection or, same thing said, unsurpassability. This is true even of Anselm's own claim, later in chapter 15 of the *Proslogion*, that God is greater than can be conceived. "Anselm's God," writes John Clayton, "is radically other, dwelling 'in light inaccessible,' eluding our senses and our understanding alike (§§17, 16), but in whose dazzle we are made aware of an overwhelming greatness and fullness of being (§14)."[13] This test or measure is how the Christian humanist avoids identifying God with thoughts about God, God with the self, God with the products of human imagination.

Take any thought about God, any idea or story or belief about God, and ask: Is that than which nothing greater can be conceived? The *religious* impulse is that only what is unsurpassable in importance *and* reality is worthy of worship. The figments of the human imagination, the authority and pride of one's community, the excess of political power or the abundance of wealth cannot withstand the test as right objects of devotion. The "proof" is best seen as a test for interpreting religious claims, a way of criticism in order to understand and purify theological thinking and religious devotion and to test distortions in belief. And in two ways, we can say. The "proof" provides a way to *criticize* ideas about God, since any idea that cannot endure the test of perfection cannot claim rightly to speak of the divine. In this way the proof might reduce us to silence and mystical awareness of God since, it would seem, every idea must always be deconstructed and surpassed. Yet the proof also shows, *constructively*, the human longing for the divine in and through degrees of imagined perfection. It shows us, what is more, the inseparability between God and a highest good.

It might seem that the Anselmic test is really just a version of the approach to God in terms of a discovery of self in God as light of the world. It has often been understood in this way. This is not quite right, in our judgment. Anselm's test presupposes a monastic community chanting the Psalms and, accordingly, addressing God in prayer and also encountering the claim of the "Fool" in Psalms 14 and 53 that "there is no God." Scripture, with its personal image of God, paradoxically announces what cannot be accepted in biblical faith, namely, the possibility of the non-being of God. It is through the encounter with that paradox inscribed in scripture that Anselm formulates his "proof." God is indeed other, as heavenly deity, and yet God is also discovered to be the very presupposition of wisdom, the light of the world. Anselm's proof functions as a test for valid theological claims that moves in and beyond the opposition of the prophetic encounter with divine otherness and the mystical discovery of self in God. It provides both critical and constructive tools for thinking rightly about the divine; it relates religion and critique.

We will unfold in greater detail this test of "that than which nothing greater can be conceived" in later chapters of this essay. At this juncture it is enough to show how it functions as an element in the bundle of ideas that characterize *Christian* humanism. For the Christian humanist, there is no opposition between God and humanity – hypertheism and overhumanization are equally false – but this also means adherence to a norm for proper thinking about God. The God that is "not far from each one of us" is the one than whom none greater can be conceived, but is also announced in the scripture as totally Other and yet discovered as the source of wisdom.

The Highest Good

According to this account of Christian humanism, the connection between self-knowledge and love of God is a way to conceptualize the core of the Christian witness. Christian faith is a trust in the living God manifest in Jesus Christ that ignites and emboldens loving service of all creatures in relation to God. Christian humanists have therefore insisted that the double love-command, to love God and one's neighbor as oneself, expresses this connection between God and self-knowledge as a maxim for the conduct of life. That maxim finds testimony in each and every human heart. In some way, every person has a grasp, no matter how tenuous or distorted, that other people are owed respect and esteem as well as having a deep longing for the divine. The task of the Christian community is to form and order personal and social existence so that people's actions and relations enact the ground and destiny of life in God. A life aimed at enacting that truth is in turn nothing other than the union of holiness and happiness, that is, the highest human good.[14] This conception of the highest good is then the third element in the bundle of core ideas in Christian humanism.

For the Christian humanist, what defines the dignity of human life, a free relation to the divine as the very life of one's life, is specified in terms of the double love-command, to love God and to love the neighbor as oneself.[15] This means that the self is not some solitary "I" in relation to itself. There is no private community between self and God lodged in the deep interiority of the "I." The self is profoundly marked by otherness; God and neighbor inhere in the love that defines existence. As Martin Luther put it in words

66

that any Christian humanist can affirm, "a Christian lives not in himself, but in Christ and in his neighbor."[16] The Christian is caught up in God through faith in Christ and also poured out to the neighbor in love. Christian existence, in other words, does not rest or resolve itself in itself. The Christian self exists in, with, and for the other: God and the neighbor.

What is more, the right intention for life appears under the form of the demand of love as the distinctly Christ-like path to the highest good. Who I am, what I can become, is defined by a project of increasing love for God and for others. The Christian self, again, is not a brute given. It is a project or task whose end is the God of life and the life of the neighbor. That is why Christian humanists speak of cultivation, education, and even perfection in Christian love. Genuine formation is to bear Christ in one's life through love of God and others.

In this vision of life, the self is not an abstract principle of identity. A human self is a concrete, specific person in community with others, seeking to live out a life of love within the complexities and realities of existence. The self is also not lost in God or the neighbor. There is no "mystical" absorption of self into the divine, nor is there a moral effacement of the worth and dignity of the individual person in praise of the priority of the "other," an idea various Christian feminists have rightly challenged.[17] A person in her or his own dignity exists within a complex set of relations with the ability to orient life responsibly.

That is, again, why Christian humanism insists on the importance of personal freedom and dignity. The same thing must be said about the neighbor. Since the love of God and true self-knowledge arise together, the command to love neighbor as self cannot mean, despite what some neohumanist detractors like Todorov think, that a Christian loves others in the abstract *as a means* to the divine. Insofar as the self is in God through faith and in the neighbor in loving acts, the same is true in principle of other people. Any actual person exists in a complex web of interrelations with others and with the living God; they must be loved concretely, not abstractly. Of course, how people live within the web of experience can take almost infinite expression. Some live in hope and courage; others live in despair and anger; still other people struggle to be faithful parents and good citizens. The ways of life that people adopt are many and part of the richness and travail of human reality.

The Christian humanist finds this variety of ways of life ambiguous. It is part of the comic but also tragic tapestry of human existence. The ambiguity of the human project does not entail an easy acceptance of the notion that somehow all ways of life are equally good and true. No way, style, or path of life ought to be adopted that violates the double love-command and thus effaces and distorts the life of others and the right intentionality of one's own life. Human sin consists in a closure of the self on itself in which relations to God and others are denied and the intentionality of life to its highest good thwarted.

If the double love-command is to guide right human relations and choices, what is the good served and sought in this vision of life? The highest good for Christian humanists, we submit, is the union of happiness and holiness. What does that mean? Here too we find Christian humanism to be a kind of third-way thinking. Much ancient Greek and Roman thought conceived of the human highest good in terms of *eudaimonia*, happiness or well-being. Thinkers debated what defines well-being. Is it (for instance) the lack of pain and the increase of pleasure, as Epicureans thought? Is happiness the contemplation of the good, as Plato and Aristotle in different ways taught? Stoics sought self-sufficiency and tranquility in the face of forces and suffering beyond human control. Conversely, Jewish and Christian thinkers shaped by the biblical traditions thought about the highest good in terms of righteousness, holiness, and obedience to God. The human good is a delight in the law or lived under the law of love, as St. Paul says. Even today, there are thinkers who insist that "morality" is mainly about fulfilling duties of justice, whereas others remain focused on flourishing or well-being, happiness.

The intuition of Christian third-way thinking is that the highest good of human existence must be the harmony of duty and well-being, holiness and happiness. Often, this truth is grasped in its denial, much like the denial of God by the fool revealed to Anselm a way to think rightly about God. The idea that the wicked should flourish or that the virtuous should suffer unjustly strikes one as wrong, hardly the highest good. The death of Dr. Martin Luther King, Jr., gunned down in Memphis while struggling for racial justice, violates moral sensibilities. The image of Job, to use a biblical example, who suffers even though he is the most righteous of men, gives rise to his own protest before God.[18] Somehow happiness and virtue ought to go together even if in this life they usually do not. The innocent wrongly suffer in this world.

In a sense, this norm of right choices and actions is just the application of the "Anselmic principle" to practical existence. Can I conceive a good greater than my sheer happiness? Yes, I can conceive of a condition in which genuine well-being is characterized by justice and virtue and holiness in me and in all people. Can I conceive of a good greater than a universal rule of justice and virtue and holiness? Yes, I can think the idea of that reality also being a state of happiness, well-being or flourishing. What is more, one could work the logic the other way around. Can any idea of God be truly unsurpassable

68

unless God is the source and end of holiness and happiness? Taken together, the Anselmic principle, and the idea of the highest good as the harmony of virtue and happiness, formulate what one can and ought to say about God and also what ought to be the good that orients human life. They are the logical demands for proper thinking and living in Christian humanism as a form of third-way thinking.

Goodness and Fallibility

We have tried to pry apart a cluster of ideas that typify the logic of Christian humanism, ideas about the human capacity for a relation to God, a norm for right thinking about the divine, and also the supreme good of human life. We have also noted that the distinctive feature of *Christian* humanism is the focus on the incarnation, death, and resurrection of Jesus Christ as the reality of God's being with and for humanity. The core of Christian humanism is "that the fullest realization of what it means to be human can be known through personal communion with Jesus Christ, the Word of God who entered the arena of human life to bring wholeness and freedom to every human being."[19]

Despite differences in conception and emphasis, this core conviction is held by Christian humanisms whether Eastern or Western, whether Ortho-dox, Roman Catholic, or Protestant. The modern Russian school in Orthodox theology, for instance, focused on *bogocheloveschestvo*, "Godmanhood" or the "humanity of God." Related, the Roman Catholic philosopher Jacques Maritain wrote about "integral humanism" even as liberation theologian Gustavo Gutierrez, following the language of Vatican II, thought that humanity is the "temple of God." Karl Barth, the Protestant theologian often seen as a strident theocentrist, wrote late in his life: "Since God in His deity is human, [theological] culture must occupy itself neither with God in Himself nor with man in himself but with man-encountering God and God-encountering man and with their dialogue and history, in which their communion takes place and comes to fulfillment."[20] Theological humanism drawn from Christian sources continues, but also revises, the core conviction of Christian humanism in order to respond to current realities.

Before turning to how theological humanism draws from these ideas to present a kind of third-way thinking for the current age, one last comment needs to be made about the bundle of ideas itself. What holds it all together? To insist that the constellation of Christian humanist ideas is held together by the conviction that in Jesus Christ "the Word of God entered the arena of human life" does not really help. It begs the question of what one means by God or the arena of human life. We have already specified the logical demands on right thinking about God, according to Christian humanism. We have also briefly indicated the supreme good: the harmony of holiness and happiness. What remains, then, is some claim about human existence that holds together these other convictions.

Actually, it was St. Augustine who first expressed the basic insight, even if it has been developed by Christian and Renaissance humanists and will be developed still further by theological humanism. The insight is deceptively simple. In his *Enchiridion*, Augustine writes:

> And I think there cannot now be any doubt, that the only cause of any good that we enjoy is the goodness of God and that the only cause of evil is the falling away from the unchangeable good of a being made good but *changeable* first in the case of an angel and afterwards in the case of man.[21]

The insight is that human beings are created for a relation to the goodness of God, but human beings are also *changeable*. No person or community has a necessary or permanent relation to the highest good. This idea, as we saw in previous chapters, was exploited by thinkers like Pico to say that human beings have no essential nature and can therefore become whatever they desire to be. For the Christian humanist, neither the goodness of finite being nor the basic changeability of human existence can ever be overcome, despite what Pico and others might think. Humans are fallible beings who can turn and fall away from their highest good. This claim about being human – that we are oriented towards the highest good but are changeable, fickle, and fallible creatures – links together the other elements of the logic of Christian humanism.

The conviction that human beings are created good but changeable has important implications that helped to shape the legacy of Christian humanism. It means, first, that one struggle of human existence is to form habits, virtues, and the bonds of conviction sufficient to keep human life steadfast in its commitment to what is right and good. This is why, for instance, education is important in the history of Christian humanism as seen in the idea of the philosophy and *school of Christ*. In a comprehensive sense, education aims to form human life around convictions about what is true and good and thereby to provide some consistency and stability to life.

A deeper insight is, second, about the human relation to the divine. Martin Luther put it well. God is, he insisted, righteousness and holiness, truth and goodness. Anyone who seeks these things seeks God. In fact, Luther insisted

70

that, "Whatever it is that makes a man do something, that motive is his god."[22] Whatever motivates and orients one's life, is, in truth, one's god, what is unsurpassably important and real in one's life. This means, significantly, that the human relation to the good, to the divine, is something that can only be lost by the person himself or herself. To be sure, human beings can be coerced, seduced, and forced into evil actions, but the real source of human failure lies not in forces external to oneself, but in one's own being, one's lack of constancy and fidelity.

This is why, one might imagine, Christian humanists have thought that the true good of human life must wed the search for happiness to the demands of holiness. Only then is the goodness of human life celebrated and the changeability of the human heart cultivated, disciplined, in dedication to what is right and good. This is, we might say, the backing for third-way thinking, linking a biblical understanding of the created goodness of human existence to the quest for human perfection in the theatre of the world found in other traditions and outlooks. The bundle of ideas that shape historic Christian humanism express a specific way of living the human adventure and also a distinctive way of being Christian. Christian humanism presents the reality and task of the "third man, the believing Gentile."

Third-Way Thinking

With the idea of the third man and third-way thinking, we reach the transition point from the work of the last chapters to a central idea of theological humanism, namely, the integrity of life. Our contention, again, is that theological humanism is yet another form of third-way thinking, but one that can be practiced by adherents of different traditions. It is a stance in life and also in traditions, freedom *within* religion. While our account of theological humanism is indebted to Christian and Western sources, we believe that the outlook and orientation finds resonance with others and finds resources in others who seek to humanize their religious tradition and to think beyond overhumanization and hypertheism.

The next step in our essay on theological humanism is then to explore and explain the idea of the integrity of life as the norm for third-way thinking about and also living out the human dimension of existence. The idea of the integrity of life will clarify the range of goods we uncovered in classical images of humanism (theatre, garden, school), but with respect to a norm of right action and a "logic" similar to the one isolated above and used by

71

Christians to transform the legacy of humanism. Further, it will build on the account of the distinctiveness of theological reflection developed in chapter 3 on the relation of religion and critique. The next chapter completes the first step of this essay by rounding out the shape of theological humanism. It will be followed by chapters which put theological humanism on trial by engaging various spheres of contemporary life, mindful of the dangers of our age.

5

On the Integrity of Life

It is a cruelly hazardous enterprise, this becoming a whole, becoming a form, of crystal-lization of the soul ..Evil cannot be done with the whole soul; good can only be done with the whole soul.

Martin Buber[1]

This book began by exploring the clash between religious and humanistic outlooks on life. Theological humanism, we said, aims to address powerful and even deadly distortions within the humanistic and religious legacies of Western civilization, namely, overhumanization and hypertheism. We intend to change the terms of debate. With some sense of the scope and challenge of this essay, we isolated features of classical humanism, theology and its critics, and also Christian humanism. This provides us with a range of metaphors which will be put to constructive work in this chapter and others. In terms of Christian humanism, we clarified its internal logic for the use and transformation of humanistic ideas of perfection, the good, and the human capacity for a relation to the divine.

Metaphors and logical analysis have been used in order to articulate the background forces that have helped to shape theological humanism as well as to isolate and to identify challenges to contemporary thought that spark the imagination and called forth reflection. In order to bring this first step of this essay to an end, it is necessary to clarify the concept that holds together theological humanism as an outlook and orientation for religion and the human future: the integrity of life.[2]

The Cruel Hazard of Life

The idea of the integrity of life signifies the truth of Martin Buber's words, cited above. The human labor of forming one's life and the life of a community is a "cruelly hazardous" thing. All too easily, human lives are formed around distorted ideals and values that mutilate one's life and the lives of others. Overhumanization and hypertheism are the main distortions in our age. The endless inflation and extension of human power to dominate other forms of life and even control the future threatens us in many ways. The fanatical demand that human beings submit to the "God" of one community as the only true active reality in the world feeds violence and stupidity around the globe. The hazard of life is that it might be fashioned on false ideas and ideals; the hazard is cruel because human beings cannot escape the labor of bringing wholeness to life but are always fallible in their perception of what is true and good.

This hazard and its cruelty were captured in Christian thought in rather stark terms by St. Augustine in his *City of God*. Reflecting on the complexity of human judgments, he writes:

> Ignorance is unavoidable – and yet the exigencies of human society make judgment also unavoidable. Here we have what I call the wretchedness of man's situation ... How much more mature reflection it shows, how much more worthy of a human being it is when a man acknowledges this necessity as a mark of human wretchedness, when he hates that necessity in his own action and when, if he has the wisdom of devotion, he cries out to God, "Deliver me from my necessities."[3]

Human wretchedness – to use an out-of-fashion term – is that human lives are always marked by ignorance and yet also the need to make judgments. The necessity is "wretched" when it becomes clear that human beings long to escape the ignorance and limitations that mark finitude and yet can never do so. We face the cruel hazard of having to make judgments about forming our souls. The idea of the integrity of life is meant to provide some response to the cruel hazard and the nagging wretchedness of human life.

Part of Buber's point was to insist that the struggle to become whole is the task of each and every human being. It is the labor of human freedom. As mortal beings we are bound to the dust of the earth even if we are also free. The challenge of human life is to rise to one's capacities rather than to fall into brutishness. The power of rising or falling is human, mortal freedom. It is what makes us changeable human beings "things in-between." The idea of the integrity of life must then tell us something about human freedom and also the kind of self-labor, the formation of self in relation to others, which has always been the adventure of human existence.

74

A third and crucial point of Buber's insight: the work of freedom fraught with hazard and even the wretchedness of existence is bound to moral distinctions. Good and evil, right and wrong, and other terms designate or name what crystallizes and makes life whole or, conversely, what demeans, destroys, and disintegrates life. Oddly enough, actions and relations that promote and ensure life in oneself and others bring a new coherence, a new form, to human life. The "good" is the elusive and tentative unity of virtue and well-being in human existence. Evil rips individual and social existence apart and, through their disintegration, brings life to an end, to death. The idea of the integrity of life must clarify the meaning of "goodness" in its various dimensions and how these cohere with the wholeness of life.

The integrity of life bundles together ideas important to religious and non-religious humanism. It does so without pitting theological and humanistic outlooks against one another. Like neohumanists, the shift is from the sole priority of self-realization found in classical humanism to the "finality of the other." Theological humanism presses that insight further. Human transcendence reaches the other, but then also to the integrity of life and the presence of the divine known within, but not limited to, specific religious communities.

The integrity of life means, first, the integration of distinct levels of goods into some livable form, always threatened and always vulnerable, but without which personal or social life is impoverished. The integrity of life also requires, second, a life dedicated to respecting and enhancing the proper integration of those goods and thereby a commitment to the well-being of other forms of life. *Spiritual* integrity is thereby the wholeness and steadfastness that is the proper aim of human existence with all of its vulnerability and fallibility. Our account of the human good proceeds, then, in terms of these meanings of the "integrity of life." That is followed with an explanation of the imperative of responsibility as the norm for right actions and social relations that contribute to the integrity of life.

Vitalities and Vulnerabilities of Goods

From Plato and Aristotle to Thomas Aquinas, moderns like Joseph Butler and current thinkers, many have noted that human beings are situated in existence through interlocking modes of life, each marked by vitalities and vulnerabilities.[4] Human beings are *living creatures* within and not against the wide community of finite life on this planet. We are *social beings* who sustain and also threaten our existence through relations with others. Human beings

75

are *reflective creatures* who seek to understand their lives, their world, and others. These aspects of human life were aptly captured by the humanistic imagination in terms of the metaphors of garden, school, and theatre, respectively. Each of them discloses the profoundly social natural human existence, the bonds of human connection. The conundrum, of course, is that these various modes of life (finite, social, reflective) are not only vulnerable to death and distortion but are also deeply interrelated in these vulnerabilities. Each mode bears its own goods. We can then identify these interlocking sets or kinds of goods.

Basic goods, as they are often called, are those goods which inhere in finite life independent of human choice, but which are necessary to sustain human agency. Motivated by biological, affective, and other vitalities, we are situated in life with respect to these goods. Our bodies, the taste for beauty, the fear of death, force of enjoyment and delight, the need for food and shelter, testify that finite life is not just vulnerable but also saturated with appraisal of its worth. The sense of basic goods places constraints on human choice; choices should respect and enhance these goods when possible. Societies must interpret, rank, and respond to these goods in some way. The saturation with worth is experienced most basically, sometimes inchoately, in the sense of pleasure and pain as motivations for human action. We are drawn to what gives pleasure; people recoil from pain.

Of course, a human vulnerability – part of the cruel hazard of existence – is that we can be deceived about pleasure and pain. We can mistake for what is pleasurable that which actually brings death and pain. The basic goods of finite life are necessarily interwoven with reflective capacities to discern what is genuine pleasure and real pain. Further, basic goods that surround finite life are interdependent with social existence, whether human or other forms of life. Disease, starvation, and the unjust treatment of human bodies around the world aptly show that basic goods are intertwined with social goods. Nevertheless, human beings are in the world at the most sensate and brute level as bodies who struggle to live and are vulnerable not only to great pleasure but to searing pain. This means that we are also bound together in bonds of sympathy, the capacity to suffer with others in their vulnerabilities, which can also be stunted, destroyed.

From this angle of vision, the labor of life, in good measure, is to stave off forces of disintegration, to forestall physical death, in the constant affirmation of life within the struggle for life. The facts of finite being provide at the level of feeling a *universality* of the claim of life upon us. All living beings, all creatures situated in being through pleasure and pain, make some claim to be respected and enhanced, even if that claim can in certain

76

circumstances and for good reasons be overridden.[5] Tzvetan Todorov gets the gist of this point, even if, as a secular neohumanist, he constricts the reach of responsibility only to other human beings. "The universality of the *they* seems, then, to be the counterpoint of the membership of all human beings, and they alone, in the same living species."[6] For the theological humanist, the most basic and most inclusive membership is not a species but, rather, the community of life, a community that evokes sympathy and reaches from the organic to the divine. The realm of basic goods exceeds what Todorov and other neohumanists usually imagine. The point is that *universality* becomes self-evident when we attend and are attuned to the dynamics of physical life.[7] Basic goods, then, situate human beings in the world at the simplest level of sensible life and yet are also linked to other levels of goods that must be properly integrated if life is to endure and to flourish.

There is also a distinct realm of *social goods*. These goods obviously depend on action and choice, and yet action and choice in concert with others. Human existence – and the life of many other creatures – is profoundly social. Human existence always and everywhere entails standards, customs, rites, practices, and beliefs, which communities develop in order to understand and to guide life. These are social inventions, the work of social imagination and labor, which guide interactions within the social and natural environments. They include such things as family, economic and political institutions (of whatever form), friendship, patterns of interaction with other species, and even the means to think, speak, and act together with others.

We call these "social goods" to denote the relation to and yet distinction from other goods. They are forms of human excellence and well-being associated with fidelity to the well-being of others, the common good. Insofar as goods must be protected, used, enjoyed, and distributed, then social norms are obviously important. Yet the realm of the social has its own status. One cannot act against social goods without endangering the conditions of cooperative thinking, speaking, and acting. There is also a vulnerability found in social goods, namely, the vulnerability to distortion, injustice, and social oppression. These vulnerabilities, and also the vitality of social existence, impinge at another level of experience or attunement to life. As social beings, we are moved by a desire for recognition and are vulnerable to shame. Recognition and shame situate human beings in social realities. The bonds of our humanity come to rise in a sense of benevolence for others. But these senses are also open to distortion, like when racist policy breeds shame for one's very being or sexism fosters hatred of one's gender. Benevolence, too, can be stunted or destroyed.

Attention to social goods requires attunement to the dynamics of recognition and shame as well as benevolence in human life and the ways these can be distorted and used to thwart communal life. An awareness of the vulnerability and also vitality of social goods exposes not the *universality* of life's claim, but, rather, what Todorov has rightly called the *finality* of the *you*. "Finality" means that the existence of others places an ineluctable claim on one's own power and, reciprocally, the self makes a similar claim on others. The "Golden Rule," found in various cultures, is a necessary norm of the social good: "do unto others as you would have others do unto you."[8] The social good is demarcated by patterns of giving and receiving respect; threats to the social good arise when respect is wrongfully withdrawn, thereby casting some forms of human life outside of the community. The finality of the "you" is bound to recognition and shame that transpire in relations of giving and receiving respect and a sense of benevolence.

We have isolated the complexity of attunements to the vitality of life that arise experientially in terms of pleasure, pain, the desire for recognition, and dynamics of shame. And these are linked to a sense of our bonds to others through sympathy and benevolence. These "feelings" situate human beings in a world of interlocking goods and evils that surround actions and relations to others. They also demarcate the kinds of vulnerability human beings face in the struggle to live and live well, individually and together. There is a certain "oughtness," an obligation to respect and enhance the integrity of life's goods in terms of the sensibility of *universality* and also *finality*. These forms of the "oughtness" of life are not artificially and tyrannously imposed on human existence; they articulate immediate senses of the vitality and vulnerability of life.

People must also take some reflective stance to basic and social goods and the motivations that arise from finite, social life. *Reflective goods* satisfy not only the drive for meaning in human life, but also open the possibility for creating new forms and ways of life. We can call these *reflective goods* insofar as they enable human agents to be knowingly responsible for themselves and others. These goods denote both a posture of interpretation and assessment toward basic and social goods, but bear worth in themselves as well. This level of good aims at truthful life, meaningfulness, and self-understanding. They are the goods of culture or civilization, that is, the entire domain of symbolic, linguistic, and practical meaning-systems.

Human beings are pictured as creatures who, come what may, interpret their lives through judgments about what to do and to be in relation to others and the goods that permeate their lives. Not surprisingly, reflective goods touch sensibilities or feelings that situate human life within the vitalities of life. Insofar as reflective goods demarcate a range of personal and social meanings, these goods are linked to the reality of people as individual agents. Pleasure and pain can and do move human beings to act without deliberation; the desire for recognition and fear of shame can provoke action without questions about the truth of those feelings. Yet human beings are also moved by the question of the truth of their self-understanding and the values and goals that orient life. As Emmanuel Levinas once pointedly put it, "we all want to know if we have been duped by morality."[9] At crucial moments in life – the encounter with someone suffering, the joy of a new child, revulsion at gross injustice – one awakens from the habitual and asks about the truth of one's life and what is held good and true and sacred. A sense of justice that exceeds sympathy and benevolence arises. From this awakening to the moral density of the world arise other feelings that situate human life, specifically our sensibilities to guilt and innocence and justice.

Self-interpreting agents constitute the coherence of their lives through judgments about what to do and to be in relation to others and the variety of basic and social goods that saturate life. These judgments gives rise to a proper sense of *autonomy*, a sense of self in relation to others, and also the sense of the gravity of one's life. In addition to *universality* and *finality*, we find, then, arising out of the range of goods that permeate human life, basic and social and reflective goods, an often inarticulate sense and demand of *autonomy*. And this sense bears within it the claim that one ought not destroy or demean one's own sense of agency or that of other human beings. The idea of autonomy is thereby infused with the sense of justice.

It is at this level of reflection, although reached in a very different way, that Immanuel Kant's humanistic motto is experientially true: what one finds *holy* within oneself and others is the freedom to be an agent, to be autonomous. Unlike Kant, since he denied that a sense of moral demand could be found in human finitude and sociality, this "autonomy" is not simply about rationality devoid of sensibilities about the goods that permeate all of life. For theological humanism, freedom situates human life within the complex matrix of basic, social, and reflective goods that saturate human individual and social existence, rather than separating the self from those relations.

Human life always takes place somewhere: in some community on some bit of earth and during some time in history. Basic, social, and reflective goods are thereby always *located* in space and time. As many philosophers and environmental scientists have noted, too often and too readily the natural and social habitats of human and non-human forms of life have been ignored in the West. The technological age endangers the "place" of life. The present time is one in which the earth and its many forms of life are endangered by global warming, species extinction, soil and land loss and deforestation. Sometimes the roots of this endangerment are found in the religions, especially the biblical traditions and ideas about the human domination of the earth. Others find the root cause deep within Western conceptions of being itself and the belief that somehow reality is a standing reserve for human use.[10] But human life, in fact, is intertwined with the goods of locality. This is true of history as well. The many processes which allow human communities to endure through time and to pass on their ways of life – language, custom, social relations – are now endangered through global processes. The earth is precious and human communities are vulnerable. These are *natural goods*. Our lives are marked by a capacity for empathy in the face of these vulnerabilities and forms of preciousness.

This preciousness of the earth and vulnerability of human communities as the space of life are often sensed in the homelessness people feel when their communities break down or are dislocated.[11] The sense of natural beauty, but also profound terror, in the face of the titanic forces of the natural world, disclose the locality of life. Not only pleasure and pain, but recognition and shame, guilt and innocence situate human beings in their world at the levels of feelings and moods about the range of goods that saturate life. The goods of *locality* of goods arises within feelings of participation and alienation amid the various spaces (natural, social, historical) where human existence takes place. A norm for right action, then, is marked not only by universality, finality, and autonomy, but also locality. We must respect and enhance the various "spaces" where life takes place, happens. In addition to basic, social, and reflective goods, we add natural goods, goods of place or locality. These goods have also found voice in the humanist imagination: the garden, the theatre, the school each denotes a space of human freedom.

We have now isolated a range of types of goods found within inchoate sensibilities and attunements to the vitality and vulnerability of life in its various dimensions, reaching from physical through social, natural to reflexive life. These diverse goods (basic, social, natural, reflective) also carry within them a felt demand or claim to obligation that we have summarized in terms of formal tests or norms for right action: *universality*, *finality*, *autonomy*, and *locality* arising within proper, developed attunements to finite being, social relations, and reflective acts of understanding. These goods and also the felt demands of life have already appeared in this book in terms of the products of the humanistic imagination.

At this juncture in the argument we confront an obvious and painful fact. The goods of life can and do conflict, and persons as well as communities often do not orient their lives by the demands of universality, finality, locality, or autonomy. Our sensibilities can be in conflict, as when (say) a demand for justice conflicts with sympathy or benevolence. The facts of finite life are such that basic goods often conflict with social goods; a range of desires arising in finite life – lust and greed no less than hunger or fear – can undercut social relations. Starvation and threat of disease lead to social breakdown. The demand for social stability, as we know from totalitarian societies, can thwart reflective goods of meaningful cultural forms.[12] In oppressive societies there is the demand to accept social and political ideology in order to survive and thereby to demean the human drive for understanding. In an analogous way, highly consumerist societies stimulate reflexive processes through the media and the market in order to heighten the need for social, natural, and basic goods – they stimulate the desire for recognition or the pangs of needs, for instance. These forms of technological, systemic, and reflexive overhumanization threaten the realm of goods needed for human and non-human life to flourish.

It is the task of the humanist, of any sort, to resist and to expose these evils. Edward Said correctly states that the humanist "intellectual is perhaps a kind of countermemory, with its own counterdiscourse that will not allow conscience to look away or fall asleep."[13] One has to combat forces that render people mute, silent, before concealed powers that structure the lived experience of reality and therefore also bring to articulation the demands of life at their most resonant experiential level. While we can isolate a range of goods that saturate finite, social, natural, and reflective life as well as discern within them the pull, the claim, of moral requirements, actual life is nevertheless riddled with conflict. The integrity we seek and desire is thwarted and thus life is wrapped in a sense of disintegration, the sense or taste of forms of death.

This provokes another level of reflection. How might the various goods and demands of life be integrated rightly? And how does this problem relate to the idea of the *integrity of life*? More pointedly, since freedom is the capacity to act as a whole within and beyond these conflicts, is there some principle of choice, an imperative of responsibility, which ought to guide human actions and relations?

Responsibility and Spiritual Integrity

The conflicts among and between basic, social, natural, and reflective goods and the conflict between the often inarticulate motivations of life (pleasure/pain/sympathy; recognition/shame/benevolence; innocence/guilt/justice, participation/alienation/empathy) that mark human wretchedness provoke a longing for *integrity* in human life. This longing gives rise to yet another level of human good. Human beings can respond to the *call of conscience* and act on the forms of obligation nestled in the goods of life. Individuals or even communities so dedicated find their lives integrated through a commitment to respect and enhance the integration of goods in others' lives and in their own life. This is, for the theological humanist, the claim of conscience, and it means that at its deepest level the integrity of life is a spiritual reality. Spiritual integrity, the integrity of dedicated life, is a specific attitude and project in relation to the other goods of life. It is the crystallization of the soul, as Martin Buber called it, and, therefore, both the highest human good and also the distinct vulnerability, risk, and freedom of human existence.

Spiritual integrity demands truthfulness *of* self and community *to* the project of respecting and enhancing the integrity of all life. The motivation for this dedication arises in and through other human motivations; it is the desire for truthful life. What that means can be formulated and directed through a specific dictate of conscience, an imperative of responsibility. Now, responsibility is about human power and freedom as well as the capacity to make choices; without the power to act and the freedom of choice and to accept consequences, one cannot be rightly held responsible. This makes the idea of responsibility extremely important in the age of technology and global dynamics. Theological humanism seeks then to meet the challenges of the various endangerments to life that define our global age. We can briefly unfold the meaning of this imperative of responsibility and its relation to conscience.

The Imperative of Responsibility

The imperative of responsibility at the heart of theological humanism is this: *in all actions and relations respect and enhance the integrity of life before God.* We can divide our comments into parts of the imperative and then show what it means for treatment of human and non-human life. First, the moral life is about actions and relations and specifically what we ought to respect and enhance in and through actions and relations. The ordering is important. One must respect self and others first and foremost. *Respect* is a way of acknowledging the worth and dignity of others; it is to extend the scope of moral consideration to include all. This is rooted for Christians and many others in God's appreciation of creation ("and he saw that it was good") and also Christ's love-command: love neighbor as self and even enemy as we were first loved. Yet responsibility cannot end with respect or even securing the needs of

82

others. It will also seek to build up the lives of others, to transform the social world, to work to end suffering and injustice, and to seek not only to preserve but also to enhance the global ecological order. Again, for Christians, the demand to enhance the integrity of life is rooted in Christ's action of healing and feeding as well as God's sustaining action on behalf of all creation.

The order of these demands of responsibility is crucial.[14] Enhancing without or before respect too easily becomes paternalistic where those with power intervene and change things unmindful or unresponsive to the will and wishes of others. Here, we can say, is the backbone, ethically speaking, of overhumanization. Respect without the demand to enhance too easily leads to quietism and an acceptance of the status quo. It assumes that if we do no harm that is all that is required. This is the moral form of hypertheism, a life in conformity to sovereign will and duty. The point is that respect draws the map of the moral community; enhancement aims to further the goods of that community. So, for instance, we can and ought to use genetic technologies only after the demand for respect is met and then only to enhance, not to create, forms of life. Designer babies whose traits are selected by parents, new forms of animal life for aesthetic pleasure, and the cultivation of forms of life as stockpiles of body parts or genetic material are not permissible.[15] We must also enhance life and this means that there is the demand to fight disease, to engage in experimentation if and when this does not violate respect for life, and labor to extend the health and welfare of the planet's ecosystem. There is the opening, then, to forms of intervention for enhancing life ranging from stem cell research to genetic technologies.

What are we to respect and enhance? As we will see later, some contemporary thinkers argue that we ought to recognize only *interests and preferences* of those beings that can suffer. This seems to make the supreme value the avoidance of suffering or the relief of pain. Another moral outlook, often associated with the reverence for or sanctity of life, risks making life into a second God, so sacred that we can never under any circumstances take life. The mistake in both forms of ethics is to believe that life *qua* life is that which is to be given respect and to be enhanced. What we are to respect and enhance is not life *qua* life, but, rather, the *integrity* of life. Integrity is a complex idea. We are to respect and enhance the integration of goods in a life: goods rooted in bodily need and well-being; goods rooted in social interaction; goods rooted in reflective structures of meaning and value; natural goods of locality. As we will see below, integrity, more profoundly, means having one's own life united, made whole, by a commitment to what respects and enhances the integration of life in others and one's self that gives rise to and enacts moral, spiritual integrity.

A focus on the integrity of life means that if one respects the coherence, the wholeness of a form of life, and yet, through technological means, can enhance it, then one is enabled and required so to act. Conversely, if technologies demean or destroy the fragile wholeness of a form of life – say, reducing a human being to a genetic code that can be cloned, or a specific ecosystem to an economic resource – then it is not permissible so to act. The value of thinking about the integrity of life, rather than sanctity or interests, is that it enables greater precision about what we are to respect and enhance. It is not biological processes or interests or suffering, but rather the integration of a specific form of life that is the object of responsibility. It is not life *qua* life, the brute fact of a kind of life, but its capacity to integrate various goods. When that capacity is thwarted or destroyed, it makes little sense to preserve life *qua* life.

Again, theological humanism not only orders duties (respect/enhance) in a way that places limits on the power of various technologies, but it also specifies when we can and ought to deploy them. This outlook clarifies the good we should respect and enhance (integrity of life and its many goods) in such a way that we do not make life into a second God or reduce life to instrumental value to serve other purposes. This brings us to a vexing question. What is the source of value of the integrity of life? Is it human power and our capacity to control life? Is physical life sacred?

Life is not a second God. Life as such is not ultimate. By the same token, life is a gift. A theological humanist needs to respect and enhance the integrity of life *before God* and, conversely, conceives "God" through the integrity of life. This means that all of finite life has value even if it does not have ultimate value; God names what is supremely important and real but cannot command what demeans or destroys the integrity of life. Further, life is never only of instrumental worth to other human purposes and technological progress. There are situations in which life can and may and must tragically be sacrificed precisely to respect and enhance its integrity. What an ethics of the integrity of life does is to dignify and yet also to relativize life. Against those who deny the sanctity of life, this ethics insists that life has great dignity and intrinsic worth. Against those who insist on the sacredness of life, this ethics argues the integrity of life, and not life itself, bears intrinsic value. Against those who argue that God and God alone is the center of value, this ethics says that religious and moral convictions must be tested by their meaning for the *integrity of life*, including beliefs about the divine. What is more, this outlook means that in living a responsible life, in respecting and enhancing the integrity of life, we are in fact loving and serving the spiritual good.

84

In terms of duties (respect and enhance), the object of moral consideration and the scope of value (integrity of life), theological humanism places strong limits on human power to intervene and change life. Yet it also opens an appropriate arena and specifies the conditions in which there can be the responsible use of technological power. This is to grant, as James Gustafson has put it, that "there is no clear overriding *telos*, or end, which unambiguously orders the priorities of nature and human participation in it so that one has a perfect moral justification for all human interventions."[16] The burden and joy of responsibility remains the human calling. Difficult and often tragic choices must be made about specific decisions and policies in the treatment of human and non-human life. The moral calling is given specificity and orientation in terms of the imperative of responsibility. That is the case, again, because the imperative provides guidance on how to order obligations (respect; enhance), clarity about the object of consideration (the integrity of a form of life), and also the scope of consideration and the source of value.

The Claim of Conscience

Insofar as human beings are creatures who must decide how to live with respect to some idea of what is good and some standards about what is right, then the "imperative of responsibility" must somehow resonate in experience. That resonance is not just in terms of the various feelings we isolated above, the feelings of pleasure/pain, recognition/shame, guilt/innocence, participation/alienation and their social analogues. More deeply, the resonance of the imperative of responsibility is denoted by the idea of conscience. And herein lies the deepest paradox of human existence. The claim of conscience signifies that the integrity of one's own life cannot be directly aimed at or achieved. Spiritual and moral integrity, the rectitude of conscience, arises in and through a life dedicated to respecting and enhancing the integrity of life in, with, and for others. We gain ourselves most profoundly in lives so dedicated.

Conscience is, then, not some specific thing in the human brain or some kind of faculty of the soul. Conscience is a concept for the totality of a human life involved in its moral and spiritual struggle; it is a name for the primary mode of being human as an agent in the world. Conscience is a way to speak about the meaning and purpose of being human with respect to the demand to orient life responsibly amid its goods, vulnerabilities, threats, and distortions. When conscience is distorted or mistaken, human life is distorted or mistaken. One should never act against conscience, as moralists throughout the centuries have argued. Yet that does not mean that one might not be mistaken, even distorted. It means that one cannot be compelled to violate the primary mode of being, one's humanness.

The claim or call of conscience is the sense of the "oughtness," presence, and reality of the integrity of life grasped under the forms of the universality, finality, autonomy, and locality. It includes intimations of basic, social, natural, reflective, and spiritual goods, intimations found in feelings and sensibilities. The dawning of conscience is an "awakening" to the depth and purpose of responsible life. Various metaphors try to explore the senses linked to conscience: it can sting, the conscience can be terrified or despair, a goad to action, it can testify to the integrity of one's life. Stated otherwise, the fourfold form of the moral claims (autonomy, finality, universality, locality) is not exhaustive of the integrity of human life.[17] These forms extend considerably beyond humans to other forms of life. The demands of universality, finality, locality, and autonomy are tests or critical markers for a valid understanding and application of the imperative of responsibility: respect and enhance the integrity of life before God. However, the four "tests" are about the *form* and *application* of the imperative rather than providing *content* to a conception of the good, the integrity of life. The content of the integrity of life includes, then, basic, social, natural, and reflective goods and also the spiritual good of conscience.

The confluence of these goods expresses both a longing for integrity and the claim of others that meet in the idea of the "integrity of life" and the claim of conscience. Conscience, the felt reality of the demand to respect and enhance the integrity of life tested by universality, finality, autonomy, and locality, is at one and the same moment an act of *conformity* to a claim beyond the self and yet also the *creative* enactment of human powers. In response to conscience there is an affirmation of self and the acknowledgment of others. To put it differently, a life dedicated to responsibility both responds to the claims of others and creates a way of life bearing its own distinctive force and tenor.

There is a certain awakening to life when the oft-silent voice of conscience arises through the dimensions of our lives as mortal beings within the wider compass of life. The voice of conscience is the call to dedicate one's life to the struggle of moral and spiritual integrity which fashions existence, paradoxically, for a good beyond what is directly achieved, immediately desired. The remainder of this book is a meditation on that upsurge of conscience undertaken to articulate, to give voice, to this claim of life upon us, thereby to awaken ever more fully to the reality of life within the power of divine life. In this way, the integrity of life present and real in the claim of conscience draws together the metaphoric clusters of theology charted before. Like the heavenly deity, there is a demand and claim on conscience. The responsible person or community beholds actions and relation in the light of the integrity of life. The reality and presence of that integrity exceeds and infuses finite life with dignity and worth. And yet, if the ideas of God and Man form the center of theology and humanism, respectively, then the integrity of life is the fount and form of theological humanism. This norm of responsibility for the integrity of life articulates the structure of actual lived experience, otherwise it is a dead abstraction. Yet it enables us to understand and work against forces of overhumanization and hypertheism. This norm is intrinsic to a right conception of divine as well as to human life.

The Human Aim and Norm

Notice that we have been able to gather together within the idea of the integrity of life the diverse range of goods found in classical humanistic images of human existence, as well as normative commitments to autonomy, respect for others, and social solidarity that find wide acceptance among neohumanists. To this we have added a range of goods in the formulation of plans of action. The question now is how, if at all, the integrity of life will give to us the means to recast the set of ideas that defined the logic of Christian humanism so that we can show its *theological* as well as humanistic meaning. Further, we need to clarify how the idea of the integrity of life provides the means for the transformation of classical humanism and Christian humanism sufficient to meet the challenges of overhumanization and hypertheism.

Recall that the logic of Christian humanism held together several ideas. One idea was about the human capacity for a relation to the divine. Another idea had to do with a rule for proper thinking about "God," what we called the Anselmic principle. The third idea was a specific way of conceiving the highest good, namely, the union of virtue and happiness, or, in Christian terms, holiness and happiness. Finally, the whole set was itself an idea about human existence, namely, finite creatures created good but changeable. This bundle of ideas enables Christian humanists to overcome the opposition between biblical revelation and the forms of philosophic truth indebted to the Greek and Roman heritage of the West. It provided a discourse for reflecting on the reality of the "third man," as we called it before, and so to practice a distinctive way of life. Insofar as that was the case, Christian thinkers used and transformed basic images of human existence found in non-Christian thought without fear of forsaking their religious commitments. They anticipated the kind of thinking required by theological humanism.

Does the integrity of life provide a similar constellation of ideas for engaging and transforming thought about human existence and spiritual longings? How might it enable one to think beyond the conflict between theology and humanism and thereby to enable a third way of human life, a way called theological humanism? We can end this chapter by trying to answer briefly these questions even while our answer anticipates later chapters of the book.

The integrity of life means the proper integration, the crystallization, of the basic, social, natural, and reflective goods of life. In this respect, the idea of integrity designates that finite human life has intrinsic worth, if incomplete. The various dimensions of goods indicated above (basic, social, natural, reflective) merely develop in greater detail humanist and Christian beliefs about the goodness of finite human existence. A central aim of human actions and relations should be to respect and enhance goodness in its diverse forms. The fact that spiritual integrity is only achieved when an individual or community acts under the demands of responsibility means that integrity is also a response to the changeability, the fickleness of human personal and social existence. The imperative of responsibility as a formulation of the claim of conscience provides a disciplined way to bring wholeness and true steadfastness to human existence. Further, because integrity spans both the goods rooted in the dimensions of finite life and the norm for responsible moral choice, actions, and relations, it links the good and the right. It joins actions and relations that lead to flourishing with the demand of duty or holiness. The integrity of life, so understood, is the name for that unity which is the goal or *telos* of third-way thinking, the goal of uniting flourishing with virtue, or, in the older Christian terms, happiness with holiness.

It seems, then, that the idea of the integrity of life articulates claims about the goodness and changeability of human existence found in the logic of Christian humanism, even as it provides a way to conceptualize the highest good, the unity of happiness and holiness, genuine flourishing and true virtue. It does so, we believe, while also holding fast to the classical insight about the range of goods that are required for flourishing, as well as the deeply humanistic affirmation of autonomy, respect for others, and social solidarity. In fact, the idea of the integrity of life expands our consideration of those goods and affirmations beyond the realm of the human species and thereby, we contend, provides the means to check within neohumanistic conviction the threat of overhumanization. That insight will be developed in the second part of this book.

Two ideas in the logic of Christian humanism remain to be addressed, namely, the means to speak of the human capacity for the divine and also the logic of perfection as the rule for proper discourse about the divine. What, if anything, does the integrity of life have to do with these ideas in the logic of Christian humanism? How might it provide the means to check the possibility of hypertheism as the inner-distortion of theistic religious and spiritual convictions? And how then to move from Christian humanism to theological humanism itself?

When we explored the Anselmic principle before, it became clear that whatever status it might have as a proof for the existence of God, it could be interpreted as a test of unsurpassable perfection for any claim about the reality of the divine. What we did not mention in that previous discussion (it was not germane) was that Anselm's argument relied upon a specific conception of perfection. The most perfect being, he reasoned, both *is* — it has being — and *necessarily* is, that is, it cannot logically, ontologically, or temporally be otherwise than it is. The unity of necessity and being, he seemed to think, is what one means by "perfection." To be perfect is to exist and to exist necessarily. Anselm further held that one cannot conceive of anything, in idea or in reality, that could surpass that unity of necessity and being; it must, therefore, name "God." His argument, it could be said, fell to the modern critique of metaphysics (see chapter 3). It is instructive, however, to turn the argument against itself in order to show how it points to the integrity of life.

Is it true that we cannot conceive of anything, in idea or in reality, which surpasses the unity of necessity and being? And, further, does the idea of the integrity of life name it? This is complicated since on the logic of Christian humanism the entire point of saying that humans are created good but changeable was to claim that the highest human good, the *summum bonum*, would have to be good and unchangeable, that is, perfect, just in the way Anselm conceived of God. God is then truly the highest good for humans and the struggle of human existence is to become united with the divine by grace and human effort. In Christian humanism there is a tight connection between the rules for right thinking about God and the idea of the highest good. The human good is to become godlike: good and real and unchangeable. Can that connection pertain to the idea of the integrity of life?

Ideas of perfection draw their force from perceptions and intuitions individuals and communities have about what is unsurpassably important to them, what is of ultimate significance and concern. These perceptions shift in the course of history. What was maximally important in ancient China is not the same as modern Europe or what had highest significance within the birth of Christianity or Islam or the wandering people of Israel. There is a history to human ideals, values, and concerns, at least with respect to their content and meanings.[18] That fact does not entail an invidious relativism of values and ideals because, as already shown, the idea of the integrity of life provides some orientation to life and the logic of perfection enables one to sort through legitimate from false claimants to human devotion.[19] What is of ultimate importance in our global age and the human future? Can it withstand the test of its claim to perfection?

The idea of the integrity of life names that perception and intuition for an age in which every form of life is endangered by forces of overhumanization and hypertheism. It does so, more pointedly, because it conceives of perfection in terms of the use of power – human or divine – not in the service of power itself, but in the service of life against forces of disintegration and death. The idea expresses the meaning of perfection as the unity of power and life, and in this way, we believe, names a central intuition and even spiritual longing of our age. Can this meet the logical test of perfection?

Consider it in this way. Is the idea of power, disconnected from the demand to respect and enhance the integrity of life, an unsurpassable idea? It cannot be, because power is always the power of something and therefore it must affirm the reality of its condition as maximal. Is the idea of life devoid of the capacity to create, respond to, or shape reality – that is, power – an unsurpassable idea? No, because life *per definition* entails that capacity and, therefore, the diminishing of power to nil is also the destruction of life. The idea of the integrity of life, in other words, captures the intuition that the capacity to respond to, create, and shape reality, a power found in living beings, must respect and enhance the right integration of its condition, that is, life. Further, any life so dedicated must be good in an unsurpassable way; it must also, as we have already shown, struggle to bind together happiness and virtue. In this respect, it is proper to say that "God" names the integrity of life even if "God" is not the sole causal agent in reality. And yet under the Anselmic principle, the idea of the integrity of life counters the forces of hypertheism. No belief, revelation, dogma, authority, or community can claim divine sanction or inspiration which in thought or word or deed violates the unsurpassable good of the integrity of life. In this way the idea bundles together both the logic of perfection and conception of the highest good, or so we believe.

What then of the last element in the logic, the claim about the human capacity for the divine? For Christian humanists, the human capacity for the divine was not a causal relation between self-knowledge or love or feeling and the divine reality. An individual who comes to know herself or himself as a moral and spiritual creature does not somehow *cause* its relation to God.

Further, the Anselmic idea of perfection, that is, the idea that perfection means necessary and unchanging being, underscores the non-causal relation between human beings and God, because humans, created good and changeable, can fall away from what is good and true, or they can seek it. The insight is that the logic of perfection, as a test about right thinking about God, and the idea of human beings as created good but changeable, are part and parcel of the belief that human beings have a capacity for the divine. On this classical Christian picture, the capacity for a relation to God is defined in terms of the possibility that a person, through the development of virtues, might become and be made like God – that is, necessarily real, unchangeably good, immortal. Further, that human possibility, the possibility, that is, that one might become unchangeably real and good, might become immortal and so escape the torment of death, seems, on many Christians' account, to find testimony in the human heart. Our hearts are restless till they rest in God, as St. Augustine put it. Human beings have a capacity for that relation even as their lives manifest a longing for the divine, for the perfection of unchanging reality.

The classical Christian humanist conception of the human capacity for the divine was a longing for completion in light of the fallibility and incompleteness of human existence. Insofar as classical thinkers thought about perfection in terms of unchangeable being, it is obvious that does not characterize actual human life, even if it names a human aspiration. We are mortal, only mortal. This is just the other side of the coin to what was noted above about perceptions and intuitions of what is unsurpassably important. For classical theologians, what was of supreme concern was conceived in relation to a profound sense of the fleetingness of human existence, whether that fleetingness is believed to be natural or, for Christians, the punishment for original sin. The human capacity for God was experienced as a longing or a mood to overcome the transience of existence into a condition of permanent and unchanging reality (say, heaven). The point, then, is just what one would expect. The set of ideas that characterize the logic of classic Christian humanism links the human capacity for God with its other ideas while inscribing itself in the deepest human desires and longing for what is of unsurpassable concern. While true about Christian humanism, the unity of being and necessity is not the core of theological humanism. Here we must strike out in new paths that take us beyond classical Christian humanism.

The real question, again, is whether or not the idea of the integrity of life denotes an unsurpassable concern of our age and then how it unfolds the human capacity for the divine. There seems to be widespread longing in our

91

age to counter forces of disintegration in forms of life amid their complex relations. Yet the same longing testifies to the ever-present sense of life's struggle to bring itself to wholeness, to integration, in spite of the pull and drag of disintegration. Most people in advanced, late-modern global societies do not seem to seek *necessary being*. It is not at all clear what that idea would mean in actual human life. There is no obvious reason why we should think that necessity is more important than what is not necessary. The oddity of actual life, in its particularity, vulnerability, and contingency, can surprise us with as much wonder and love as what is permanent and necessary. People tend to have a sense for vibrancy, changeability, the aliveness of reality. What is desired, then, is more aliveness. William James, the American philosopher, wrote in his book on religious experience that "life, more life, a larger, richer, more satisfying life, is, in the last analysis, the end of religion. The love of life, at any and every level of development, is the religious impulse."[20]

James is only partly right. What seems of unsurpassable importance is not simply life, even more life. If that were true then life itself could pass the Anselmic test of perfection; life would be a kind of God. Theological humanism would thus require pantheism and vitalism, the belief that the world is alive and is divine. That does not seem right, and for the same reason that traditional Christian humanism did not just seek only being or mere necessity, but some state of perfection that unified those other goods.

What a theological humanist seeks, we submit, is the right integration of the goods of life around a commitment to respect and enhance this integrity in others and oneself. What seems to be of unsurpassable importance is the right and responsible unity of power and life as the integrity of life. There is little wonder why that should be so in an age in which the radical extension of human power through technology threatens all forms of life. It is also an age in which forces of disintegration show that any one form of life cannot claim ultimate importance unless gathered up and linked to a commitment to respect and enhance the integration of those goods needed for life to be sustained and to flourish. The integrity of life connotes for our time the deepest longing and the most profound claim on human life. That is the contention of theological humanism.

How might one speak of that longing and claim as a felt sense in human existence and as a capacity for the divine? What images or metaphors and symbols would a theological humanism drawn from Christian sources use to name this "God?" That is to admit that a form of theological humanism arising within other religious resources might be developed through different metaphors and images and might even reject the idea of God itself. The answer to the question was intimated in our discussion of conscience. As a picture, image, or metaphor for our whole being as moral and mortal creatures, conscience is both the longing for integrity, a desired crystallization of the soul, and a claim, a demand, to respect and enhance the integration of goods in other forms of life. Insofar as "God" is the integrity of life – that is, the power of life towards its ever-renewed integration of power and life sensed and held as ultimately important and real – then conscience is a sense of the divine, a capacity for what we can call or name God. Of course, this sense, this capacity, can be vague, fleeting, and distorted; human life is riddled with fallibility and fault. As Christian thinkers have always known, the fact of conscience is insufficient to ground valid reflection on God. The claim of conscience does not *cause* a relation to the divine. Yet the sense and longing of conscience, that is, the longing for and sense of the claim of the integrity of life, arises through the dimensions of life conjointly with the sense and longing for the divine. It must then be constantly tested to ensure that this is a right sense, a true longing, a valid idea of the divine. That test, we can now see, is provided by the whole constellation of ideas found in the notion of the integrity of life. Insofar as that is correct, then we formulate the imperative of responsibility rightly to reflect the human capacity for God in and through the sense and claim of conscience: in all actions and relations, respect and enhance the integrity of life *before God*. That imperative, we submit, clarifies what is ultimately important and real and also the way in which the human capacity for God can be conceived within theological humanism.

The Next Step

In this chapter we have completed the first step of this book by outlining theological humanism aimed at the integrity of life. Next, we will show what light theological humanism sheds on various domains of existence in response to the twin challenges of overhumanization and hypertheism.

Part II

The Task of Theological Humanism

6

Our Endangered Garden

Challenges to Natural Life

The following chapters focus on challenges within the contemporary global age. These chapters put theological humanism on trial to see where thought leads us. The present inquiry is about basic and natural goods. In terms of classic humanist images, the following pages explore the garden, those given features of life which must be rightly cultivated in order to flourish. The garden, this fragile blue-green orb called planet earth, is now gravely endangered. The place of life, the good of locality, is threatened. What is needed, we argue, is clarity about the moral standing of all forms of life, as well as the specific responsibility of human communities.

Of course, human beings have always intervened to alter their environments for the sake of survival. Nevertheless, in the present age the expansion of human power has increased the impact of human action on life. Nuclear energy, farming and fishing techniques, tall-stack factories, and automobiles threaten future life on this planet, most obviously through global warming, but also in the loss of species and the destruction of lands and forests. Those threats are deeply interwoven with economic forces that generate wealth but also leave a trail of poverty and misery in their wake. As the Christian ethicist William French has noted:

> No previous generation has faced the array of ecological concerns that now command attention: habitat destruction, global warming, aquifer overuse, deforestation and erosion, species endangerment and extinction, air and water pollution, acid precipitation, and nuclear waste. Some biologists warn that the

synergy between habitat destruction and climate change may well usher in the sixth extinction spasm in the Earth's long history, the first for which humanity bears responsibility.[1]

The endangerment to human life is no less real and pressing. The hideous and ongoing violations of human bodies, especially women's and girls' bodies, around the world takes many forms. Rape, human trade (mainly children), sex tourism, honor killings for the violation of (patriarchal) sexual codes, and the fact of the global spread of HIV/AIDS testify to the many ways human flesh is demeaned and destroyed and the integrity of people's lives violated. Insofar as basic and natural goods are necessary conditions for any other goods humans can and might pursue, then forces that threaten them endanger the future.

The world's religions have at best an ambiguous record in their teachings about care for the earth and the human body. At worst, the religions too often picture the physical world as the domain of death and sin that must be escaped, by (say) enlightenment from karmic cycles, or as a means to heaven through salvation. In these outlooks, reality is enfolded in a vision of divine power or ultimate reality which can demean the domain of goods and thereby threaten the possibility of a livable and sustainable future. The origin and destiny of the world, it is believed, is "in the hands of God" or under some logic of karmic cycles which can relieve the demand of human responsibility for protecting and sustaining finite life.

A popular criticism of religion is usually leveled against the monotheistic faiths. Based on a reading of the creation story in Genesis, a male creator God supposedly rules like an ancient despot and demands that human beings subdue and exploit the earth. This idea of God, it is argued, forms the background to the ecological crisis and the development of technology in the Western world. To be sure, the idea of a heavenly deity who has little regard for earthly matters is deep within the monotheistic religions. Yet to reduce those religions to this idea is obviously a distortion of the monotheistic religions, not to mention bad biblical studies and theology.[2] Still, forms of hypertheism threaten fragile basic goods.

This is also true of human bodies. Too often, the world's religions have demeaned bodily existence and also legitimated the unjust treatment of human bodies. Virtually every religious community has tragic and sad legacies of sexual abuse. Some conservative religious communities want to deny lesbians and homosexuals a range of civil liberties, and in other cultures traditional religious practices (cutting; female circumcision; marriage customs) contribute to the spread of diseases. Additionally, the prohibition of contraceptives among some religious traditions too often leaves women with newborn children but limited means for proper care and nutrition, while also contributing to the ecological burden of increasing human populations. The plight of the human body is interwoven with endangerments to our shared, planetary garden.

Theological humanism must provide a way to orient human life within world-shaping dynamics. How to proceed? First, we will explore briefly the reality of globality and globalization and the possibilities and endangerments these introduce to the human future. After all, the locality of present life is truly global. That discussion will provide background for other chapters.

Global Dynamics and Global Locality

Some people like to speak of globalization as the McDonaldization of the world.[3] Global dynamics, on this picture, obliterate previous markers of identity and draw new ones; they define the world's peoples within the logic of the consumer market. Others disagree. The condemnation of economic globalization as market tyranny is not so easy. Behind the supposed "sameness" of globalization are surprising forces of difference. People around the world are fashioning lives in new and different ways. Additionally, there are extensive debates about the so-called clash of civilizations and also the collision of faiths. The idea is that the forms of conflict that will characterize the age of globality are cultural, ideological, and religious, and that one cannot expect an easy resolution to these forces. The age is described not in terms of the dialectic of sameness and difference within global economic and cultural flows, but rather as the titanic clash between incommensurable forms of human civilization.[4]

Scholars note that globalization is not a new phenomenon. Some trace the earliest phases back to the spread of hunters and gatherers and the rise of agriculture around 10,000 years ago.[5] It is helpful to isolate several dynamics at work within the current wave of globalization that make the world our shared "locality:" deep connectivity, global reflexivity, and recognition. Taken together, these dynamics lead to the "deterritorialization" of identity and authority and also to what is called the "compression of the world."[6] Our world is becoming "smaller" and is also increasingly seen by people around the planet as a whole, a shared destiny. These facts of locality alter identities.

John Tomlinson notes that globalization "refers to the rapidly developing and ever-densening network of interconnections and interdependencies that characterize modern social life."[7] "Deep connectivity," as he calls it, is forging, for good or ill, the future of planetary life. There is an increasing sense of shared planetary destiny even as global dynamics foster powerful senses of cultural, religious, and ethnic difference. Clear examples include globalized cities such as Berlin, Hong Kong, or Mexico City. These are "places" in which people's identities, sense of others and the wider world, as well as values and desires, are locally situated but altered by global dynamics. Saskia Sassen writes that the "city has indeed emerged as a site for new claims: by global capital which uses the city as an 'organizational commodity,' but also by disadvantaged sectors of the urban population, which in large cities are frequently as internationalized a presence as is capital."[8]

One element in the current structure of human life is the quickening pace of deep connectivity that drives the compression of the world. Yet these dynamics also mean people's lives are increasingly shaped by how they are perceived by others. This brings to light a second dynamic. Theorists call it "global reflexivity," and it profoundly influences both social and reflective goods. Reflexivity is the many ways social entities act back upon themselves to adjust to information about their internal and external working.[9] It is rooted in the distinctive human capacity to be aware of oneself while interacting with and adjusting to others. Political entities, for instance, have to adapt reflexively to developments in the market or world opinion. Individuals and groups see themselves in terms of how others see and react to them. Reflexive dynamics shape how people react, often violently. Think of the massive global response to political cartoons that depict religious leaders. So, one can decode the structures of experience amid global dynamics in terms of deep connectivity and reflexivity. These bring about the compression of the world along with the expansion of consciousness and the deterritorialization of identity.

Deep connectivity and global reflexivity are closely related to a third dynamic, one that brings us to more obvious religious and moral features of globalization. Recognition, as we know from chapter 5, is the perception and acknowledgment of moral standing in social relations, that is, the rightful claim to respect and enhancement. People's identities and self-understandings arise within or are effaced by patterns and structures of recognition. This is of course not a new idea. It is found in debates about multiculturalism and "identity politics" and also among feminist theologians who chart the effacement of women's agency within patriarchal systems.[10] Patterns of recognition are also central in discussions of truth and reconciliation after intolerable acts of violence and war and abuse. One of the crucial conditions of such acts of intolerable violence is the breakdown of capacities of moral perception and imagination needed to recognize the moral standing of human beings.[11]

100

The dynamics of recognition are interwoven with the other processes of globalization. The global media, for instance, intensify but block recognition. Global markets forge patterns of deep connectivity, but can efface recognition of distinctive ethnic and cultural identities. The spread of disease is a reflexive process that compresses the world in much the same way that global warming does; the horror of epidemic and the fear it breeds often deprive those who suffer of moral recognition. It would take more pages than we have available to sort through the connections among these dynamics and processes, as well as to address the many moral and political challenges they pose at the intersections of basic, social, natural, and reflective goods.

The current locale of lived social reality – the processes and dynamics of globalization – poses a fundamental challenge, namely, how can human consciousness be transformed in order to foster recognition of and responsibility with and for others that does not devolve into the horrific celebration of power? On many fronts, the challenge is to recognize and respond to the moral claim of diverse forms of life within the actual process that structures global reality. This raises the question of fundamental attitudes towards natural life, as well as deeper reflection on basic goods. We turn to that question now and then explore social and reflexive goods in the following chapters.

The Status of 'Nature"

Three challenges define the topic of basic and natural goods.[12] First, increasingly, human beings can alter forms of life from the genetic to planetary levels; we can communicate globally even as we can probe life at its most minute levels – map the genome. This technological explosion has had profoundly good and profoundly destructive consequences. By technology is meant not just tools people use to accomplish things, although it includes that. Technology, as thinkers like Heidegger noted, is a structure in our lives. It implies a way of seeing and valuing the world, a whole worldview. Reality is increasingly perceived as subject to human power and what many value is the extension of control over life to serve the ends of human control.[13] People seek, for instance, to end disease and to relieve physical suffering, and that is good. Yet this implies a worldview that is sometimes stated as the technological imperative: because we *can* do something we *ought* to do it. Some even define morality in this way. "Morality," Brian Wicker puts it, "is essentially concerned with the exercise of those capacities which make us more self-aware, and so more in control."[14] Is that right? *Are there things we ought never to do, even if we can?*

101

Developments in genetics and also the Human Genome Project are a powerful instance of this technological outlook. When Dolly was cloned in 1997 – a sheep cloned from the udder cell of a 6-year-old ewe – an article in *The Economist* noted:

> This makes her [Dolly] trebly significant. She brings closer the time when it may be possible to clone a human. The technology that produced her will probably make it far easier to alter the genetic make-up of animals … and she answered some questions scientists want answered about the role of DNA as creatures develop into fully grown adults.[15]

Subsequent cloning of a black bull from a stem cell (a cell without a specialized function) furthered the process. At the far end of these developments are questions about human cloning. These questions about human life accompany the modern developments in genetics, from the discovery of DNA (1945–70) through the developing of recombinant DNA techniques (genetic engineering, 1970–95), to the developments in the 1990s and the Human Genome Project: a detailed map of the human genome that will reveal the basic "instructions" for the development and functioning of the human. Our technological capacities now shape our own nature. As the theologian Paul Ramsey once put it, "those who come after us may not be like us."[16] We must ask: What is our responsibility to a future species of humans that is genetically different than us? What do we owe future life?

Technology bears on conceptions of "nature" itself. This is the second challenge. Throughout much of Western history, "nature" was a term for what defines something as what it most essentially is. For example, the nature of a human being, in the classical Aristotelian definition, is to be a rational, social animal. More specifically, while human beings are social creatures and linked to other animals, it is "reason," classical thinkers held, that denotes the specific difference between humans and other creatures. In a connected sense, nature represented a domain of reality, opposed to "super-nature," that was the condition for temporal existence but also the limits on existence. The regularity of seasons, of light and dark, the subtle balance of ecosystems, sustain life on this planet, and yet natural creatures are also limited, they are mortal. The idea of the human, we know from previous chapters, inscribes within the name the idea of mortality, earth-bound.

Each of these senses of nature may now have come to an end. Together, they constitute a threat to locality, basic goods, and the preciousness of the earth. The capacity of human beings to intervene and change forms of life at the most basic genetic level or to alter ecosystems seems to imply that "nature" is no longer a viable idea in traditional senses of the term. The human power to alter reality suggests that there is no "essence" to any form of life – in fact, we can alter the genetic code – and, further, that the "limits" nature once implied no longer pertain. Not surprisingly, this has led some authors to speak about the "end" of nature or the "reinvention" of nature.[17] Certainly, it means that moral norms cannot be easily grounded in nature and that we have to forgo the longstanding idea that somehow the nature of some form of life clearly indicates what will bring it flourishing.

The debate about nature in our technological age leads to the third challenge. It is about *what is valued and how much it is valued*. There is the challenge of how people around the world are responding to the many threats to the viability of life on this planet. Consider the worldwide environmental movement. Will we respect the fragile web of life that sustains us and is the condition for any viable form of existence in the future? How is one to explain the "value" of the natural world in an age in which technological rationality and consumer demands reign over forms of thought? Without a sense of the goodness of natural life, a perception of the fragility and vulnerability of non-human life, it is not clear that changes in environmental policy will actually work. Some thinkers, like Hans Jonas, believe that we need a "heuristics of fear" about the threat to future life in order to energize responsibility for the natural world, the cry of mute things, as he calls it.[18] Likewise, there are debates about "exit ethics," that is, the moral issues that surround the end of life, euthanasia, abortion, capital punishment, and war. How is one to think about conflicts between forms of life, between mother and fetus, the suffering and medical responsibilities, the justification, if any, of death as a means of punishment? There are debates about the moral requirements on peoples, governments, and even economies to provide with some modicum of justice the basic needs necessary for human life to flourish. Do we have rights to basic goods like food and shelter and bodily integrity? What is the status of those rights in terms of sprawling global market systems?[19] Ecology, life and death issues, political and economic realities, the question of the Human Genome Project, must also and more particularly be seen in terms of debates about the extent to which we can and should alter any form of life.

In the face of these moral and political realities, pervasive attitudes towards life have come to light. The Zen Buddhist monk, peace activist and scholar, Thich Nhat Hanh, argues that the first precept for any contemporary ethics must be "reverence for life." He writes:

Life is precious. It is everywhere, inside us and all around us; it has so many forms. The First Precept is born from the awareness that lives everywhere are being destroyed. We see the suffering caused by the destruction of life, and we undertake to cultivate compassion and use it as a source of energy for the protection of people, animals, plants, and minerals. The First Precept is a precept of compassion, karuna – the ability to remove suffering and transform it. When we see suffering, compassion is born in us.[20]

In the Western ear this passage harkens back both to Albert Schweitzer's argument for an ethics of a reverence for life, and also to many themes in Christian faith about the care for life as created by God and redeemed by Christ. Some concern, compassion, or reverence for life is widespread in the religions and among peoples of the world. How one values life – and what life is valued – orients other decisions, say about cloning or genetic testing.

The claim that life has a special worth, that we ought to dedicate ourselves to actions, relations, and policies that respect and enhance life, is precisely what is now being debated, even at the level of fundamental attitudes. Pope John Paul II talked about affirming life in a culture of death – a culture of war, devaluation of the aged, euthanasia, and abortion. Other thinkers talk about the need to affirm "deep ecology," that is, seeing how ecosystems are valuable. Peter Singer, we know, insists on "unsanctifying human life." As he notes, "we are going through a period of transition in our attitude towards the sanctity of human life."[21] He argues for an open policy of euthanasia, especially of the old, the possible justification of infanticide, and a denial of any morally decisive difference between human beings and non-human forms of life. What matters is the relief of suffering in sentient beings. Similarly, there are discussions among theorists of various sorts on "cyborg existence," the melding of the human and the machine, creation of virtual life, debates about computer intelligence and forms of life – both in the lab and in popular TV programs like *Star Trek*. The deepest challenge is not only technical or procedural or global, but also *evaluative*: it is how we understand and evaluate the "worth" of life. How one responds to this third challenge shapes more specific discussions about the goods of natural life.

One needs clarity about the idea of value when one says that life has value. There is, first, the difference between value (or worth) and price. To speak of something having *moral worth* or *moral value* means that it is to be acknowledged and respected in and of itself without reference to other ends or purposes it might serve. I say, for instance, that my son has worth and by this I mean that he is to be acknowledged and respected for what he is and not because he might make a lot of money or be a good citizen or a fine doctor. For theological humanists, the idea of the integrity of life denotes the source and term of moral worth, of value. This means, second, that we can also speak of *instrumental value* versus *final value*, meaning by this those things that we value as a means to some other end. My car has instrumental value to me insofar as it gets me to where I want to go. But what of human genes and body parts and euthanasia to get us what we want, say relief from pain? And what of ecosystems?

Now we can *define* the issue before us. The technological imperative – because we *can*, we *should* – risks reducing everything to instrumental value, to price, in the pursuit of technological goods as a final value. Actions and policies, forms of life and ecosystems, are then enfolded within the reach of human power conceived as a good–in–itself, a final value. This is the project of overhumanization. In the current situation it is extremely difficult to artic-ulate and to defend a conception of worth that is not easily reduced to price or instrumental value. There is the increased willingness to assign a price to body parts, wetlands, air and water, and genetic advances to alter species. We are not, thankfully, quite to the point of the complete banishment of moral argument about final or intrinsic value from the public arena – although we are on that path. That is one reason to insist that social and political policy remain open to moral criticism.

We ought not to resist all forms of technology. That would be humanly impossible and actually immoral. Still, people must morally assess the power at their disposal and how that power is to be used. With that insight we can now turn more directly to the debate about basic and natural goods in our global situation.

Mapping the Moral Landscape

We have been sorting through a range of issues in trying to *define* the moral challenges involved in thinking about how to assess and rightly value the garden, that is, the goods of natural life which human power can intervene to cultivate, change, and destroy. Let us now map some widespread argu-ments. The aim is to clarify the moral debate and to sort out what might be a properly theological humanist position.

Ethics for the Enhancement of Life

One common ethical stance in the West holds that the moral task is to promote those aspects of life deemed most important and to counter or change what impedes life, (say) disease, physical and mental suffering.

105

The accent falls on what we ought to do in order to further what we value in life. This ethical position affirms the technological imperative in the service of greater control of life. The aim is to fashion a better, stronger form of human life; it is to free us from pain and suffering. The ethics for the enhancement of life (as we call it) is found among secular and religious thinkers and movements. In terms of theory, it is rigorously utilitarian: the right thing to do is defined by the consequence of action measured by some idea of utility. This ethics too often fails to question technology as itself a moral worldview, a way of seeing life and value. In this view, the primary ethical task is to minimize suffering through the development of medicine and technology, and also ending moral qualms about end of life issues (say, abortion or euthanasia). For this outlook, anyone who wants limits to experimentation and discovery rooted in claims about human life's sanctity or dignity seems cruel. One needs to focus on the good consequences that can follow from procedures. This is overhumanization within the realm of human and non-human life.

On the plane of human existence, practical questions arise. Will the procedure relieve suffering and serve the interests of those involved? Are scientific procedures and results undertaken, attained, and distributed in a fair manner? Is the cost of life and other public goods – including economic ones – acceptable with respect to the utility, i.e., the promotion of interests and relieving suffering? If space allowed, we could go through these specific issues surrounding ethical analysis. For our purpose the most crucial thing to see is that this ethic *requires* the denial of the sanctity of life. Some, like Singer, insist that ideas about the sanctity of life are specifically religious and thus have no place in multicultural and religiously neutral nations. Others argue that ideas like the sanctity of life are fictions, since there is nothing called "human nature." Human beings are plastic creatures, shaped by their cultures. The only task is to avoid suffering and respect cultural differences.[22] And still other thinkers argue that ideas about the sanctity of human life are anthropocentric because they falsely place human life at the center of what we value.

By denying the inviolability of life, this ethics shifts the weight of moral analysis to what will "enhance" life through means that relieve suffering and promote interests. If we can use some forms of life, from stem cells to fetuses and newborns, to that end, it is ethically warranted. This moral outlook, if not the precise ethical position, is one of the dominant voices heard in the discussion of the Human Genome Project, stem cell research, and also debates about ecological holism where whole ecologies, not human beings, are morally central.[23]

Ethics for the Reverence of Life

A second view says that the moral task is to *reverence* life as it has developed on this planet. This ethics is usually found among religious and non-religious people, often conservatives. Ethically speaking, this position is deontological: what is good and right is defined in terms of duties to moral laws and others, not consequences. The ethics of the reverence of life asserts that human existence, the *humanum*, is given by God and reflects God's image in the world. Technology is a tool rather than a worldview. The ethics thereby misses the depth of the challenge as well as the positive side of *homo techno-logicus*. The outlook is hypertheistic, even if not explicitly cast in religious form. Morality is not about making life better by overcoming pain, sorrow, and loss, but protecting it from destruction, even the destruction caused by human action. This widespread ethical position, including secular people and religious leaders from popes to Buddhist monks like Hanh, denies the tech-nological imperative in favor of insisting on the intrinsic sanctity of life. For theistic traditions, the idea is that moral goodness is about discerning God's will for us and then living in conformity with God's will. Insofar as human beings are created in the image of God, we ought not to seek to alter or change that image. Limits must be placed on experimentation when those limits are intrinsic to human nature. To deny those limits is, for this position, immoral insofar as it leads to actions that deny the duty to respect the lives of others. There are some things we should never do, and these are rooted in the inviolability of life.

For the ethics of the reverence of life, practical issues are of various kinds. Will the procedures respect the sanctity of life as it is given, and are they con-sistent with a range of other life-issues? Are scientific procedures and results undertaken, attained, and distributed in a fair manner? Are the procedures part of the formation of a "culture of life" in which other goods – like sci-entific research and economic goods – are put to the service of what fosters life and cares for the least advantaged? If space allowed, we could go through more specific questions surrounding ethical analysis of genetic technology.

For our purposes, the most crucial thing to see is that this ethics *requires* belief in the sanctity of human life. Some thinkers, like Pope John Paul II, Paul Ramsey, and others, ground this claim in their religious convictions and hope to show how those convictions can resonate in public debate. Other thinkers, philosophers, and theologians argue that ideas like the sanctity of life are grounded in human freedom, consciousness, and relation to others. Human beings are cultural creatures, to be sure. But we are also the members of a species with attributes we value.[24] And still others – and this includes some religious thinkers – argue that only by holding on to the intrinsic worth of life can we place limits on technological power in the name of future life on this planet. By insisting on the inviolability of life, its sanctity, this ethics shifts the weight of moral analysis to what "respects" life and so evaluates any technological means that claim to relieve suffering and promote interests. What is intrinsically good is life; the relief of suffering for living beings is not self-justifying.

The Human Calling

In the face of technology and the spread of human power, certain neohumanists argue that we must see humans as the "Shepherds of Being," or, theologically stated, assume stewardship for the earth. The central moral issue is not just power or technology, but, rather, attitudes for life, as these neohumanists have seen. On this point the ethics for the enhancement of life and the ethics of the reverence for life are off the mark. The ethics for the enhancement of life recognizes only *interests and preferences* of those beings that can suffer. This seems to make the supreme value the avoidance of suffering or the relief of pain. The ethics of the reverence for life risks making life into a second God, so sacred that we ought never to take life under any circumstance. The mistake in both forms of ethics is to believe that life *qua* life is that which is to be given respect and to be enhanced.

For a theological humanist, the human calling is to bear responsibility for the *integrity* of life. What we are to respect and enhance is not life *qua* life, but, rather, the integration of goods: goods rooted in bodily need and well-being; goods rooted in social interaction; goods rooted in reflective structures of meaning and value; goods of locality. In terms of duties (respect and enhance), the object of moral consideration and the scope of value (integrity of life), theological humanism places strong limits on the power to intervene and change life. It combats the full- scale acceptance of the technological imperative. And yet it also opens an appropriate arena and specifies the conditions in which there can be the responsible use of technological power. The burden and joy of responsibility remains the human calling. Difficult and often tragic choices must be made about specific decisions and policies in the treatment of human and non-human life. As noted in chapter 5, responsibility orders the demands of *respect* and *enhancement* and so signals third-way thinking about actions and relation, including basic and natural goods.

It would be possible to explore specific cases and challenges surrounding the responsibility human beings have for the garden. Rather than enter into particular cases, it is important as the final step in this chapter to address a question especially salient for any form of *humanism*. What is the relation between human and non-human forms of life? Are there any valid reasons to grant human distinctiveness without thereby demeaning the status and stature of non-human life? Why not join some form of neohumanism, Heideggerian or ecological, in response to the challenges of our technological and global age? While the following chapters of this book set forth a picture of human responsibility in exemplary domains of life, a few words are needed at this point in the argument. These thoughts focus, again, on the differences between hypertheism, overhumanization, and theological humanism.

Classical theism holds that God is supremely important and real and the one in relation to whom the rest of reality draws its being and its worth. Classical theism is, accordingly, radically *theocentric* in its conception of what has worth. In most theistic traditions, especially the great monotheistic faiths, human beings have distinctive worth because of their special relation to God, say, created in God's image, as it is put in the Bible, or, according to the Qu'ran, God's viceregents. In a theistic outlook, intrinsic value derives from a relation to God, and human beings (however defined) have a unique relation to the deity, unlike the rest of the created order.[25] Theism defines the point of life in terms of *conformity* to God's will, and, further, human beings share in a distinctive way in God's future.

Classical theism has been under relentless attack throughout the modern period. The theistic outlook linked God as the highest value to human beings as possessing unique worth in relation to other forms of life. Theism seems to denigrate the natural world and pictures non-human animals as instrumental to human flourishing. With the breakdown of this theistic outlook there emerges both anthropocentric value orientations, usually associated with humanism and overhumanization, and, conversely, non-anthropocentric outlooks that have taken religious form, in hypertheism, and also non-religious expression, say, in ecological holism. Many contemporary people believe that human beings alone possess intrinsic worth, and, accordingly, the natural world and non-human animals have their worth in relation to human beings. Conversely, others argue that the value of human life is interdependent with larger patterns and processes of reality and it is the larger wholes, not human life, that have intrinsic worth. If that is the case, it is justified to put limits on human flourishing for the sake of the patterns and processes of which we are a part.

This chapter has already charted some of the arguments of these two positions in the various ways they appear within the current debate about

109

natural life. What then about theological humanism? While it will take a good deal of the following chapters of this book to explain the point, it is warranted, we contend, to speak of human distinctiveness. We say *distinctiveness* in order to stress that human beings are not absolutely unique within the realms of life. Other creatures face the unrelenting task of integrating their existence against forces of disintegration and death, have capacities for action and forms of consciousness, and, in some primates, have "moral" emotions and sympathies. Yet human beings are distinctive, we contend, because of the extent of the demand and capacity to exercise power in order to respect and enhance the integrity of life. Neither earth nor being is the ethical focus, but human responsibility for the integrity of life. Human distinctiveness is a way of speaking about the depth of moral responsibility and not moral privilege, and in two respects.

The range of goods that must be integrated in life shows the ways in which human life is embedded in and interdependent with other forms of life on this planet. Human beings exist within and not against the realms of life. And yet human beings confront the task of integrating their personal and social life as a *moral task* rather than a simple biological need or instinctual given. The integration of human existence (personal and social) is chosen and achieved with respect to ideals and norms that orient life. Being human is a distinctly moral and spiritual project. Human beings are things "in between;" we exist in between features of given life and the ongoing task to achieve the integration of existence. This means, in terms used before, that humanity is both an origin and a destiny, something received and something achieved. Human distinctiveness is, ironically, the burden of fashioning our existence, tending our garden.

With the radical expansion of human power that characterizes the technological and global age, human distinctiveness is intensified. The fate of the earth, other species, and also human well-being falls within the scope of collective human responsibility. This is the second respect in which human beings are distinctive. Human power is both the problem and the possibility for a livable future. What values and ideas and norms will guide the exercise of human power, individual and social? Ought we to seek the continual maximization of power in order to further human purposes, as over-humanization contends? Is the human calling to live in conformity to the will of God and God alone, as the various kinds of hypertheism contend? Theological humanism holds that the distinctive calling of human beings in our global age is to respect and enhance the integrity of life. If that calling is forsaken, then the powers of this age are unleashed from any purpose other than their own advancement or these same powers are shackled to those who claim to speak in the name of God. From the perspective of theological humanism, the distinctive calling of human beings is to turn power into responsibility and thereby to assume the commitment to tend the fragile garden of this earth.

Conclusion

The rest of this book clarifies various aspects of human responsibility for the integrity of life. In this chapter we have tried to provide a context for that discussion in terms of the condition and dynamics of globalization. We have also noted the specific contribution of theological humanism to combat various endangerments to human and non-human life. At the heart of that contribution are duties and their relations (respect and enhance), the good that can and ought to be served by responsible action (the integrity of life), and, finally, an inclusive scope of concern. People have the hard task of deciding in difficult cases how responsibly to meet the challenges and conflicts of the age. That difficulty, we conclude, is another way of speaking about the distinctive calling of human beings in our global times of endangerment to life.

7

A School for Conscience

The previous chapter centered on basic goods and the debate about natural life. The kind of good explored in this chapter is the "social" good. Again, we are putting theological humanism on trial with respect to other ideas and positions now dominant in public discourse. In terms of classical humanist images, we are exploring the school.

The school is a crucial idea in humanistic social thought for several reasons. First, humanists – religious and otherwise – have always held that the purpose of social life is not only to maintain order, to advance power, or to secure wealth, however important those tasks might be. The wider social purpose is to contribute to human well-being and the formation of people's moral identities through free, creative action. Second, humanists believe, in ways that some others do not, that the bonds of society, the links of human social life, extend beyond the locality of any specific community, whether a nation, religion, race, or empire. The idea is that human life must be freely formed and, further, that it is rightly formed by engaging the most profound expressions of human insight, intelligence, and creativity. No culture or tradition possesses the sum total of knowledge and insight; we have much to learn from others.

A third reason why the idea of the school is crucial is perhaps the most pressing in our current context. Humanistic thought is dedicated to the victory of understanding rather than force in confronting human conflicts. There are cases when coercion and force are justified as the means to the ends of new understanding, responsibility, and genuine persuasion. Still, a humanist believes that social life proper aims at intelligence and peace, not belligerence. There is a finality of the other, as we put it before, and therefore one is necessarily committed to a cosmopolitan outlook. Later, we will call this the *cosmopolitan conscience* as a distinct idea about the *task* of theological humanism in thinking about the formation of social identities. Here too we draw on and yet think differently than certain types of current neohumanism.

In order to educate the cosmopolitan conscience, we must begin this chapter with a problem now found on the global field of social interactions. Our concern, recall, is not just with the freedom *of* or *from* religion, but much more with freedom *within* religion as a dictate of conscience.

The Conflict of Powers

The importance of identity for social and political thought is not difficult to grasp, especially on the world scene.[1] Human beings are born unformed and, accordingly, through processes of social formation and self-cultivation, "education," receive and achieve a view of the world, a sense of belonging (or alienation), and an identity. Identity markers like religion, gender, race, or class specify how individuals and communities see themselves and others. What is more, there is the constant desire and pressure by individuals and groups for *recognition*. People want to be recognized and acknowledged to have standing with and before others. As we saw in chapter 5, recognition, shame, benevolence, and other sensibilities are motivations in human life. Not surprisingly, there are worldwide struggles for recognition among those who are ignored or effaced by dominant social powers. The struggles for recognition among women and colonized peoples (to name just two forms of struggle) are forms of resistance to forces of dehumanization. The question about human identity and the kinds of freedom people have in their social lives is thereby important in our context.

The debate about identity is often cast as a collision between political and religious outlooks. On the one side are thinkers like Daniel C. Dennett, a philosopher at Tufts University. In his book *Breaking the Spell* and elsewhere, Dennett argues that protecting democracy must come before promoting any faith. In fact, protecting democracy might require policies that act against specific religions. Religion thwarts human freedom and forms identity around superstitious beliefs that derail democratic societies.[2] Religion robs people of the choice about how to live by demanding mindless conformity. On the other side are those who insist that the public square is "naked," as Richard Neuhaus put it.[3] Citizens in "secular" liberal democratic societies are required to bracket their faith-convictions in order to participate in free and open political debate. In doing so their ability to provide robust reasons for their political commitments is endangered.

113

Each side of this debate is being played out in the popular media, in religious institutions, and also think-tanks in the United States and elsewhere. It surfaces, for instance, in debates about Muslim women wearing headscarves in schools and public offices. Seen globally, the extremes are more extreme, ranging from the State suppression of religions to recent attempts to establish theocratic regimes.

These debates find expression *within* religious communities. Buddhists, Hindus, Christians, Jews, and Muslims argue among themselves about what it means to be a member of the Church, a Jew, part of the worldwide Islamic community, a Hindu, or a Buddhist. Take Christianity, for example. In the United States, the United Kingdom, and elsewhere, there is a theological movement called postliberalism or narrative theology or, we think best, Christian particularism. This outlook holds that the primary task of the Christian community is to enfold Christian identity within the story of God's actions in Jesus Christ, and that story alone. Christians need to develop virtues and traits of character, that is, form their identities, in ways to live within the Church as an alien reality to the "world." The Church is to witness to the "world," a realm of violence and sin, about the possibility of peace made possible in the Church and only there. The Church exists in opposition to the "world."[4]

There are, unsurprisingly, equally powerful voices within the churches that challenge Christian particularism. These Christians believe that the purpose of the Church is to be inclusive, to extend the embrace of Christ. It is to overcome the identification of Christian faith with an invidious patriarchy that effaces the experience of women and the legacy of virulent racism and Eurocentrism that denies the importance of the lives of peoples around the world, especially those formerly enslaved or colonized. These movements form Christian identity in the Black Churches, within local communities important for liberation theology, in feminist and womanist movements, and also in the Latino/Latina communities. Sad to say, there seems to be a clash of civilizations *within* the churches. The same could be said of other religious traditions as well, say in conflict between Sunni and Shi'a Muslims.

Theological humanism is poised at the intersections of two "powers" that have often dominated social existence, namely, the religious community, the Christian Church in our case, and political community, the State. These two powers have battled for supremacy in social existence throughout time. How could it be otherwise? Each claims to represent the unsurpassable good of human life: God's will or the human community. The tactic of theological humanism lodged between these two powers is to articulate that good, the integrity of life, that human communities can and ought to serve.

The remainder of this chapter is the working out of that proposal and its relation to social freedom. This chapter cannot offer an entire theory of the State and political authority, a complete vision of religious community, or an account of all social goods! We need to show that theological humanism provides a perspective on how responsibly to inhabit political and religious communities in ways that ensure a religious and humane future. The next step is to engage the debate about the relation of religion, morality, and politics in current thought.

Politics and Moral Substance

Historically, some thinkers tried to sever social and political decisions from moral ideas or religious ideals. Politics is the realm of power and power alone. What is right and good, holy and just, are taken to be secondary, at best, to political considerations. The purpose of politics, as Machiavelli claimed, is to attain and keep power. Some forms of Marxism believe that "morality" is an ideology that blinds one to the real material conditions of a society. Moral beliefs do not have critical leverage to challenge and alter political reality; they reflect social reality.

Each of these positions implies that there is no resolution to political conflict that can transcend political means. Insofar as that is the case, human beings are always potentially in a war of all against all, as Thomas Hobbes put it. Religion is used to further political purpose and to achieve political loyalty. Machiavelli, for instance, writes that religion is useful in "directing armies, in animating the people, in keeping men good, and in shaming the wicked."[5] A brief glance at the current world scene seems to confirm his observation.

Thankfully, there have been others who sought different ways to resolve political conflicts and to consider the place of religion and morality in social life. What are these positions? One form of political theory important in the modern West, but now found elsewhere, argues that "morality" is the domain of embedded convictions and values, *Sittlichkeit*, as the German philosopher Hegel called it. These values and convictions are about what counts as good conduct, just social relations, and a good life presupposed in the existence of a nation. Traditional values, the moral substance of a community, are the necessary background to any political structure, whether those beliefs are about tribal relations (as in some African nations), about the proper role of women, or religious beliefs. Explicit norms for public decisions must articulate but also draw from that moral substance. Without "moral substance,"

115

political norms are powerless and lack social validity. The rise of democratic nations seems to mean the inevitable destruction of ideals beyond bare political equality, especially ideals about human excellence.[6] The task of social and political discourse is not only to meet the usual demands of political life, say, the creation and distribution of power. The more basic challenge is to articulate the moral substance of a people in order to warrant and sustain political action.[7]

This vision of the relation between morality and political existence is apparent in the American context. Like all previous presidents, George W. Bush, in his Second Inaugural Address, made repeated references to "the American heritage." Conservative evangelical Christians insist on "Christian values" as the backbone of the nation. There is also constant appeal to the vision of the Founding Fathers. The articulation of moral substance can and must motivate and direct political policy. More recently, a host of thinkers, such as Alasdair MacIntyre, Stanley Hauerwas, and others, have been called "the new traditionalists."[8] In their attack on political liberalism, new traditionalists, much like conservatives in the White House and evangelical Christians, appeal to some "tradition" or moral substance that should guide communal life, political or religious.

Conservatives rarely note that the articulation of the "moral substance" of the nation is in many respects the product, not the cause, of the political founding of the United States in the Declaration of Independence and the Constitution or the Church in the story of Christ. Those who appeal to "Christian values" forget to note how those "values" have always been contested, especially among Christians. The precise character of the Founders' ideas about religion and statecraft remains in dispute. However one wants to assess the content of these political and moral outlooks, they manifest the belief that the political order must draw its sustenance and vitality from some moral substance. The debate is about the content of that substance and how to articulate its meaning for political existence. That is why there is considerable ranker over, say, the meaning of marriage or family values and public policy.

Those who worry about moral substance bemoan the "naked public square." Substantive moral and religious commitments have been banished from public discourse. The reason for this banishment is a specific liberal interpretation of the separation of Church and State and also the general inarticulateness of citizens about their moral heritage. In the face of this challenge, neoconservatives in the United States have set about rethinking the separation of Church and State and also the "free exercise" clause in the

Constitution, as well as seeking to rearticulate the supposed religio-moral substance of the Republic. These rearticulated beliefs revise inherited convictions from the perspective of contemporary concerns. The glorious faith of the "Founders" is partly an invention of present discourse. The pristine Gospel of many American evangelicals is actually a theological construction in reaction to the realities and ambiguities of modern life. Ironically, advocates of "articulation" miss the ways in which rearticulating the moral substance of a culture is an act of invention which changes the commitments they seek to express. The conservative is unwittingly an innovator.

There is a genuine gain but also a problem in this kind of social thought, especially when we cast the discussion in terms of identity. Communitarians, as we will call them, insist on the priority of a specific bounded moral substance in the formation of identity, whether that substance is the will of the people or religious beliefs and stories. They grant the complexity of identity (say, American, Female, Christian, etc.) and yet want to organize people's identity through the priority of *one identity over others*. The freedom to make choices about identity is best when it endorses an identity that stops the demand of ongoing choice. The position thereby risks making identity into destiny, as Amartya Sen names it. If moral substance is the condition for identity, then it would seem impossible to use reason and choice to challenge and change those identities when they run into conflict with others. "Many communitarian thinkers," Sen rightly notes, "tend to argue that a dominant communal identity is only a matter of self-realization, not of choice."[9] Christian particularists — as a religious version of communitarianism — want to conform identity to the Church's story. This means that among true believers, a person has really only the choice to conform or live in sin. But that misses the importance of the freedom to make choices about what to give *priority* in our identities without assuming that this choice must be once and for all. That kind of freedom, we will see in a moment, is important in the social contract tradition.

There is an insight in the communitarian argument. Human freedom, if it is to be more than mere license, must be infused with substantive commitments about what is a good human life and just society. As historical beings we form our lives with others and for ourselves; we never can nor should escape the bonds of community, the legacies of tradition, that sustain and make possible meaningful life. The question, for any humanist, is not freedom versus tradition, but, rather, freedom as a way to *inhabit* traditions and communities. What that means will emerge in the remainder of the chapter.

117

Morality and the Social Contract

The other major conception of the relation of morality, religion, and politics in the modern, Western world is found in the idea of the social contract. Deeply rooted within Anglo-American thought, it is also found among modern continental thinkers like Rousseau and Kant. The idea is seen in the earliest moments of birth of the United States and draws inspiration from ideas in Protestant thought, for instance, the famous Mayflower Compact. Human beings freely and rationally form political associations (compacts, covenants, or contracts) in order to sustain certain goods (property, peace, the pursuit of happiness).[10] The legitimacy of the State rests upon the social contract.

This vision is quite tolerant of divergent moral and religious outlooks so long as citizens abide by the social contract. As John Locke famously noted, only two commitments cannot be tolerated: (1) atheism, since this meant in Locke's mind a lack of respect for moral order, and (2) allegiance to a foreign power, which he saw in Roman Catholic relations to the Holy See that might thwart the claims of Parliament and the Crown. Beyond those limits, the constitutional state is morally neutral in terms of citizens' moral and religious convictions, as well as ideas about happiness. John Rawls, a recent exponent of this position, contends that political liberalism seeks an overlapping consensus among citizens and does not rest on any comprehensive doctrines, especially religious and metaphysical ones.[11] Citizens must abide by their moral judgments and remain committed to the political community they create. Moral ideals can and do enter political discourse, since they may function as regulative ideals for political action. However, in public action the validity of those ideas must be established politically and not religiously or metaphysically. The aim is to form an inclusive political community that allows the maximal diversity within the bonds of social peace and security.

The contractarian outlook, as we call it, is deeply entrenched in the American context. From the so-called Social Gospel movement at the end of the nineteenth century to many other reformist impulses, the attempt has been to bring moral ideas of human equality and justice to bear on political realities. A stirring example is Martin Luther King, Jr.'s sermon "I have a Dream" (1963). King aimed to express a moral ideal sufficient to move the nation towards racial equality and social justice.[12] His inspiring rhetoric drew upon the African-American Baptist heritage, but also philosophical ideas about democracy. Granting the religious and philosophical character of his comprehensive doctrine, King still appealed for validation to the democratic process and the social contract expressed in the Constitution and the Declaration of Independence. King sought to envision a just and inclusive social order, the "beloved community" (as he called it).

While the contractarian vision admits that high ideals can enter the political arena, there is also the constant insistence on the neutrality of the State towards those commitments. The political process that *validates* ideals for political purpose cannot and ought not define the *content* of ideals. In recent years, public debate in the United States about gay marriage, prayer in schools, and the public posting of the Ten Commandments in state and federal court houses, bespeak the power of this vision and its ostensive neutrality on comprehensive commitments. Little wonder, then, that versions of the liberal account of the relation of morality and politics were in open and rancorous conflict with those dedicated to articulating the moral substance of the social order.   .

As we have seen, the main problem facing advocates of "moral substance" is a loss of the means to express commitments necessary to sustain political stability and form national identity. Among religious folks this same challenge takes the form of trying to reclaim "orthodoxy," or the story of Jesus, or (among Muslims) the desire to have the dominance of *Sharia* in political life. For the social contract model, the main problem is related and yet different. Given the ostensive neutrality of the State about religious and moral commitments, the worry is that this position forces citizens into social duplicity. The identity of citizens is torn asunder wherein their personal moral and religious convictions, including how they justify those beliefs, are barred from impinging on the political process. Political action which is, obviously, motivated by a host of ideals, values, norms, and interests becomes unexplainable or profoundly deceptive. This has the effect of instigating a break within persons' identities. It is hardly surprising that various forms of "identity politics" (women's rights, the rights of indigenous peoples, etc.) are rife among those dedicated to the social contract resolution of the relation of religion, morality, and politics.[13]

The idea of the social contract holds real insight, but also problems. By prying apart the question of the *validity* of substantive commitments from their *content*, the contractarian outlook seems to require that citizens validate, show to be true, their religious and moral convictions on grounds different from those convictions. This entails two troubling claims: (1) that the standpoint for the validation of convictions is itself *neutral*, and (2) that it is possible, in principle, to *suspend* belief in one's various convictions until they are properly validated, since it is the whole bundle of convictions that must orient action. These demands seem humanly impossible to meet. They give

119

rise to the justified complaint that modern, liberal democracy, while claiming neutrality, is really an imposition of a political ideology on deeply held religious and moral beliefs and therefore must be resisted. Religious fundamentalists within various religions decry the notion that their convictions can or should be validated on any terms other than the convictions themselves. What is missing in the social contract argument, it would seem, is some way to show that the commitment to the public validation of *political* policies entails a moral and even religious outlook.[14] One needs to clarify that it is right and proper to hold some beliefs while testing others. While these problems clarify the central weakness of the social contract tradition, they also expose its greatest insight.

The force of the contractarian argument is to insist that human beings have the ability to step back and ask about the truth and justice of their commitments and accepted identities. Of course, these positions often overestimate the extent of that capacity to step back and imply that we can put all convictions that sustain our identities into question at once. That is obviously not the case. Nevertheless, the stepping back, whatever its scope, is an act of freedom, reason, and choice. It is an act of freedom because the capacity to put one's ideas and ideals into question means that one is not bound by them, determined by them. Identity is not a destiny. Anytime we ask if our beliefs and forms of identity are ones we want to continue to inhabit, we exercise freedom. That is why oppressive social orders, religious or political, seek to suppress the quest for truth and the criticism of accepted beliefs and practices.

This act of stepping back is also an act of reason and choice. One is seeking the most intelligent set of beliefs and values to guide social life. What will define and justify those beliefs and values are not internal to them, as communitarians insist. Valid beliefs and values for orienting social existence have to be demonstrated within the public order in the thicket of debate and deliberation. What makes a belief valid is both recognition of an identity received and also forward-looking to what will respect and enhance social existence rather than just conformity to inherited ideas and forms of identity. This only makes sense, we contend, if it can be shown that the commitment to free, rational, and open determination of the *validity* of social ideas and ideals is itself part of the *content* of one's identity. If that is not the case, then one claims a stance of *neutrality* that seems humanly impossible to adopt.

Like the communitarian argument, revisions will have to be made in arguments about the social contract. There are also insights in both of these outlooks on social existence that theological humanism will want to preserve. Yet we need to change the terms of the debate.

Responsibility and Identity

In the present time people's identities are too often circumscribed within one description and this fosters what Sen helpfully called the "illusion of destiny." Within the whirl of global dynamics there are powerful forces at work seeking to shape people's identities in order to provide solid boundaries between communities. There are also forces working to persuade people of their sovereign power to shape at will and whim who they are and who they will become.[15] These strategies of identity-formation usually fail because of the reflexive interaction among peoples on the global field, noted in chapter 6. No community is free from interaction with others within the space of its life; no one is sovereign over the forces, natural and social, that shape her or his existence. The failure to control the formation of identity often leads to harsher and even more violent means to retain the boundaries or to reassertions of the right of self-formation. That is the engine of a clash of civilizations. Is it really surprising that when interactions among peoples increase in the global age, so too does conflict and violence? What is needed, we believe, is a vision of the internal complexity of identities and the various ways one can and ought to live with that complexity in self, in community, and in the world. The sovereignty over self that a human being actually has and the degree to which social identities can be freely created are more limited and yet also more important than usually understood.

In the global situation one needs to articulate the complexity of persons' or communities' identities in order to find non-coercive points of contact among people without loss of distinctive ways of life. In this light, communitarians and contractarians are bedeviled by opposite problems that express hypertheism and overhumanization. Communitarians seek *conformity* to some social identity and see the point of social life in the realization of that identity. This underestimates the freedom we possess as social beings to step back and assess our beliefs, values, and even identity, precisely because these are multiple. Contractarians, conversely, understand the importance of freedom and the rational assessment of ideas and ideals in social existence aimed at the *creative* fashioning of new modes of life, new identities. Yet in their desire to secure the realm of freedom, they risk enfolding every belief and value within freedom's domain and thereby enact overhumanization. Freedom is never neutral, and one cannot and need not simultaneously test every belief. Sometimes we are justified in living by beliefs and identities untested through free, rational reflection. All that is required is the willingness to test them, if that becomes necessary.

Actually, we have already hinted at what needs critical revision in ways similar to neohumanists like Todorov and Levinas, who stress the finality of the other. *The revision is the subtle but important shift to the problem of identity from its unquestioned good.* Neither the "I" nor my community's identity and it alone is final. In our global age, the question of the conflict of values and the supposed clash of civilizations is more deeply a matter of the social and cultural proliferation of identities and the claim to sovereignty of those identities. The struggle is in the human soul. The problem is how we are to *live through* the communities and traditions that have formed our lives and, therefore, how rightly to *inhabit* our identities in freedom.

If conflict among peoples is to be lessened and managed, then it must be possible to decide in specific situations which of several identities provides contact with others and thereby supports cooperative action. One's identities can and ought to serve a good beyond themselves. This is not a facile optimism or naïve idealism. Genuine realism about possibilities for action acknowledges that in particular situations human differences might not be overcome and conflict ensues. The idea that conflict will cease if people just consider what priority to give their several identities is naïve and dangerous. When conflict does erupt, violence can be blunted, if not escaped, when some bond of commonality places a limit on force. Testimonies from Truth and Reconciliation Commissions around the world note that acts of horrific violence require seeing another human being as *lacking humanity*.[16] The strategies to dehumanize others, the social mechanism needed to engender ongoing violence, are many, sadly. Tribalism, revenge, terror, racism, the eroticizing of violence and power, and the will of God (to name but a few) have all been used, are being used, to dehumanize others and thereby to drive social life into the fury of unending violence.

Aside from the use of justified force to stop violent slaughter, what is most important is the capacity to see the other as a human being with multiple identities, some of which are shared. No specific identity, including one's religious identity, can trump the whole of existence and claim exclusive right to orient social action. In some contexts I need to see myself as a human being who faces death, who loves his family, and who bleeds *just like, in principle, every other human being*. I need then to see that the one suffering before me is also a human being. In this case, more distinct identities (say, Christian or Indian or Communist or White or Female) are set in the background and are only judged valid when believed to support shared humanity. Call this the Good Samaritan principle. That commonality can and must delimit the scope and extent of violence, because, again, unending conflict requires the *dehumanization* of the other. Of course, there will be other situations where one must stress more particular identities, say, in the midst of theological debate with fellow Christians or among members of one's political group. Even in those cases, something shared is the condition for cooperation and persuasion and thus should limit coercive interaction.

Notice something key about our argument. At each point of encounter with others, the task is to find the relevant *commonality* that is the condition for cooperation and the limit on coercive interaction. This procedural rule requires that no specific identity be deified, having finality, as the singular description of one's existence because one's life can and ought to be dedicated towards right relations with and for others. This is true of the religious community as well. The Church, for instance, is not only the gathered body of believers or the body of Christ (as Christians believe), but also a human community, a treasure in *earthen* vessels.[17] The various beliefs, values, and traditions that shape identities are enlisted in the project of fashioning social life dedicated to what respects and enhances the integrity of life with and for others. Anyone who can grasp the intelligibility of the rule thereby endorses, at least implicitly, a coordinate stance in life. And the argument applies to persons and to communities insofar as the idea of identity is analogically applied to individuals and communities.[18]

This strategy for orienting social life is deeply embedded in theological humanism insofar as it signals the complexity of a life: one is a religious person (of some sort) and a humanist (of some sort) and has other identities, too. Yet the possibility of that outlook is found at the crossing point of the goods that constitute the *integrity of life*. And this is why theological humanism extends the finality of the "you" beyond the human other, so dear to neohumanists, to the community of life. Human beings are bound together in their mortality, their fleshliness, with other creatures, but also because we are social beings and persons who desire meaning in our lives, reflective goods. In other words, a theological humanist inhabits her or his more particular religious, ethnic, gendered, cultural, and racial identities deeply and yet with a light touch, as it were. While shaped by these identities one is not, finally, a slave to them.

Freedom and Conscience

The right and responsibility of people to make decisions of priority about their identities denotes another aspect of theological humanism. It is a distinctive form of *freedom*. This was a point that divided the two major outlooks in political thought explored above. Communitarians and Christian particularists see identity constituted through conformity to social authority (Church or political association). Freedom unmoored from moral substance or tradition is understood by them as little more than license or unfaithfulness and so the sad and troubled legacy of modern individualism.[19] The contractarian position implies that freedom means that a citizen is supposedly able to assume a *neutral* position in relation to their various values and validate them as needed. The idea of freedom consistent with theological humanism is different. Freedom is the capacity of an entire person or community to labor responsibly for the integrity of life in oneself and in others. It is the ability to give priority to and reasons for orienting life in specific situations. One's identity is neither an undeniable destiny nor, in theological terms, a foreordained election; it is also not chosen or reinvented willy-nilly. Whatever the ultimate end of existence might be, in this life human beings can, may, and must responsibly orient life in ways that foster life and delimit destruction. One does not take a neutral stance in relation to one's identities, nor assume that they can all be tested at once. Freedom is the capacity to make decisions of priority about one's identities and commitments with respect to the good of the integrity of life.

How then is one to speak of freedom as intrinsically linked to the joys and demands of responsibility? Conscience is a term for human beings as whole creatures with multiple identities and in whom the capacity for choice and action is infused with a sense of responsibility that arises through our many senses of goodness that saturate life. It is the call to orient the self and one's identities towards actions and relations that respect and enhance the integrity of life. For precisely this reason, a basic right of human beings is *freedom of conscience* and that just means the freedom to be a responsible agent. No human being can rightfully be coerced to conform his or her identity and life to any power, no matter how seemingly legitimate or how divinely authorized, that denies the capacity of conscience as the labor of human life.

In this light, one can be less anxious about the uniqueness of her or his identity than many communitarians and Christian or religious particularists. One can also be less worried than contractarians to keep comprehensive beliefs out of the public square. The concern of the theological humanist is different. It is the fear that religious and cultural and social forces will stunt conscience and demand unity rather than integrity of identity. And to be sure, complex social systems, especially within the whirl of global dynamics, always encumber and stunt conscience. This is why appeals to "responsibility" or "social justice" or "love" unmindful of the dynamics of social life never alone orient action or bring about social change. The concern is about human freedom, the failure of conscience, or a weakness of will (to put it in different ways), so that our commitments and responsibilities with and to

others become constricted by petty identities and blocked by social processes. When this happens there is the deadly risk of dehumanizing others and
thereby unwittingly opening the possibility of unconstrained violence. The
answer to that problem is not to try to seek some neutral standpoint as if
one can leap out of those forces which have shaped what and who one is.
The challenge is to make space within social life for the labor of conscience.

Within social life, one task of conscience is to make decisions of priority
about identities for the sake of the integrity of common life. In situations of
social conflict, identities that indicate shared *commonality* with others have a
claim to priority as the condition both for cooperative action and to delimit
acts that dehumanize the other. Of course, the relevant commonality can
shift. Among Hutu and Tutsi in Rwanda what was needed was the commonality of shared humanity rather than identities imposed by colonial powers.
In the clashes among Christians and Muslims around the world what is
needed is (say) the commonality of monotheistic faith. Other identities one
happens to have (Tutsi or Sunni or Protestant) must then, in that situation,
be made supportive of commonality. No one is asked to give up his or her
particular identities; particular beliefs and values do not need to be validated
all at once. What is required is some flexibility, some freedom, to make
decisions in specific situations with respect to a commitment to the integrity
of life. That commitment means an openness to have one's identities changed
towards a good beyond one's present form of life. Interactions with others is
the school of conscience for the formation of identities.

Theological humanism entails two further things especially important in
the relation of the political order and religious communities. One is the rule
of law. Just laws are meant to block social processes that distort or stunt conscience. Social conflict can only be resolved if there are non-coercive means
to settle conflict fairly and justly, and, additionally, the fair and equal treatment of all members of a community. The specifics of a legal and judicial
system are of course beyond the scope of this book. Yet, from this perspective,
a legal system is just and legitimate if it embodies the workings of conscience
in the realm of social life. A legal system despite its complexity must aim at
the integrity of social life and enable the mechanisms for resolving conflict
without dehumanization by free decisions about priorities in identity.[20] This
means, additionally, that the coercive or retributive use of law, and so the police
function of the State, is only warranted and just when it seeks the restoration
of social integrity as the rightful balance within the body politic of people's
identities and flourishing social life.

The same would be true in relations among political powers. While some
wars might indeed be just, they are so only as a last resort, when aggression is

stopped through appropriate force, and are undertaken without the dehumanization of combatants and non-combatants.[21] The presumption of just law is the same as just war: the social order can and ought to aim at the integrity of life and thus protect human beings from unwanted desecration of humanity. The desecration can take many forms, of course: torture, oppression, unending poverty, and on and on. At the core of all these forms of intolerable acts against human beings is the denial of a human being as a creature with the *right to have rights*.[22] They deny the claim on a person's part to be a creature who can rightly claim against the community that other rights ought – all things being equal – to be fulfilled, rights rooted in the various goods that need to be integrated in order for personal and social life to flourish.

All things being equal: while a human being (on our account) has the right to claim the right (say) to participate freely in the social and political life of a community, the *form* and the *extent* of participation can and will vary from community to community. What cannot be justly violated (on our account) is the standing of a human being as one who has the inviolable right to claim other social rights. Political and social power as well as the distribution of social goods are limited and tested by the standing of human beings as moral creatures. Here is the proper domain of human rights discourse, that is, claims against political and religious coercion and rights for social goods. What then grants a human being this right to have rights? Is it God? Is it the political community? Is it custom and tradition? What grants a human being the right to claim other rights is freedom of conscience as a necessary, if not sufficient, condition for living a life of integrity, even while, as theological humanists, we also insist on the religious depth and force of conscience. What grants legitimacy to a political or religious community is the extent to which it respects and enhances that "right" and therefore in its structures, policies, and procedures fosters conscientious social life.

Many questions must remain unanswered or not fully addressed in this short essay. The decisive idea to grasp is that social identity finds its good not in itself but in the project of conscience and so in responsibility for the integrity of life. On reaching that conclusion we return to the question of the central social good in our age. We can speak about the *cosmopolitan conscience*.

The Cosmopolitan Conscience

In the light of the deep tensions we have charted above between accounts of the relation of morality, religion, and politics in the US context, one can grasp something about the global scene as well. If one looks at military and

126

diplomatic actions, humanitarian relief aid, or global economic and environmental policies, it seems obvious that nations are motivated by national
interest. Take the United States, for example. In some situations little if any
action is taken to stop forms of obvious genocide, while in other cases military force is used to wage the so-called war on terror. In both cases the driving impulse is what advances national interest and state security. This is true
of all of the nations on this earth.

Depending on the way in which the "moral substance" of the Republic or
the scope of rights and freedoms are understood, differences of foreign policy
occur. If the rights of freedom and self-determination are understood to hold
for human beings as human beings, rather than just for members of a specific
state, then the nation may have moral cause to spread democracy around the
world, as President George W. Bush believes. On the same grounds, as former
Secretary General of the United Nations Kofi Annan said in his last speech at
the Truman Presidential Museum, "respect for national sovereignty can no
longer be used as a shield by governments intent on massacring their own
people, or as an excuse for the rest of us to do nothing when such heinous
crimes are committed."[23] The idea of human rights can warrant intervention in
the affairs of nations. Of course, the political shape and force of US action to
spread democracy will always be formulated as an attempt to further national
security. Conversely, conceptions of national sovereignty rooted in the heritages
of nations have constrained intervention even for humanitarian purposes.

The tensions found in the US domestic situation are now writ large onto the
global stage. People worry that the spread of liberal democracy requires the
alteration of the moral substance of cultures, as, for instance, in the debate about
the possibility of Islamic democracy. Still others wonder about the disregard for
the rule of law. While the United Sates insists that nations abide by the terms of
international law, especially the agreements of the United Nations, it frequently
rejects those same laws and agreements as binding on policy. Finally, the discon-
nection of political participation from personal and cultural comprehensive
beliefs is reflected in the failure of the United States to consider the cultural
forms and beliefs of other nations when executing foreign policy objectives.
Hot button issues, like the war in Iraq, environmental policy, or international
legal tribunals, reveal but also conceal deeper tensions and problems.

How then is theological humanism to think about the social challenges of
the global field? Along with some other contemporary neohumanists, we
advocate a cosmopolitan outlook.[24] The idea is not the ancient Stoic one
that somehow a person can be a "citizen of the world." As we have stressed
throughout this book, our social lives are always located in time, place, and
community. The idea of citizenship only makes sense in local communities.

The "world" is not a politically relevant concept with respect to citizenship. Indeed, one of the problems in our current situation is the plight of "stateless persons" who, for various reasons, are denied the protection of actual citizenship. In the global age, it is important to insist that while we might indeed understand the world as one, human existence is always situated in particular contexts and communities. This fact gives rise to the multiple identities that make up any one person's or community's existence.

While that is the case, the point of theological humanism is to orient identity by an aim beyond itself, namely, the aim of what respects and enhances the integrity of life with and for others. It entails a cosmopolitan outlook where the scope of *human* community extends beyond the boundaries of any specific community, political or religious, to others and to the whole community of life. The task of theological humanism, accordingly, is to help foster communities in which conscience, the basic mode of moral and spiritual being in the world, can be educated and formed towards a cosmopolitan outlook. One inhabits a specific community, political or religious, from within this wider perspective in ways in which freedom is infused with a sense of responsibility. The term for that stance in religious and political life is the *cosmopolitan conscience*. This form of conscience, we have been arguing, must be the touchstone for freedom and identity if social life is to have a future in the global age.

The cosmopolitan conscience is the answer to the orienting question of this chapter. It names the way a theological humanist *inhabits* their social identities: political, ethnic, religious, cultural, gendered, economic. One has the responsibility in specific situations to make choices of priority about one's identity for the sake of the integrity of life from a cosmopolitan perspective. This is not, we stress, a denial of any specific identity, but, rather, a project of integrating life with and for others. A person's or a community's form of life is oriented beyond itself in ways that respect and enhance the integrity of life rather than contributing to the endangerment of life. The cosmopolitan conscience is an answer to hypertheism and overhumanism in the domain of social life. Neither human nor divine power alone orients and integrates existence. Rather, the complexity of identities backs choices meant to fashion lives and communities that make possible the ongoing adventure of communal life and in doing so enliven the social good.

8

Masks of Mind

This chapter explores reflective goods and the human quest for meaning, recognizing that everywhere basic, natural, social, and reflective goods are intertwined. These goods arise within domains of conceptual, symbolic, linguistic, and practical meaning-systems. As noted in chapter 5, reflective goods aim both at truth *in* life and at a truth*ful* life. More simply, reflective goods are distinctive to self-interpreting beings. In acts of reflection, human beings bend back on their immediate relations to life in order to think about them, to express them, and to assess their worth under standards of truth and knowledge, goodness and right, beauty and meaningfulness. Reflective goods are thereby bound to human consciousness and judgment.

The link between consciousness and reflective goods is the problem we seek to address. In our view, consciousness is the ground, art is a medium, and modeling is a method of articulating reflective goods. The chapter begins by putting an account of reflective goods on trial with respect to a spirited debate over the nature and origin of human consciousness raging in the academy and the wider society.[1] How does theological humanism enter the debate about consciousness, its origin and good? What does that have to do with reflective goods?

Terms of the Debate

The question of the relation of mind and matter is longstanding in Western thought. With the advances in modern biology and genetics, the old debate has been reopened. Some thinkers have tried to isolate the "God" gene, that is, the biological origins of religious sensibilities. There are discussions of the natural roots of our moral sense of right and wrong. The question also reaches into the theory of evolution and all the controversy surrounding it. The debate about consciousness highlights a collision of basic outlooks.[2]

Materialists (also called "physicalists" or "reductive naturalists") contend that the only reality that exists is material or physical reality. Consequently, human consciousness can be comprehensively reduced to physical states of some kind, namely, the firing of neuronal impulses.[3] Undoubtedly, research into neuronal activity in the brain is making tremendous progress in showing the physical basis of mental activities. But can scientific materialism reduce consciousness without remainder to its material substrate? If so, reflective goods would be reducible to natural goods. The human experience of an inner life of freedom would be an illusion that can be explained away by scientific materialism. Materialism is historically connected with secular humanism, but in our view, materialism oversteps its limits in claiming that it can fully account for subjectivity in terms of objective reality. Its weakness is its inability in principle to account for the conscious experience of "inner life" as the qualitative aspect of subjectivity.[4]

Dualism stands at the other end of the debate. For dualists, consciousness has an entirely different nature and origin than our bodies, as Descartes famously demonstrated: the method of radical doubt (*cogito, ergo sum*) discloses the non-objective yet real existence of the "I."[5] Plato, too, was a dualist. Consciousness is an immaterial, immortal "soul," which wings its way back to the divine from its exile in the perishable body.[6] Contemporary dualists drop the language of the immortal soul, but they preserve the "explanatory gap" between matter and mind.[7] For dualists, human consciousness is really not at home in the world. Reflective goods are disconnected from bodily and natural goods. What is more, dualism is historically and conceptually linked with theism. The theistic image of God as the light of the world finds its human correlation in consciousness that reflects the divine light. For many dualists, souls and bodies exist because God created them. The strength of dualism is its demonstration of the real existence of subjectivity. Its overriding weaknesses, however, include the mind–body problem, namely, its inability to account for causal relations between body and mind, given that the two are altogether different kinds of substance, and its lack of scientific warrant.[8]

Emergentism (or "biological naturalism") attempts to articulate a third option between materialism and dualism. It holds that the phenomenon of consciousness is irreducibly subjective and is thus *ontologically distinct* from objective, neurobiological states. However, consciousness is nonetheless altogether *caused* by neurobiological processes in the brain. Consciousness emerges in biological organisms out of non-conscious neurobiological constituents, just as, for example, the conscious feeling of thirst arises from physical processes which activate neuron firings in the brain.[9] But how can such an enormous jump occur from non-conscious physical processes to the fullness of conscious life? To appeal to the theory of emergence *seems* like pulling a rabbit out of a hat, even if counter arguments can be made.[10] Something conscious has to emerge or evolve out of something non-conscious.

The question of the nature and origin of consciousness, and so reflective goods, quickly divides thinkers into these camps. The conflict between positions fills the popular media, academic conferences, and think-tanks that explore religion and science. What can theological humanism contribute to reflection on consciousness? We introduce our reflections through the metaphor of the theatre. Classical humanists used this metaphor to explore how human freedom can assume various "masks" on the stage of the world. Drawing on that metaphor, this chapter enters into the debate about consciousness and reflective goods by exploring two ways in which "mind," or consciousness, appears in reality.

First, we explore the appearance of the nature and origin of consciousness. At this level of argument we, like many others, are trying to move the debate beyond the conflict between materialists and dualists, but also in a different direction from the emergentists. To that end, we develop an elementary model of a fundamental property of consciousness, namely, *embodied freedom*. With a model of consciousness in hand we turn, second, to an exemplary "mask of mind" that is a distinctive reflective good, namely, visual art. Our account of consciousness is on trial to see if it enables us to make sense of this crucial type of reflective good, and, conversely, to see what art discloses about human consciousness. Our claim is that art discloses the "inner life" of consciousness to reflection. Art has the structure of *embodied meaning*. We limit the discussion to visual art; other arguments are needed to explore different forms of art and reflective goods. Visual art is chosen as a test case for a specific reason. It has to do with the question of religion and the human future.

Currently, various depictions of religious leaders (say, Muhammad or Christ), sacred texts (the Qu'ran), and groups, in cartoons, dramas, novels, and performance art, have caused uproar among hypertheists in various traditions, especially fundamentalist Christians and Muslims. Artists, authors, and satirists have been killed or had their lives threatened. Conversely, radical secularists of various stripes argue that nothing is sacred and thus no human artifact can make a claim to disclose the sacred.

There is an endless banalization of culture. Many postmodern churchly and post-theistic theologians look to the realm of art as a way to explore the aesthetic character of the Christian message or the religious dimensions of cultural life.[11] In a word, the question of art is at the intersection of religion and cultural forces around the world.[12] True to theological humanism, we will see that some forms of visual art can awaken us to the integrity of life in its depth, freedom, and beauty. Art is a reflective good, namely, a meaningful and true grasp of the integrity of life. We address it to show its connection to the larger debate about consciousness within the context of theological humanism.

How then to begin? Any account of consciousness presupposes the work of consciousness in providing the account. Prior to these two steps we need then to reflect on what it means to provide a model of consciousness or of art. The act of making a "model," we think, is a reflective form of art itself.

On Modeling

Among other things, theological humanism is a mode of reflecting on the goods of life, including life's reflective goods. But what happens when one reflects on reflection? One is then exercising *reflexive* consciousness, which is reflecting on acts of reflection. Thought bends back on itself to adjust to new information and for the sake of gaining insight into, or even knowledge about, goods. Human self-consciousness is marked by this capacity for reflexivity, as we noted in chapter 6. This self-reflective capacity invites debate and disagreement about how to account for consciousness.

One way to think about the process of understanding and knowing consciousness is by constructing and testing *models*.[13] Modeling is the methodological motor driving the quest for knowledge in the natural and social sciences. For example, the widely known model of the DNA molecule assists anyone to understand it better, and it has explanatory power in analyzing genetic differences. While humanists are less familiar with the language of modeling than are scientists, they in fact construct models when they interpret, for example, the meaning of Tolstoy's story *Father Sergius*, or a painting by Jackson Pollock. Models are constructed for the purpose of explaining observable patterns within a domain – why the things we observe appear or behave as they do. Models can be made up of anything. They may be physical entities (plastic, wood, and the like), mathematical formulae, verbal descriptions, images, stories, or anything else. The model should clearly specify the *domain* it is modeling, along with the elements of that domain that are relevant for the model. Every domain is made up of a set of elements that make the domain be what it is. The goal of modeling is to present the *structure* of that domain so that we can understand why observable elements behave as they do. As we use the term, a *structure* is what integrates elements that constitute a determinate domain. When the model enables us to understand the integration of life on or within the structure, it is possible to respond theologically to a domain. At least, that is our contention.

Models compete with each other to explain and interpret some phenomenon under investigation. Some models are more successful than other ones. In time, one model among many may come to give superior insight and to provide better explanations over a wider and wider range of phenomena. In that case, the model takes on the character of a *theory*. Theories are broadened models, which are extended over a wider and wider range. Theories take their place within an overarching conceptual framework called a *paradigm*.[14] Paradigms provide the means to extend or modify theories into entirely new domains. Shifts in paradigms occur when anomalies appear that defy successful modeling on the basis of the reigning paradigm and thus suggest radically new models with features that do not come from the reigning paradigm to explain them. In this book, we have actually been advocating a paradigm shift from the clash between humanism and theism into the outlook of theological humanism.

Constructing models, whether in science or any other discipline, requires imagination and creativity. The activity is akin to making works of art, writing poetry, or composing music in its use of hunches, intuition, and experimental play.[15] Viewed as a creation of language, models, like metaphors, are phenomena of "semantic innovation" or meaning-creation. Models, like metaphors, have the capacity to provoke the mind to think something new by seeing a resemblance previously unnoticed. They display humility of mind because they invite criticism and ask to be refuted in the name of a truth that the modeling activity always imperfectly approaches and never actually reaches. Constructing models fits theological humanism, precisely because modeling combines epistemic humility with testability. Models are fallible constructions of the imagination, but the best models give partial insight into the nature of some domain of reality. The history of modeling in any domain allows for a progressive, albeit limited approach toward objective truth, which is their ultimate yet unrealizable goal.

We now propose some beginning steps toward constructing a model of the capacity of human beings for reflective goods.

Modeling Consciousness

Reflective goods require consciousness. We can *experience* things, and we can *reflect* on them as good or beautiful, for example, only if we are conscious of them. Yet, what *is* consciousness, and how does it arise within the material universe? These questions point to a genuine mystery for human beings. Nothing is more familiar to us than our own consciousness, yet nothing is more elusive to thought.

Levels of Consciousness

In its broadest sense, consciousness "includes *all* experiences."[16] Some important distinctions must be made, however, among three levels of consciousness which the human mind traverses as a "thing-in-between" (chapter 1). Most basically, *immediate consciousness* is direct acquaintance with some state of affairs – a physical object or a mental state – and as such is interdependent with that reality ("There is a painting over there" or "my seeing a painting over there"). Call this "spontaneous awareness." Second, *reflective consciousness* arises when consciousness reflects on the contents of immediate consciousness and its many relations ("I know that I see a painting over there – a painting of a man and a woman standing by an ancient tree, contemplating the moon; I choose to call it beautiful").[17] This is the level of conscious choice. Third, *reflexive consciousness* advances by reflecting on reflective consciousness in its complexity and internalized otherness ("I call this painting beautiful, but I mean that it stops me in my tracks, its *otherness* makes me feel 'other.' I am freely responding to an image, freely constructed by the artist, of two people contemplating the enormity of death"). This level is marked by integrative freedom – always, of course, within the limits of human finitude.

These forms of consciousness are progressive, but also interactive. In each case, consciousness is embodied in a living creature with senses and feelings, the capacities to act and to speak with and for others. Interestingly, each form of consciousness adds more complexity and richness in engaging the world that consciousness illuminates. With each new layer of consciousness, awareness also increases of its embodiment in a multi-dimensional matrix of sustaining relations. These relations include what we have called basic or natural goods in immediate consciousness, social and reflective goods through reflective consciousness, and the spiritual good of respecting and enhancing the integrity of life. The power of consciousness is one rising power of integration in life; its falling is into disintegration.

Traits of Consciousness: Qualia, Inwardness, Otherness

Crucial traits of consciousness show themselves in all forms. First, consciousness has a *qualitative* dimension. In immediate consciousness, one does not see a painting in general; one is conscious of *this* particular painting, with its own unique quality, and hence its own unique meaning and value. This immediate sense of quality is prior to any inferences that one may make or additional knowledge that one may invoke. The mysteriousness of immediate consciousness has to do with the fact that when we bend back on it in order to reflect what it is, we lose its immediacy. The immediacy of consciousness moves from the initial state of consciousness, on which I am now reflecting, to that very act of reflecting. Reflection transforms the initial immediate state of consciousness into a mediated object of inquiry.[18] This trait of being conscious of a unique quality extends into the other forms of reflective and reflexive consciousness. In reflection, one is aware not only of the quality of the painting, but also of the singular feeling of what it is like to be judging the experience of the painting as beautiful. In reflexive consciousness, one is additionally aware of what it is like to be free to weigh and assess the value and worth of many competing feelings and thoughts in the give-and-take of responsive thinking.

Consciousness also has a deeply intertwined *subjective* dimension marked by otherness. In being conscious of something, one is also immediately aware that this act is "mine," that "I" am conscious of it. Immediate consciousness *per se*, of course, is not reflectively aware of the "I" as its source and origin, else it would not be immediate. Nonetheless, a pre-reflective sense of "mineness" amid otherness accompanies the spontaneous act of selecting something to see or to feel. At the reflective level, one is conscious of self-relatedness: "I" am *seeing*; indeed, "I" am *choosing* to see; "I" am *deciding* what it is I see and what it *means* to me. But there is something there to be seen, to decide about, to have meaning. At the reflexive level, the "I" of consciousness appears in freedom and responsiveness to others and its world. As we said earlier, what is remarkable about ascending levels of self-consciousness is that the more "I" become self-conscious, the more "I" understand my profound embeddedness in a complex world of multiple goods, a world, and other human beings and non-human life. I understand myself, in my inner life of subjectivity, as enmeshed and embodied in a matrix of competing forces and desires – free to assume responsibility to respect and enhance the integrity of life.

135

An Elementary Model of Consciousness

We now present an elementary model of a fundamental property of consciousness with all the epistemic humility that informs the true spirit of modeling. *A fundamental property of consciousness is embodied freedom.* Let us examine the elements of the model.

The first element is the *irreducible capacity for awareness* and so presence of otherness in self. By "irreducible" we mean that consciousness, in its subjective and qualitative dimensions, remains an anomaly for the materialist view of the world, even with the advent of neuroscience. The immediacy of first-person experience is not a sensibly observable neuronal process, but an "inner life" that accompanies activities of consciousness. This "inner life" is constituted by an awareness of "what it is like to be" a conscious organism.[19] Any attempt to objectify inner life misses the phenomenon, which recedes behind the effort to objectify it and thus systematically eludes objectification.

This irreducible capacity for awareness manifests itself as a complex potency or power-to-be in actualizing possibilities in life. In human beings, this capacity for awareness assumes the forms of feeling, acting, and thinking at the different levels of consciousness. Immediate consciousness, or awareness, is a capacity to make spontaneous selections in perceiving and responding to *this* rather than *that* in a complex perceptual field. In directing its "mental look" toward selected contents, immediate consciousness makes choices among possible alternatives.[20] Reflective consciousness has the capacity to deliberate and to choose among multiple possible goods within the natural and social worlds. The reflexive power of consciousness expresses itself as the embodied freedom in the thickest sense while contemplating different approaches to resolving conflicts among competing goods and to envision a path along which life's goods may be integrated around the integrity of life.

The second element is the *embodiment*. Consciousness is always embodied in a material system. In the human case, consciousness is embodied in the complexity of the human organism with its highly developed nervous system and brain. The human organism is embodied in the infinite set of worldly interdependencies on which it is dependent for its basic goods of nourishment, clothing, and shelter from the elements. The operative causality of the entire embodied sphere is natural causality – the inviolable laws of the natural world.

The third element is the connection between consciousness and embodiment, freedom and nature. This relationship is *interconnectedness* or

136

co-dependence. Each of the first two elements is an ingredient in the other. Consciousness, we say, is necessarily embodied, but it is not reducible to the body. Human consciousness cannot exist apart from neuronal processes in the brain and central nervous system, which constitute a necessary material substrate for human consciousness. However, conscious states are not merely neuronal processes, as, for example, materialists argue when they identify the immediate consciousness of pain with C-fiber stimulation in the brain, claiming that pain is utterly reducible to C-fiber stimulation. Likewise, the healthy human body with a functioning brain and central nervous system is necessarily conscious, but it is not reducible to an idea in the mind. The fact that consciousness registers its awareness of the body in thinking does not mean that the body is merely a thought.

Beyond Emergentism

So far, we have distinguished our rudimentary model from the materialist and dualist models. How is our model different from emergentism? Recall that emergentism has to explain human consciousness as an "emergent property" of an evolving biological system that is not itself conscious. That leap, we have said, is so enormous that the emergentist model gives rise to reflection. What if, just as the body is not utterly material, *matter is not utterly devoid of consciousness, at least in some primitive form as a potentiality for freedom in nature?* Try a thought experiment.

It is important to focus precisely on the fundamental property of bodily movement that signifies the presence of consciousness. What is that fundamental property? It is the capacity of a material system *to opt* among alternatives, such that this individual outcome is neither simply random (probabilistically predictable) nor wholly determined.[21] In perception, for example, among multiple possibilities, one may spontaneously attend to a painting – and not to the wall, the light fixture, the sound of the room, the crowd gathering at the entrance, etc. A selection is made in immediate consciousness. At other levels of consciousness, this pared-down moment of opting is enormously enriched in the complexity of deliberate choice and reflexive freedom in human existence, as we have discussed. "Opting" refers only to the most elementary manifestation of freedom; it provides the simplest possible test for the analogous experience of another embodied consciousness – namely, the behavior of actualizing one possibility among others such that the event is individually unpredictable yet intentional. Opting so defined exhibits a causality that is interconnected with, but not reducible to, natural causality.

What other kinds of material systems exhibit opting behavior? Consciousness can assume various "masks," as it were. One need not believe that human beings, or even higher animals, are the only conscious beings or that an inexplicable gulf exists between conscious and non-conscious beings. Here we extend the barest property of spontaneous opting to *matter itself*. Amazingly, the quantum behavior of elementary particles – the ultimate constituents of matter itself – and the spontaneous life of immediate consciousness in human beings share the fundamental property. In each case, one finds the capacity to opt among alternatives in ways that are individually inscrutable because they are neither random nor determined. Admittedly, it is a gigantic stretch from embodied human freedom to the behavior of subatomic particles. The implication is nonetheless staggering: could elementary matter reveal some kind of proto-consciousness? If so, an interesting line of inquiry opens up beyond emergentism: instead of pulling rabbits (consciousness) out of a hat (non-conscious matter), it may be rabbits all the way down.

We have already considered the human side of the analogy. Humans opt among given alternatives in immediate consciousness, they choose deliberately among interconnected layers of goods in reflective consciousness, and in reflexive consciousness they exercise freedom in contemplating a variety of possibilities for integrating basic, social, and reflective goods in the unity of a coherent life with and for others. On the side of elementary physical particles, we see opting at a primitive or proto-conscious level, with none of the complicated material systems that support human consciousness, such as an organic body with a nervous system and brain. Nonetheless, in the famous two-slit experiment, among others, elementary particles display the fundamental structure of opting among alternatives. All quantum behavior is of this kind. Quantum theory makes astoundingly accurate predictions in terms of the probabilities of how particles will behave in the aggregate, but it cannot predict the outcomes of individual events. The quantum behavior of elementary particles is neither random nor determined.

The model of consciousness as embodied freedom leaves open what kinds of material systems can embody consciousness, or some kind of proto-consciousness. As such, we are open to the possibility that consciousness is not a unique property of human life, nor even that of higher mammals, but is potentially present in matter in a primitive form from the beginning. The model postulates a scale of matter, starting with fundamental constituents such as electrons and nuclei, passing through atoms such as the hydrogen atom to molecules (such as the water molecule), and moving on through inorganic life forms to more complex systems within organic life forms. At each level more alternatives are in principle open to the system.[22] Richer and richer forms of freedom arise as we go up this hierarchy, with deepening awareness of the entanglement of consciousness in the interdependencies of life and increasing realization of the responsibility that comes with freedom for the integrity of life.

This model of embodied freedom as a fundamental property of consciousness steers between extreme tendencies of overhumanization, expressed in materialism or reductive naturalism, and hypertheism, found in dualism. Accordingly, it is no longer possible to think of an absolute division between matter and spirit, mind and body. Matter already bears the elementary traces of consciousness, and consciousness is always materially embodied. Moreover, humans share with other things the structure of embodied consciousness, although inorganic life forms admittedly possess only a proto-consciousness at the level of elementary particles and cannot otherwise be called conscious. Nonetheless, the unity of matter and consciousness expands the scope of human responsibility. Think, for example, of the double love-command to love God and one's neighbor. When someone asks, "Who is my neighbor?" the answer is not merely "anyone in need." Under the terms of this model, our responsibility to love and care for the other extends to life in its integrity. Human beings are indeed distinctive in terms of the sophistication of capacities to exercise freedom. This distinctive capacity is the responsibility we bear for our own species, other species, and the earth on which we all live.

The model of consciousness has theological implications. The ability to envision the real connection, the interrelatedness, between consciousness and matter enables a deeper comprehension of the integrity of life. Drawing from Christian and other sources, God's being is taken to be manifest in the integrity of life. A theological humanist freely feels and sees the real presence of the divine in all realms of life, and we formulate that presence as "the integrity of life." God is neither a supreme being – a heavenly deity or the light of the world – nor the nothingness of critical negation. God's being is imagined and sensed in the integrity of life. The masks of mind reach from subatomic matter through human and non-human life to divine life itself.

At this point in reflection we turn to visual art as a mask of the mind. By engaging visual art we want to show how this model of consciousness helps to understand the reflective goods expressed in art, but also how art so conceived provides the means to grasp the dynamics of consciousness.

Visual Art as a Mask of Mind

Art is one medium through which the deepest possibilities for self-understanding are transmitted to people within a culture. We now want to try out a model of visual art. The model of art proposed here incorporates these elements into the structure of *embodied meaning*: artworks are (1) humanly made (or chosen) works that (2) visibly embody consciousness (3) in relation to some viewer (4) under aesthetic, moral, or spiritual forms.[23] Art in this view is a mask of *otherness* as embodied freedom. Art is the visual expression in the form of an image of the inner life of embodied consciousness, which includes of course awareness of the interrelationship of inner life with an expansive world of basic, social, and reflective goods. Whereas anyone who says "I" experiences their own consciousness as embodied freedom, "I" experience a work of art by analogy as an embodied meaning. The mask of freedom and the mask of meaning are spiritual twins. As embodied meanings, works of visual art have a distinctive sensuous capacity to propose reflective goods for the sake of respecting and enhancing the integrity of life. That may be true of other forms of art and culture as well (we think it is), but our claims here are rightly limited to the visual arts.

A piece of art is externally *embodied* outside the mind of the artist. Artworks are physically "there" in the world with us, much like other human beings, things, or animals. Just as human beings, animals, and things have bodies in which they are located, so do artworks present themselves in the materiality of a painted canvas, a sculpted stone, or the like. The artwork is also embodied *meaning*, the product of opting as performance. Works of art embody conscious meanings at two different levels. At the *representational level*, works of art present an image of something (e.g., a landscape) that is empirically absent.[24] In addition, at the *expressive level*, artworks enable another meaning (or set of meanings) to appear in, on, or through the representation.[25] Through the perceived image, we feel or sense new meanings, through a "metaphoric twist," which speaks from the work and strikes us with its significance. In this way art enacts or displays features of consciousness under its mask.

A metaphoric twist can happen in at least two different forms, each of which has a religious root.[26] Expressive meanings can appear in the first mode of "manifestation," which means that a second meaning shows itself naturalistically, as the mystery or even glory of things in their sheer givenness. The expressive meaning illuminates a hidden depth, as if from behind. A famous example might be Vermeer's painting, *The Milkmaid*. In this painting, we have an utterly commonplace scene: a young woman pouring milk from a jug. This ordinary scene is infused with a sense of the extraordinary, partly because the woman is wholly unified with her task, and partly because the interior light in which her resolve shows itself transfigures the entire scene and imbues it with a sense of sacredness. This mode of expressive meaning has theological significance in the Christian West in the liturgical experience of Eucharist. The elements of bread and wine are transformed into the Body and Blood of Christ. It is also connected to the image of God as the light of the world.

On the other hand, expressive meanings can also appear in the mode of "proclamation." A second meaning can break into the form and content of a representational meaning, disrupting and disturbing it. This mode of expression is often seen as the privileged one for the twentieth-century experience of dread and anxiety about the possibility for ultimate meaningfulness. This mode has its theological form in the Christian sermon. The word of God as heavenly deity breaks through ordinary human words, accusing and condemning, as well as uplifting and edifying, those who are morally and religiously serious. A famous example of art conforming to the mode of proclamation is Van Gogh's painting *Wheat Field with Crows*, in which a power breaks through the form of a landscape painting and the content described by the title, unsettling and judging the viewer.[27]

Next, art has a *relation to some viewer*, who must connect with the artwork. We can distinguish three kinds of relations between the viewer and the artwork, which can either coexist in the same experience or may occur singly. At each level, the artwork can open the imagination to new possibilities of reflective goods. So, the work of art can open up a shared world of meaning for the imagination. Artworks project worlds for the imagination to inhabit and in which it can discover its own possibilities to be. Call this capacity the *aesthetic dimension* of the work of art. It is the ability of art to open a world that engages interest and commands attention, so that the viewer may lose herself within it. By "world" is meant what the work is about, that is, a particular way of connecting experience into a meaningful whole.

In viewing a work of art one may also feel the presence of another being, a "you" to whom respect and admiration is owed. One feels under the watch of another consciousness, as if a light has been turned toward one. The work of art assumes a personal presence with a moral status. It is not merely the opening of a world for the imagination, the work of art becomes a "you" to whom I must answer. The work of art as embodied meaning arouses the viewer's conscience. The work may address the viewer: "Who are you?" "What do you want from your life?" "What do you do with your time?" Call this the *moral dimension* of the work of art.

The work may not only challenge one's world and one's sense of subjectivity, but also empower one to be something more. If, for example, I sense that the work of art undercuts or overturns my own sense of self and world, and presents me with a higher standard of integrity than I had previously known, then the work of art presents a *sacred or spiritual dimension*. In this case the work of art confronts my world and sense of self with a meaning that I must admit is superior to the views with which I have been living. The work not only challenges one to change one's life and fills one with the sense that life cannot continue as before, it also concretely gives a new sense of the integrity of life. This gift fills one with feelings of awe, humility, resolution, and gratitude. If these feelings, along with accompanying intuitions and visions of possibility, can form a new basis of motivation in life, then the art is sacred.

The experience of a sacred or spiritual dimension to the work of art is paradoxical, because it embraces two opposite meanings. The new sense of selfhood is donated to one through the work of art as something that is *most my own*; it enables one to become the one I truly am as a human being. Second, one experiences the gift of consciousness in the work of art as at the same time *not at all one's own*. Through the work of art one receives one's own life as a gift from another – from God or the universe or the artist – but not from oneself. In such a case, the work of art manifests and enables spiritual presence experienced in and through a material object that is an embodied consciousness.

How does this model of visual art relate to current debate?

The Plight of Contemporary Art

In our time, art is in a crisis that is at once a blessing and a curse. If anything can be art, then nothing is art or everything is art. Visual art is free to relate in new ways to its own history and to the traditional materials of art. In this way, the situation of art is analogous to the current condition of theology, as explored in chapter 3. How so? According to Arthur Danto, there are four major eras in the development of art toward its "end."[28] To review these eras is helpful, because they reveal how reflective goods may appear in art as a mask of mind, and it has an analogy to the crisis of theology in the West.

The first period spans the ancient and medieval worlds, lasting until approximately 1400. This period is called "pre-art."[29] In the era of pre-art, objects that we would think of as art objects were produced and venerated not as "art" objects, but as media of the gods. Art was indistinguishable from religion, and even religion was not identified or conceived as such. In this stage, meanings appear directly *on* given objects, which were felt and sensed as powerful and awesome.

The second period is the era of art properly speaking, where "art" primarily meant an image endowed with beauty, the sensuous presentation of truth. The rough dating of this period is from approximately 1400 to the mid-nineteenth century. During this era, painters strove to present the world in their artworks the way that the world presents itself to the eye – whether the chosen world was biblical, mythological, historical, or natural. This was the era of realism, or even of an enhanced realism, as artworks became over-saturated with the qualities of the real, as the Dutch masters remind us. Reflective goods appear in the viewer's act of seeing truth and beauty in humanly made works of art, which weave their magic in creating the illusion of three-dimensional space, perspective, etc. The form of consciousness for realistic art is reflective; beauty or sacredness appears in an embodied meaning that is constructed *by* the artist and *for* the viewer.

Modernism, the third period, brought about a genuine revolution in the conception of art and a new reflexive level of artistic self-consciousness. Modernism can be dated from approximately the mid-nineteenth century until the early 1960s. The focus was on the artwork's ability to evoke reflection on the mystery of creative imagination as the ground that makes art possible. Giving up the pretenses of visual illusion, modernist painters highlighted the real conditions of visual art: the two-dimensional flatness of the canvas surface, its rectangular shape, awareness of paint and the brushstroke, and the like. For modern artists, the painting is to be looked *at* rather than *through*.[30] The agenda of modernism was to produce a more honest art – one that reflects critically on inherited understandings of what it means for an artwork to be judged beautiful or sacred. To understand a modernist work means to grasp what it says about *what makes* something a work of art, in light of all previous answers to the question. It also means to understand *who one becomes* if one enters the artist's vision of the world. Embedded in a modernist work of art is philosophical orientation, as well as a spiritual discipline for transforming embodied subjectivity.

Modern artists were committed to a kind of spiritual alchemy. For example, Van Gogh painted peasants, landscapes, interiors of rooms, and portraits to reveal how embodied human life is touched by the eternal and how his own tortured consciousness could affirm life in the midst of suffering and death.[31] Kandinsky insisted on the "inner need" of the artist to express, in abstract forms of intense color and strong painterly gestures, the spiritual path of consciousness toward the divine.[32] When one sees a cubist Picasso portrait, a dreamscape of Miro, or an image of a devastated mythical landscape by Anselm Kiefer, one says: "I understand what the work says about the inner truth of art, and how the artist's vision transforms body, soul, and the whole meaning of the world to which we relate."[33]

These eras in the history of art on Danto's account are held together by a single grand narrative: art emerged out of primordial religious origins, developed through realism under the idea of beauty, and culminated in self-critical expression of the inner life of artistic consciousness in the modernist period. These turns are analogous to the path of theology charted before. And like in the case of theology, in the early 1960s with the advent of pop art this narrative seems to have come to an "end." Pop art was the anomaly that broke down the modernist paradigm because it violated all the rules of modernism yet was stunningly successful within the art world. Pop art had the affect of liberating artists from the modernist paradigm, so that art could henceforth be anything that the artist fancies it to be. It did so by producing works of art which are visually indistinguishable from real objects in the world.

Consider *Brillo Box*, which Andy Warhol exhibited as art in 1964. It consists of a set of painted and stenciled wooden cartons which closely resembled the cardboard cartons of brillo pads which could be bought in any grocery store. Until Warhol showed those boxes as artworks, who could have imagined them as a possible subject of an artwork? Pop art's appearance showed that anything can be art, and that there is no dominant style or approach in making art.[34] The question now becomes: "Why is one thing art and another thing not-art, when there is no significant visual difference between them?"[35] Nothing is disallowed; everything is possible. Non-art could be art, just as much as could more traditionally identifiable works of art such as paintings or sculptures. Pop art ends where theology in the twentieth century ended: God is not God; art is non-art.

As a result of this revolution in art, a profusion of different styles appeared in the 1960s – color-field painting, hard-edged abstraction, French neo-realism, minimalism, new sculpture, conceptual art, neo-expressionism, and the like. None of them could lay claim to defining the new stylistic direction in art. At this level, aesthetic reflective goods appear precisely in the confusion about what counts as art. The art world is thrown into a creative state of chaos in which much is at stake. Will art survive as a distinctive medium of reflective goods?

Theological Humanism and the World of Art

What does theological humanism have to say about the condition of art as a reflective good? In today's world, as we have said, anything whatsoever can be art, and art can be anything. Under these chaotic and unstable conditions, two strong impulses compete for the soul of visual art: didactic art and commercial art.[36]

Didactic art refers to any art that minimizes its own embodied status and exaggerates its ability to deliver a message. Didactic art diminishes the embodiment-side of the work of art, so that the freely created art object, with its potential for opening a superabundance of meaning for interpretation, is nullified in favor of conveying an easily catchable "meaning," like a message in a bottle. Very often in current "postart," the conveyed meaning is banal to the extreme. Consider, for example, *Solid Sea*, an installation at Documental II (2002) by Multiplicity, an Italian group of postartists. "It deals with the death of some 200 Asians who drowned when their overcrowded boat sank between Malta and Sicily." The installation includes a collage of video images and interviews "spliced together in a chorus of lament and anger." The problem with the work is that it provides no insight into the event. We are simply given "managed imagery with no aesthetic relevance, that is, with no transcendental import that would turn it into tragic art."[37] The public art of Jenny Holzer and Barbara Kruger is another example of didactic art. This "art" projects word-messages into public spaces, with messages such as "I am because I shop."[38] The slogan ended up on New York City shopping bags.

If the main purpose of the artwork is to proclaim political or social propaganda, then the artwork fails as art. The expressive level of meaning is reduced to a banal message, and the vocation of art is trivialized. The richness of human freedom, in its reflexive interpretation of the meaning of being human in a globalized and contentious world, is flattened. Rhetorical pandering replaces creative imagination. In general, didactic art suppresses rather than liberates the inner life of consciousness. It flattens human experience through an ideological cause.

Commercial art stands on the opposite extreme from conceptual art. Commercial art exaggerates the power of the image to stimulate desire or to provide entertainment without having an adequate meaning embodied in it. Much Hollywood film, pulp fiction, and advertising fall under this category, but the shocking thing is that commerciality has overtaken much fine art as well. Commercial art finds its purpose in *profit* and its means in

145

marketing. Observing the price of "artworks" go through the roof in recent decades, shrewd marketing experts have turned to art. Why not, if anything can be art? So-called artists calculate how to sway an audience in order to cash in on sales or popularity of some kind. Art turns into a commodity, purely and simply. One strategy has been to market everyday objects as artworks, as in Jeff Koons' exhibition of new vacuum cleaners ("New Hoover Convertibles, New Shelton Wet/Dry Displaced Double Decker," 1981–7).[39] Another is to market pornography or scatology as art, as in Jeff Koons' "Made in Heaven." Damien Hirst is another example of a highly successful commercially driven artist. His *Home Sweet Home* (1996) is a porcelain ashtray filled with cigarette butts. The apparent meaning is the same as in other works by Hirsh: "that everyday life is more interesting than art, and art is only interesting when it is mistaken for everyday life."[40] Even when this work is exhibited in an art museum, and thus is called art, it loses its identity as art. There is no productive relationship between representational meaning and an expressive meaning in the embodied image. Commercial art engages the imagination, but only to distract it in order to convert the value of art into economic value. Here too human experience is flattened, concealed within the mask of art.

Didactic art and commercial art both fail to realize art as an embodied mask of consciousness for a viewer. The work of art is reduced either to a trivial message or to a marketable commodity. Theological humanism seeks and promotes art that respects and enhances the integrity of life. From this standpoint, good art integrates embodiment with meaning so that meaning and medium fuse together into a living, free unity. In that way art is a mask of mind displaying consciousness so that it can *partially* be understood and thus contribute to the integrity of life. This is possible because genuine art integrates three dimensions that bear the traces of goods and formal norms noted above: (1) the aesthetic dimension, which opens up for the imagination a world, a locality, that reaches beyond immediate interest; (2) the moral dimension, which presents the viewer with a living subjectivity and finality of the other over against my own; and (3) the spiritual or sacred dimension, which challenges and transfigures one's autonomy and one's world. Of course, this account entails a reflective *judgment*, a choice for some works and not others. That simply means that theological humanism is a way of *inhabiting* the domain of reflective goods different than commercial or didactic art in order to respect and enhance the integrity of reflective life.

Each of us would have candidates for the renewal of art beyond the end of art. Consider one example, the intermedia artist Hans Breder. In addition to many incredible digitized works, prints, and photographs, Breder has done a series of paintings called *Liminal Icons*, one of which dons the cover of this book.[41] The image is that of an abstract yet tangible and concrete doorway, which hovers in the unbounded universe, framing the unframeable expanse, inviting entrance yet repelling it at the same time. Through the door is palpable nothingness as a sacred presence. To enter the door is to enter the alchemical space of transmutation; it is the locality of *nigredo*, the blackening, the place of initiatory death and rebirth. The colors of these paintings are extraordinary and intense. Deep blues and riveting reds change and deepen with an incredible purity in different lights. The lights, the colors, seem to come from some otherworldly source that is somehow the very soul of this worldly life. Hints of new life beyond death appear through the dark passage; we receive intimations of rebirth from a cosmic womb.

This painting, and others by Breder, is humanistic and theological, on our account. It discloses a world of mystery and awe for the imagination. One is freed to feel the presence of a spiritual reality. It empowers one to embrace a destiny beyond the moment. This painting is grace embodied, material grace.[42] It opens human existence to the integrity of life beyond material conditions or the boundaries of social and reflective existence. This opening, in which one can freely dwell, is the possibility and the power for the meaningful integration of life. Here art embraces and evokes the integrity of life because it opens to consciousness a range of reflective goods that contribute to an integrated existence. That kind of art enacts the complexity of the integrity of life as it comes to light in human existence. It presents human life beyond the flatness of materialism or the implausibility of dualism and into the richness of integral consciousness. In this way, the experience of art masks — reveals and conceals — the depth of our inner lives.

Inhabiting Reflective Goods

The force of our argument turns on the connection between how consciousness is conceived and the ways one can and ought to inhabit the realm of reflective goods, including the domain of art. Dualistic and reductive accounts of consciousness threaten to render banal reflective goods because of what they imply about inhabiting cultural forms. These positions conceal the reality of consciousness as reflexive, embodied freedom aiming at a meaningful integration of life. In a sense we have then changed the debate by turning around the question. Rather than seeking the *origin* of consciousness in matter, as in emergentism, or the *end* of consciousness in divine spirit, as

147

dualists contend, we have sought to develop an account which is scientifically plausible but also captures the in-between freedom of consciousness. Human consciousness is at the intersection of matter and the power of mind creatively to mask itself in works that enact the integrity of life. A theological humanist inhabits reflective goods and cultural forms in ways that combat banality and deepen the world. One does so knowing that art is not a second god but a mask of the all-too human mind.

9

Religion and Spiritual Integrity

If one casts a glance on the global scene, it becomes obvious that religion is a force of goodness in the world and is a power of evil as well. Throughout the centuries, people have appealed to religion in order to motivate and justify destructive and gracious deeds. How many people have killed others or have been slain in the name of religion? The number is countless. How many people have been helped by others or have been redeemed from evil in the name of religion? Again, the number is countless. Historically, religion has a mixed legacy. The task of religion and the human future, then, is to resolve that every religion foster responsibility for the integrity of life. That is the contention of the present chapter. To live that vision is the great spiritual struggle of our time, a struggle raging in the hearts and minds of people around the world.

So, this chapter wades into the troubled world scene where the debate between religion and secularism is exploding everywhere. We can begin by clarifying the direction of our inquiry.

Spiritual Integrity

In our global time, religion is resurgent in nearly all places, even within Western Europe, although some Christian churches continue to lose influence. In the United States, evangelical Christianity is growing, but so too is secularism.[1] Fading in strength and influence is the religious middle composed of moderates or religious liberals, traditionally associated with the "mainstream" Protestant churches and post-Vatican II Catholicism. The situation is polarized. Defying the predictions of nineteenth- and twentieth-century social scientists, strident forms of religion thunder above the earthly landscape. Some people take the thunder as the promise of victory. Religious militants engage in holy wars – real or virtual – with the heathens of the world, thinking that God will smite the enemy. Other people hear the thunder as a sign of torrential floods that will encompass the whole world. Secular humanists close ranks to pray for a world with no religion.[2] The extremes of hypertheism and overhumanization, respectively, present real dangers to the human future. Will religion bring us life or death?

The aim of this chapter is to make clear the excesses in both directions that afflict and limit religion today. We want to put theological humanism on trial, again. Our hope is to set forth a vision of "true religion" in relation to the spiritual discipline required by theological humanism. The task is to protect the integrity of religion in a world that is both obsessed with religion and weary of it. The strategy is to show how to inhabit religious forms critically so as to transform them and place them in service to the integrity of life. The step needed to approach the future entails nothing less than a revolution in thinking. Theological humanism seeks to educate conscience in the realm of religion and thus to advance freedom *within* religion.

More specifically, this chapter is about the good of *spiritual integrity*, which aims at the right relation among the other goods which together constitute human life – basic, social, reflective, and natural goods. The irony is that one cannot aim directly at spiritual integrity; it is a good of human existence that is only realized through dedication to responsible existence with and for others. In this way, spiritual integrity is never the product of direct striving for self-fulfillment; it is received, if at all, indirectly, mysteriously, while seeking to live a life dedicated to all that respects and enhances the integrity of life. *Spiritual integrity* thus unites flourishing and virtue, or, as we put it before, happiness and holiness.

Traditionally, people have turned to religion (or its functional equivalent) as the enabler of spiritual integrity. For theological humanism, spiritual integrity entails a life dedicated to respecting and enhancing the integrity of life in all actions and relations – before God. It is a life responsive to the call of conscience. In this chapter, we explore how this form of integrity enables one to inhabit religion and critique to make them mutually constructive powers in the human future. As part of globalization, religious diversity and multiculturalism will continue to grow, which means that we live among a plurality of languages, literatures, customs, traditions, ways of organizing time and space, social groups, professions, and faiths.[3] Theological humanism must include a coherent response to the religious and secular otherness in our midst.

What is Religion?

While it was mentioned in chapter 1, we want to be clear about the meaning of "religion." Scholars in the modern West attempted to identify the "essence" of religion as a universal human phenomenon by focusing on the structures of religious experience. Friedrich Schleiermacher, founder of modern Christian theology, writing in the early German romantic movement, defined religion as the feeling and intuition of the infinite in the finite.[4] In his magnum opus, *The Christian Faith*, he construed the essence of religion as the "feeling of absolute dependence" on an unknowable ground (the "whence" of this feeling), which he called "God." The Romanian phenomenologist of religion Mircea Eliade defined religion as the experience of a hierophany, that is, a manifestation of the sacred as wholly other than the profane.[5] Paul Tillich, an émigré from Hitler's Germany who became a distinguished theologian in the USA, thought religion was "ultimate concern" – that is, concern with what is of ultimate importance in life.[6] *Universalist* definitions of the essence of religion capture something significant about religious experience: human consciousness is implicitly directed toward ultimacy of meaning, what is unsurpassably important and real. Human consciousness potentially includes awareness of an infinite ground and horizon of meaning alongside its awareness of discrete objects or other human subjects. This is denied, as we will see, by secular humanist critics of religion. This makes their positions morally committed to human well-being, but strident in the denial of religious transcendence.

Against universalistic approaches to religion like those mentioned, many current scholars concentrate on the particular religions as historical phenomena occurring within human cultures. Religion in general does not exist, they claim. Particular historical communities are what exist, and they abound with dazzling complexity and difference one from the other. It is wrong-headed to attempt to define the "essence" of something as historically complex as "religion."[7] The *particularist* view is that each cultural tradition is unique, and that its uniqueness is lost when we subsume that culture under general categories. According to the particularists, we falsify the data, we lose the particular meanings of cultural events and developments, when we coin general theories of such things as "religion," especially where representatives of the living traditions do not recognize the concept. The denial of any shared religious quality to existence is, as we will see, crucial to the outlook of religious exclusivists. They insist on the religious dimension of life, but too easily stunt the scope of moral concern to their communities.

151

Several traits of "religion" in its historical, particular manifestations commend themselves for reflection.[8] The concrete historical religions (Buddhism, Christianity, etc.) tend, first, to have foundational myths that relate original events about how people in this particular tradition came into the real presence of divinity as a formative force in their lives. Embedded in foundational myths are symbols and metaphors, which incorporate moral, cosmological, and theological meanings. A second trait of historical religion is its intellectual tradition, that is, a pattern of reflection, born from interpreting the foundational myth and its central symbols, practices, and metaphors, which leads toward theology and ethics. Third, religions have rituals that enable practitioners to enact the meanings of the myths. Fourth, the use of myth, reflection, and ritual aims at inculcating tradition-defined religious experiences, such as those of divine grace, *nirvana*, or *moksha*. Fifth, religions inculcate artistic forms and styles which express and communicate the meanings of myth, ritual, theology, and religious experience. Art, ritual, myth become gateways to the soul, meeting points for the divine and the human. Finally, religions have an institutional structure with a hierarchy of leaders who are especially adept at interpreting the myths, performing the rituals, and displaying the intended religious experiences.

Religion, we contend, is neither simply a universal structure of human being nor a set of unique and relatable culturally embedded events within particular traditions. *Religion is the human longing for and awareness of the divine (what is taken to be unsurpassable in importance and reality) experienced and expressed within the concrete cultural life of particular historical traditions.* There is no religion in general, apart from its concrete historical manifestations. There is no particular religion which does not display the general traits of the concept "religion." The challenge is to avoid making any one specific religion into an end in itself, thereby circumventing the claims of responsibility for the integrity of life. We can see the depth of this challenge, and the dangers that come from making any religion an end rather than a means, if we turn to patterns of religious life within our own culture (the contemporary United States) and reflect on the situation of religious diversity. Diana L. Eck writes that "America has always been a land of many religions."[9] In recent decades, diversity has exploded in magnitude and complexity. One sees a conflict between *true believers* and *secular humanists*, as we note in the introduction to this book. And everywhere are the puzzled, open, yet uncommitted who bemoan the situation. How should we respond religiously to this unprecedented diversity for the sake of the human future?

Christian Hypertheism

One persistent response to religious pluralism in American history has been Christian exclusionism, the troop of *true believers*. And as everyone knows, there are virulent forms of exclusionism found in other religions around the world, (say) Islam, Hinduism, and others. At the political and social level, Christian exclusivism asserts that the United States is in fact, and should be by law, a "Christian nation."[10] Non-Christians should stay away or go home; they are not welcome. Christian exclusionism in its evangelical version asserts that one can only be saved if one holds certain beliefs about Christ as personal Lord and Savior, or, in the conservative Roman Catholic version recently asserted by Benedict XVI, if one participates in a specific way in the sacramental life of the Catholic Church. There can be no doubt that a high percentage of the approximately 217 million adult American Christians hold exclusionist views, which are commonplace among evangelical and fundamentalist Christians (comprising 38 percent of the total American population), as well as among conservative Catholics. It would be folly to ignore this right-wing Christian movement, which is a potent force in American cultural, political, and religious life.

Religious exclusionism has many benefits to offer people. Exclusionist churches of true believers integrate basic, social, natural, and reflective goods into a quest for what they consider to be the highest good, defined as personal salvation. What is this salvation? In its extreme forms, Christian exclusionists understand salvation as redemption *from* a world drenched in sin, decadence, and chaos. Salvation is the promise of bodily assumption into heaven. This view exemplifies "hypertheism" in religion. Hypertheism surrenders human freedom of moral and theological reflection in service to absolute truths, divine decrees that are beyond criticism. It contradicts the good of spiritual integrity, namely, a dedication to the proper relation among goods in the integrity of life. Human basic, social, natural, and reflective goods cannot be rightly pursued or integrated when one seeks redemption *from* this world rather than *for* the world, because that quest violates the integrity of life as life *in* the world.

Consider now an extreme form of Christian exclusionism. Fundamentalism in the United States is a particular form of traditional, Bible-based Christianity. Fundamentalism in particular constitutes a subgroup under the larger umbrella of evangelical Christianity. All fundamentalists are evangelicals, although not all evangelicals are fundamentalists. Indeed, not all Evangelical Christians are exclusionists. Fundamentalism represents a loose confederation of churches and individuals without a central institution or

153

self-defining structure. It is a growing presence and force in American society, reaching millions of people with its combative message. One central trait of fundamentalism is its self-proclaimed militarism.[11] Fundamentalists fight back against "overhumanization."

Decrying the rise of modernity, with its faith in scientific reason and its technological drive to subdue the world, fundamentalists choose not to rely on human intellect but on the revealed will of God. They witness to Christ's work in the saving of souls from a world besotted with evil. There can be no compromise with the opposing forces of overhumanization. Mainline churches, which have traditionally sympathized with liberal Christian theology in various forms, are part of a secular humanist heresy. Fundamentalists do not consider "liberal Christians" (i.e., non-exclusionist Christians, who consider salvation to be redemption for the world on behalf of social justice) to be Christians at all. Liberal Christianity makes accommodations to modern thought, culture, and social structures; it adapts the message of Christianity to current trends and practices. For a fundamentalist, such accommodation is betrayal of Christ and the Bible.[12] Fundamentalists choose to fight humanistic threats to their core identity as Bible-believing Christians. They march under the banner of Christ. They struggle for a vision of the world shaped by a highly selective reading of the Bible.

The foundational myth of many Christian fundamentalists is that of "dispensational pre-millennialism."[13] According to the myth, there are seven stages of God's activity in history. History is the drama of a heavenly deity's actions. The current age is that of the church. It is decisive for true believers to belong to a true Christian church as a bulwark against the evil world outside, a church where faith is taught and lived. The stage to come is all-important: the rapture. Satan is still alive and well in this world, which grows increasingly corrupt. Christ will not tolerate the Evil One much longer. Christ will come to take up true believers into his heaven above. All non-believers will be left behind to suffer the tribulation when the forces of God confront the forces of Satan. Following the final victory, Christ will institute a thousand-year reign. The purpose of the Christian life is to prepare oneself, to be ready, for the rapture. This vision is widely propagated in the pulpits of fundamentalist churches and in the hugely popular *Left Behind* books written by Tim LaHaye. For the fundamentalists, the Bible is inerrant; its literal sense is utterly trustworthy as the direct word of God to humans.[14] They find symbols and metaphors of both the rapture and the tribulation of non-believers in such texts as Daniel, Revelation, Matthew 24 (esp. verses 37–41), and most importantly, Paul's First Letter to the Thessalonians 4:15–18.

The key rituals of fundamentalists are Bible study, preaching, testifying, and missionizing. The promise of the rapture provides certainty of salvation for the true believer, offers support for faith, gives an absolute standard of moral and spiritual judgment, extends comfort in suffering and persecution, and enables freedom from fear of death.[15] To show one's worthiness as a true believer, however, one must win souls for Christ, according to the great commission in the Gospel of Matthew 28:16–20. The resurrected Jesus meets eleven disciples and instructs them to "go forth and make all nations my disciples." Fundamentalist Christians take this injunction seriously; their war is one to win souls for Jesus in the cosmic battle against Satan.

Fundamentalists, in concert with evangelical Christians, are active in the political domain for the sake of combating secularism.[16] True believers like the late Jerry Falwell insist that the United States has a special role in God's plan. The United States is to be a Christian nation and a leader in saving souls for Christ. To foster this goal, Falwell founded the "Moral Majority" to promote Republicans with fundamentalist leanings running for political office at all levels. Huge successes were realized with the election of Ronald Reagan and George W. Bush as Presidents of the United States. Tom DeLay served as Speaker of the House under Republican congressional control and went public with remarks like these: "Christianity offers the only viable, reasonable, definitive answer to the questions of 'Where did I come from?', 'Why am I here?', 'Where am I going?', 'Does life have any meaningful purpose?' Only Christianity offers a way to understand that physical and that moral order."[17] Christian exclusionism in its political form reaches the highest levels of US government with this militant evangelical-fundamentalist movement, which also harnesses the most up-to-date technology on its behalf. Sophisticated websites and television broadcasts help spread the Christian exclusionist message throughout the country and the world. The same use of hi-tech resources is found among hypertheists in other religions.

The institutional structure of fundamentalism is marked by separatism. Fundamentalists and right-wing evangelicals picture themselves as living separately from the corrupt world of secular humanism. They promote home schooling, associate as much as possible with fellow believers, and inculcate an "us" versus "them" mentality. Right-wing Christians carefully integrate life's basic, natural, social, and reflective goods under the protection of Christian exclusionism. United with others in the community by belief in the imminent rapture, led by a pastor who is a spokesman for God, and fortified in their faith by the ritual of personal witnessing, fundamentalist Christians attribute everything to God, the real agent in the world. Everything that

155

happens can be traced back to divine activity, where "God" is caught up in a life-and-death struggle with Satan. Anything good that happens is the direct result of God's intervening grace. Anything bad that happens is either because Satan is not finally defeated or because God is testing one through suffering.

This kind of hypertheism confers blessings on a true believer: a strong sense of identity in belonging to a special community, a set of secure beliefs by which to live one's life, and certainty of redemption from a fallen world in the promise of God's heaven. The marks of salvation include unwavering trust in God, surrender of one's life to Jesus Christ, removal of sin and doubt, and right behavior. These things satisfy human desires and sensibility, ranging from fear of damnation to forgiveness for guilt and also divine recognition. They also unify basic, social, natural, and reflective goods through conformity to a biblical principle of obedience to Christ and his Church.

The cost of these satisfactions is high, however. Genuine freedom and responsibility for the world are sacrificed on the altar of hypertheism. The notion that only Christians (or Jews or Muslims or etc.) have access to the absolute truth of God, and that all others are in error, is prideful to the extreme. The conviction that salvation is redemption *from* the world, and not for it, can cultivate a tolerance for injustice and environmental degradation, because this world is but a temporary testing-place of no intrinsic value. The Church of true believers has become an end in itself, and other forms of life are means to that end. In the end, hypertheism distort the integrity of life in their denial of the goodness of finite existence, and they warp the conscience into a voice of a tribal creed. In this way, religion endangers the human future.

Is there a way to preserve what is powerful and good in the hypertheistic versions of exclusionism, while transforming the spiritual good around the norm of the integrity of life?

Secular Overhumanization

A second, competing response to the reality of religious diversity comes from the side of secular humanists. At a political and social level, secular humanism delivers a fearsome critique of religion: religion ought to have no part in American social and political life. Religion is, in this view, deeply entangled with superstitions, and religious belief is the root of evil. Secular humanism aims to liberate humanity from the tyranny of religious absurdity in order to actualize goods that constitute true ideals for humanity. The target of animosity is theistic belief and practice, whether Christian, Jewish, or Muslim.

At a philosophical level, secular humanism promotes versions of scientism, reductive naturalism, and materialism. Scientism means that only scientific inquiry is rational and that science is the only way to a better human future. Reductive naturalism and materialism are similar stances. They hold that what is real is natural (there are only natural events with natural causes), that what is natural can be construed in terms of the organization of matter and is, as such, a proper object of scientific inquiry. There is no telling how many Americans hold these views, although the 1990 ARIS poll showed 23 percent declaring that they subscribe to "no religion." It seems plausible that many, maybe most, scientists are naturalists or materialists, and that the scientific worldview pervades contemporary culture.[18]

"Secular humanism" names a general tendency toward cultural forms. It defines education, art, politics, literature, economics, etc. in such a way that they owe nothing to religion and cannot, in principle, disclose experiences of religious transcendence. In this broad sense secular humanism is strongly allied with the appearance of critique in modern culture, as discussed in chapter 3. Yet according to our definition of religion in both its general and particular dimensions, secular humanism, ironically, qualifies as a functional equivalent of a religion. Ingredient is the mood of joy in exercising the liberating power of free and rational inquiry in order "to bring out the best in people so that all people can have the best in life."[19] Secular humanism is committed to solving human problems in practical ways, to moral principles, to constitutional democracy and protection of the rights of all minorities, and to the maximization of human potential. Redemption is *from* religion and *for* the world.

There is much that is admirable and noble in secular humanism. It provides an orientation capable of integrating basic, social, natural, and reflective goods under a principle of what it considers to be the highest good. But what is the highest good according to secular humanism? In its extreme forms, secular humanists believe in humanity as the master of its own destiny and source of its own moral law. This view we call "overhumanization." It gives up any sense of genuine transcendence in human consciousness other than intrahuman transcendence. It makes human flourishing an end to which all other actions, relations, and forms of life are possible means. Overhumanization thereby contradicts the good of spiritual integrity, or so we contend. Secular humanists endorse a cosmopolitan outlook with genuine passion and commitment and yet they delimit the range of experience in ways that stunt the integrity of human life. The world becomes flat and the future of life is thereby threatened. In order to elaborate this point, we consider the recent literature of new atheism as an extreme version of secular humanism.

157

Recently, books by Richard Dawkins, Daniel Dennett, and Sam Harris, among others, have become bestsellers and have engendered a debate about the relative merits of religion and atheism. The "new atheism" presented by these authors is in many ways the humanistic counterpart to fundamentalism. The new atheism, like fundamentalism, is militant to the extreme. New atheists fight back against hypertheism.

Lamenting the resurgence in religion and the new holy wars that threaten human existence, Sam Harris declares that "religion is as much a living spring of violence today as it was at any time in the past."[20] Harris insists that human slaughter is principally about religion, which is understandable because "intolerance is intrinsic to every creed" and religious belief leads directly to action.[21] If you believe that certain texts are written by God without error, and if these texts include the duty of leading holy war against infidels or heretics, you will act accordingly. The new atheists define religion as an extreme and crude version of theism. According to Dennett, religions are "social systems whose participants avow belief in a supernatural agent or agents whose approval is to be sought."[22] Unless you can talk directly to your god, and unless you belong to a dedicated community, you are not in a religion. Harris adds that "every religion preaches the truth of propositions for which no evidence is even conceivable."[23] Just as fundamentalists do not believe that moderate Christians are truly Christian, new atheists consider religious moderates to be anathema. "Religious moderates are, in large part, responsible for the religious conflict in our world, because their beliefs provide the context in which scriptural literalism and religious violence can never adequately be opposed."[24] Against the religions of the world, the new atheists have declared war. They fight for a world without the irrationality of religious beliefs and commitments. There is a dread of an impending apocalypse induced by religion in the new atheism. Their greatest fear is that religious fanatics might obtain nuclear weapons. A world without religion, they assert, might have a chance of surviving. A proper cosmopolitan outlook is thereby bound to ideas that stunt the scope of human transcendence and so flatten the world.

Consider the new atheism in terms of the characteristics of historical religion. The new atheists each have a functional equivalent to a foundational myth: namely, a grand narrative of biological evolution in which they present a naturalistic theory of religion. In the beginning is the Big Bang and the creation of stars, followed by the formation of planet earth and the emergence of living creatures, and the evolution of human beings with their advanced neural, reflex, perceptual, learning/memory, emotional, cognitive, and symbolic (cultural) systems.[25] The individualizing force of culture works in tandem with the universal structures of human nature to produce the manifold of human societies. In Loyal Rue's account, religions arose within each culture in the course of biological evolution. The roots of religion are the general need to maximize reproductive fitness through the strategy of achieving personal wholeness and social coherence by means of educating the emotions and unifying the worldview.[26] Religious traditions thereby exert a decisive influence on human behavior by engaging and organizing human neural systems for the sake of human survival. The problem with the religions today is that they no longer produce adaptive benefits. Religions sow the seeds of discord and violence. They have become an obstacle to human survival.

The new atheism has its own intellectual tradition of those thinkers who have reflected on the natural history of religion, including Kant, Feuerbach, Strauss, Nietzsche, and Freud, all of whom we explored before. The new atheists tend to be ignorant of this tradition of critique. They write as if they were the first generation to engage in the frontal assault on religious belief and practice. Their lack of communal rituals is what most separates the new atheists from traditional religious communities. At best we can say their rituals are reading, writing, and discussing. Enlightenment is the experience at which their practice aims: freedom from religious superstition and the courage to assume responsibility for their own lives. The chief artistic form is rhetorical. The new atheists aim to persuade. They seem intent on building up institutional structures to compete with those of the religions. Dawkins includes "a partial list of friendly addresses, for individuals needing support in escaping from religion" as an appendix to *The God Delusion*.[27] It includes contact information for 19 groups, such as the American Humanist Association, the American Atheists, and the like. These groups are the functional equivalent of churches for new atheism.

True Religion

We have examined extreme forms of religion within the situation of exploding pluralism in the USA. It is hardly surprising that in this situation of the scathing criticism of religion by secular humanists colliding with the religion of true believers many people are open but simply uncommitted. Apathy and exhaustion now seep through the culture and into the souls of people. Theological humanism must fashion a response to this complex situation. Taking exclusionist Christianity as a form of hypertheism, and secular humanism as a type of overhumanization, we can ask two questions. What is

159

true religion? How can we produce a third way of thinking about religion that respects and enhances the integrity of life and thus the human future? In response to the first question, a glance back in time might help.

What is true religion? Any and every religion (including functional equivalents to religion) is true religion, when it both *preserves* its own unique, particular, historical traditions and *opens* them up through critical interpretation, directing them toward the true ultimacy expressed in the words "the integrity of life," an ultimacy which some religions construe as God. To understand this point, recall for a moment Jean-Jacques Rousseau's novel *Émile* (1762), and its famous chapter "The Creed of the Savoyard Priest."[28] Rousseau provides a *speculative* version of religious humanism, as we called it before. What can we learn from him?

Émile, a young man who had fallen into cynicism concerning his religion, seeks out a priest from Savoy to receive guidance about religion. The priest responds by telling his story about how he broke his vow of celibacy. In being honest about his transgression, rather than covering it up, he was disgraced and condemned. He fell into melancholy and from there into radical doubt about his faith. Needing some resolution to his despair, and unable to find it in church doctrine any longer, he turned to the philosophers, but found them too proud and haughty. The priest resolved instead to think for himself by following the "inner light" of his own experience and conscience. This method led him to develop a "natural religion" by deducing the self-evident truths of the being of God and the existence of the self as finite freedom. From these truths, he derived a series of theoretical and practical principles applicable to human beings. Proper worship of God is through wisdom and love; and the highest good for humans is the worthiness to be happy. But is this natural religion true religion? Not according to the priest. In the abstract universality of its message, natural religion lacks concrete and particular symbols, myths, rituals, and community as the medium of its expression.

So what about "revealed religion," such as Catholicism?[29] The priest says that revealed religion possesses an abundance of concrete and particular symbols and rituals. This particularity is precisely its problem. Revealed religion is based on particular revelations of God that are entrusted only to particular people, and that are handed down through narratives, rites, dogmas, and institutions. Revealed religion, for the priest, cannot be true religion; revealed religion is intolerant and exclusive. All revealed religions claim to be the one true religion, such that those who believe in a special revelation will be saved and those who do not believe will be damned. Revealed religions tend to make themselves ultimate goods. Many religions make this absolute claim, and it is humanly impossible to adjudicate among them and to discover which of them is really true. The problem is the confusion of the particular medium of God's revelation with the universality of its message. It contradicts the nature of God, who is One for all, the Truth open to all. So what is true religion?

True religion, according to Rousseau, is neither natural religion on its own nor revealed religion on its own. Revealed religion without natural religion is blind; natural religion without revealed religion is empty. Each needs the other. Every person, like Émile, grows up in a culture, with a set of sacred stories, images, symbols, rituals, and a community, that is natural to us. To each of us, the priest advises that we return to our own sacred tradition (or find out what it is), and discover true religion within it in a non-exclusive and tolerant way that is open to the same truth that appears in other, different revealed traditions.

Taking a cue from history, theological humanism thinks something like Rousseau, but with a *crucial difference*. True religion is *any* religion, whatever it may be, when its concrete, historical symbols, rituals, and meanings are opened up and interpreted in light of the integrity of life and the responsible conscience. Many religions have this idea. The Buddhists have a nice term for the relatedness of things: dependent origination. We awaken to the true nature of things in its ultimacy and to genuine compassion for others when we understand the co-dependence of all things, including the co-dependence of religions. Christianity, to use another example, found the ultimate relatedness of things in the very being of God, since God is a living Trinity. The love of God extends to the love of others, including the enemy. The insight is that a "religion" is true when it is a means to a more ultimate end, namely, the inner-truth of life itself, otherwise it is an idol. From this perspective, religions are true religions when they refer their own particular meanings to the ultimate meaning of mutual interrelatedness, the deep structure of just order. The spiritual struggle of life is thereby to inhabit one's religious identity for a good that exceeds that identity, namely, the integrity of life.

Yet just on this point theological humanism is markedly different than Rousseau's form of religious humanism. Particular religions are not merely the historic expressions of a universal natural religion, as he seems to suggest. We cannot peer through the religions in their wild diversity and expect to find the same "natural religion" at their core. The actual religions are profoundly diverse as well as different ways of seeing and interpreting reality and the point and purpose of human existence. Theological humanism does not and cannot deny those profound differences. What it seeks, rather, is a shared way of inhabiting or living through radically different ways of being religious and being human.

How can we produce this third-way thinking? By measuring and reforming the actual religions according to the idea and norm of the integrity of life. Just as the integrity of life transcends mere life, so does true holiness transcend any particular expression or revelation. This does not mean that a vague spirituality or synchronism is possible. The holiness that Christians experience does indeed appear on or with the person of Jesus Christ. The fact of this one appearance, however, does not place a limit on other possible appearances of the holy, which other religions can experience in other places. The holy is not understandable outside actual religions. Christians – and all other religious people – should contemplate the transcendent being of God, revealed in the integrity of life. They should glorify God by rejecting an idolatry of their own symbols, that is, a reduction of God's being to the medium in which they receive it. Christians also should measure themselves by an experience which tends to be lacking in Christian exclusionism. This requires the independent capacity to consider the nature of spiritual experience as one basis for solidarity, but not unity, with other religions. The same is true of any other historical religion. In this way a cosmopolitan commitment is actually lived.

Similarly, secular humanism in general, and new atheism in particular, should measure themselves by the integrity of life. Secular humanists rightly point to the limits of scientific reason in knowing the world, and they pledge not to violate them. However, life is not exhausted by the natural, material objects of scientific inquiry, as scientism holds. As one example, self-consciousness is not and in principle cannot be an object of scientific inquiry, as we saw in the previous chapter. The very core of human identity and thinking is an irrefutable reality that systematically eludes materialist explanation. So, too, does the *whole* of being transcend scientific investigation. Yet, without an understanding of being as such, we could not imagine ourselves as inhabiting a *uni*-verse. By respecting the human capacity to understand what it cannot know, namely, the awareness in human consciousness of an ultimate horizon of meaning and reality, secular humanism can legitimately develop its own powers of spiritual life.[30] Secular humanism contradicts itself when it claims, on one hand, that human reason emerges from a blind process of natural selection in biological evolution, and, on the other hand, that human confidence is rightly placed in reason alone. As Leon Wieseltier wrote, "The power of reason is owed to the independence of reason, and to nothing else ... Evolutionary biology cannot invoke the power of reason even as it destroys it."[31] Secular humanism should also understand that its attack on religion is only an attack on a crude form of supernaturalistic theism. In that way the full scope of human transcendence is grasped.

162

The extreme tendencies of hypertheism and overhumanization share not only militancy but also certainty in their propositional beliefs. They both seek and find hard-and-fast answers to life's most profound questions. Theological humanism, by contrast, changes the terms of the debate. It offers a stance and orientation of passionate and open questioning toward the integrity of life. The mystery of life's integrity eludes complete human grasp. Humility must replace certainty in the religions. True religion is the willingness to live in the open, in freedom, guided by one's own religious symbols and rites, without the need to reduce ambiguity to certainty.

By calling on the religions, including the secular opponents of religion, to measure themselves by the idea of the integrity of life, we are calling for a revolution in thinking. We advocate freedom *within* religion. The revolution is long overdue.

A Revolution in Thought

As we know, for centuries, theologians have worked out concepts for thinking about human experiences of the divine. It is time for the religions to catch up with theology. Theological humanism poses the integrity of life as the source of a sense of ultimacy that is both theological and humanistic. The integrity of life is definable by specifying its basic structure within dynamically related wholes. Obviously, people will disagree and have disputes not only about the content of this ideal, but also about how to apply it to real situations. We need this debate, and we need participation from all sides, both theological and humanistic. This debate will have scientific, political, aesthetic, economic, educational, and religious components to it, as people reflect on what the integrity of life means in any particular real situation. In fact, we have been engaged in this many-sided debate throughout part two of this book.

Our view of religion and the human future does not draw its warrants for humanistic claims exclusively from specific religious resources. That would be religious humanism, as we called it before. Religion is also not just a natural phenomenon explainable by theories of evolutionary biology. Those positions, we have seen above, often value religion in promoting social coherence and personal wholeness, but judge theistic modes of religious thinking false, scientifically speaking. These positions are forms of religious naturalism and continue in current terms the enterprise of natural theology or, as we called it, "speculative" religious humanism. Theological humanism, to repeat, is not a version of religious humanism in these customary forms, traditional or speculative or, for that matter, spiritual form.

Human beings possess capacities to sense, understand, and respond to events of transcendence manifest in everyday existence and that a transcendent reality exceeds intrahuman and infrahuman relations. This is one way in which theological humanism differs from the forms of neohumanism we have also explored throughout this book. The "divine" is not merely a trace "between" human beings. The sense of the transcendent, or an instinct for the divine, responds to real disclosures within the natural, historical, and linguistic orders of reality. "God" names what is actually present in the power, depth, scope, intensity, and claim of the integrity of life when it is sensed as unsurpassably important and real.

These disclosures of divinity within the natural world and the historical realities of peoples need to be read, interpreted, like one reads a text. They have a semantic autonomy which enables them to address humans as a countervailing subject and agent manifest in and through a text. Humans can gain real intimations of the divine via signs of sacredness in the world around them and the timeliness of existence, insofar as the transcendent reality shows itself through matter, time, and language. A theological humanist freely decides to sense, attend to, and reflect on those intimations of divine presence. No supernatural deity or divine action is posited, however. Naturally, critical thinking – moral and scientific reflection – remains a necessary and desirable moment of the interpretation of divine disclosures. But "God" is also more than a regulative ideal, as Rousseau and Kant claimed. "God" is also not a supernatural agent whose actions determine all reality. For theological humanism, "God" names the presence of the transcendent reach of the integrity of life manifest in various dimensions of existence which claims human beings and empowers them to respect and enhance life's integrity.

Theological humanists embrace a commitment to a cosmopolitan conscience both in their self-assessments and in their interpretations of the integrity of life. One affirms that "there is within our souls an innate principle of justice and virtue by which, in spite of our maxims, we judge our acts and those of others as good or bad, and it is this principle that [is] conscience."[32] We should cultivate a conscience that is self-critical by developing our powers of thought in all areas. To become people of conscience, we adopt spiritual and religious practices that actualize capacities to be open to the integrity of life in fundamental moods and feelings.

This truly is a spiritual struggle. The benefits of religious exclusivism and secular humanism we have noted continue to beckon heart and mind even as weariness with the conflict about religion in pluralistic societies fosters apathy and lack of commitment. There are resources for this struggle. Theological humanism drawn from various sources aims at inculcating a vigilant faith, a resolute hope, and an abundant love, as modes of openness to the integrity of life. Similarly, it fosters the feelings of heartfelt gratitude, steadfast humility, and demanding compassion. These deep moods and feelings disclose shared humanity and bring the transcendent divine into awareness and experience. On the basis of a well-formed conscience, grounded in religious moods and feelings, theological humanism calls for a willingness to act for the common good expressed in the integrity of life. Such a path will help to ensure a human future. It is a life of spiritual integrity.

Conclusion

This chapter has sought to engage the debate about religion in current pluralistic and moderns societies like the United States. We have shown how theological humanism responds to the conflict between secular humanists and true believers. But the chapter ends on an inconclusive note. When all is said and done, can we give reasons that might inspire and move people – even the uncommitted – to adopt this outlook on religion and the human future? That question sets the task for the final chapter of our essay.

10

Living Theological Humanism

Recollection

Some of the most ancient and yet always pressing questions in human existence are how we ought to live as individuals and communities, and, further, what ways of life are really worthy of a human being. Those were the questions raised throughout this book. Our essay has charted the global debate about these questions and also various proposals for how to answer them. We have presented theological humanism as a fundamental stance and orientation in life dedicated to the integrity of life. Most of the book has been spent making sense of how this stance and orientation enable people to inhabit their religious convictions freely and humanely. We have done so by engaging a welter of images important to the theological and humanistic imagination, but also by isolating and refining a specific "logic" that is meant to hold together the bundle of ideas that characterize theological humanism. This strategy has allowed us to draw from the rich conceptual and symbolic resources of traditions, but also to revise them in light of the current situation and trends in neohumanism.

We have also argued that theological humanism resists powerful cultural tendencies on the extremes of human possibilities. Overhumanization is the result of radical self-assertion as the hallmark of the modern age, religious and non-religious. It appears in many forms, including the secular humanist agenda with its quasi-religious faith in unconstrained human freedom or post-theistic religious forms. The problem of overhumanization is forgetting an ineluctable truth: human beings are interrelated with each other and with all living beings in their struggle to integrate their lives. In overhumaniza-tion, we find the hubris of enfolding life forms into the rapacious greed of an instrumental thinking for which nothing has intrinsic worth. Over-humanization has brought our planet to the brink of catastrophe. Global climate change, for example, is now generally recognized as caused by unrestrained use of fossil fuels for escalating energy demands. Human expansion drives into extinction more and more animal species and endangers all life on earth.

Hypertheism has engendered virulent religious conflicts around the globe. With the advent and availability of weapons of mass destruction, religious extremism tied to political ambitions threatens the very well-being of humanity. More and more people seem to be ready and willing to die for some religious cause, even ones that mistakenly think they are not religious. Hypertheism is the product of abdicating human freedom in face of a perceived divine will, the word of God in some particular religious form. It dominates the religious agenda today by identifying a religious community with divine authority, forgetting human interpretation. The problem of hypertheism is its self-righteous idolatry in thinking that its own particular image or idea of God is identical to divine reality itself and that its particular community of believers constitutes the one true religion. In hypertheism, in religious or secular form, we see competitive tribalism, with each religion embracing exclusionism in hostility to the others.

Current thought about religion and the human future is too readily straddled between these outlooks that pit religionists against secular humanists. Theological humanism envisions the possibility for a flourishing future for humanity in its interconnectedness with all other life forms.

Exploring the metaphors and images of the theological and humanistic imagination, we have isolated resources for responding to our troubled times. From the humanistic traditions, both classical and modern, theological humanism summons the love of freedom, human equality, the cultivation of community and character, and also learning, languages, history, and letters at all levels of study. These values are embedded in the humanistic images of the theatre, garden and school which we have used to unfold the meaning of theological humanism. The humanistic traditions have been specifically concerned with cultivating the abilities both to produce and to understand meanings in language, along with the reflective art of thinking systematically within dynamic historical contexts of culture. In order for humanity to have a future, the love of liberal learning must once again flourish.

Humanistic education promotes thinking about noble and worthy ends and purposes for human pursuits, and not merely the means for achieving unreflected ends. With advances in technology and expansions in global economy, patterns of thought and evaluation increasingly become calculative

167

or instrumental, which perfects ever more efficient and profitable means to achieve the bottom-line goals of corporations or nations. Humanistic learning, as theorists ranging from Said to Sen and Todorov note, is desperately needed to counteract the predominance of technical and economic pursuits in thinking. Humanistic criticism aims at liberation from the spell and power of words and slogans. Learning foreign languages, studying history, and reflecting on the nature of human understanding free one from the bondage that comes from too closely identifying well-known signs or names within one's native language with the meanings they signify. And from the traditions of critique, theological humanism draws on the emphasis on intellectual rigor, open and unrestricted inquiry, and a willingness to challenge and criticize authority for the sake of the truth, wherever it leads. From within the legacy of Western humanism, theological humanism is a kind of counter-memory, to borrow Said's term. It witnesses to the transcendent reach of the human spirit to counter the forces of overhumanization. But it also opens human existence to a depth and reach denied by too many contemporary neohumanists and their limitation of transcendence to intrahuman, lateral relations.

Drawn from Christian sources, theological humanism as we have presented it calls on the history of ideas and images of God as "that than which none greater can be conceived." The idea of God thereby designates the reach of human transcendence to include but exceed later transcendence. The idea is about a transcendence that cannot successfully be reified into the idea of a supreme being. The idea of God surpasses expressions (signs) of God, which attempt to convey it. That self-surpassing element in the idea of God opens the mind to what is truly mysterious in the integrity of life. Idolatry is precisely the identification of the transcendent God with the signs or symbols adopted in history to signify the divine life. By the same token, the human spirit reaches beyond the confines of communities and traditions into a freedom of genuine spiritual transcendence.

The idea of God is crucial to the integrity of humanity, because human being and thinking are intrinsically open to transcendent otherness and a force of mystery. The importance of theology to humanism is thereby clear: although we begin from the human in its ambiguity, human being is not self-sufficient and not self-grounding. The human quest for integrity is always also a quest for what lies beyond human power and striving. Human being, as a being "between" the complexity of goods that saturate modes of life, and human thinking, as a mediating between perceiving, conceiving, and interpreting, are rooted on the earth within an open horizon of transcendence.

Theology is the language that testifies to the approach of this transcendence and its conferring the grace of ultimate meaningfulness onto human understanding. Only with a schooled sense of the openness of human being to the integrity of life can humans resist the temptation to elevate and exalt their own freedom into an ultimate position, which it does not deserve and which it cannot sustain.[1] From the closely related religious traditions, theological humanism draws on the crucial notions of religious experience and religious communities. Our ideas of transcendence and of human worth arise and are sustained within the myriad particular religious communities and so various and even conflicting ways of naming the divine.

Religion plays a crucial role for theological humanism in securing a genuine human future, but it must be a religion tempered by the convergence of both humanistic and theological sensibilities just outlined. Theological humanism affirms the interconnectedness of theology and humanism, and it expresses that in the ultimate affirmation that all our thoughts about God and all human aspirations must cohere with a due respect and enhancement of the integrity of life. Such is the conceptual framework of theological humanism.

How then to *live* theological humanism?

A Way of Living

A theological humanist lives *through* the religions rather than apart from them. One undertakes the discipline of living freely *within* a particular religion. The human future needs the contribution of the religions, but it needs only self-reforming religions that are dedicated to the integrity of life as the manifestation of divine life and the human good. Religious people should undertake the free and serious work of reform that will enable them to live more fully, completely, and responsibly. Why, given all of the problems that currently afflict the religions and which so often set them against each other in spiteful antagonism, do we propose to work through and not against or apart from the religions?

Theological humanism is not a specific philosophy or a new kind of religion, although it implies philosophical commitments and religious sensibilities. As mortal and time-bound creatures, human beings live, think, love, worship, and die in specific communities. Accordingly, to be a theological humanist cannot mean that somehow one must stop being a Christian, a Muslim, a Buddhist, a South African, an American, a German, or some combination. At issue is how one inhabits, lives through, the many identities that

169

shape any person's or community's actual life. This is the work of freedom and responsibility under the dictates of the cosmopolitan conscience, as argued in chapter 7. As a theological humanist, one freely decides to inhabit openly and critically the social and religious forces that have shaped one's life for the sake of respecting and enhancing the integrity of life. One cultivates the goods of life in oneself and in others, works to educate conscience, and also undertakes reflection on how meaningfully to orient existence, personal and social. A theological humanist undertakes that way of life within an abiding commitment to the imperative of responsibility with its complexity and in dedication to life with and for others.

It would take another treatise to enumerate the specific practices and disciplines involved in a theological humanistic way of life and the spiritual struggle it requires. What is more, these practices and disciplines would change depending on the religious tradition one inhabits. For example, a Roman Catholic theological humanism might find in the practice of the Eucharist a pattern for cultivating a principled love for the human garden rooted in Christ's actions of feeding and healing that in the power of the Spirit has become the very life of the Church. A Protestant might look to the Eucharist, but also to the study of scripture and the proclamation of the Word as the school of Christ in which conscience is formed and reflection developed in order to see all existence as the theatre of God's glory in the integrity of life. A Buddhist or a Muslim or a Hindu theological humanist would undertake different practices and disciplines as part of their way of inhabiting freely a religious outlook. Some would not want to use the word "God." It is not the task of this essay to explore these disciplines, especially those that arise within religious traditions we do not actually inhabit. We hope that others will do that work as well.

More important for the conclusion of this book are the *reasons* for adopting theological humanism as an outlook and stance within religious life. Providing those reasons transforms our essay into a manifesto. What are the reasons?

One basic reason to adopt theological humanism is a matter of sensibility which we have tried to communicate throughout this book. It is captured most generally in the idea that human beings are "things in between." But human beings are not simply a composite of animal and angel. The complexity of existence is greater, deeper. We have isolated at several levels the sensibility consistent with the idea. From the perspective of theological humanism drawn from Christian and Western sources, human beings exist in between basic feelings or senses that arise within and through the levels of goods that permeate life (pleasure, pain, and sympathy; recognition, shame, and benevolence; innocence, guilt, and justice; participation, alienation, and empathy). Our lives transpire in this field of feelings and passions that motivate action and also the profound desire for the integration of life. Freedom is the ability to inhabit that field with responsibility for its integrity.

Disciplined attention to this "field," this affective location of human existence, discloses that in spite of sorrow, pain, and agony, human life is nevertheless saturated with worth and is driven, moved, to draw together that goodness into a complete life with others and for oneself. At the root of theological humanism is therefore a deep sensibility of affirmation for life, a yes to existence, despite its loss and terror. It has been said by Socrates and many others that philosophy is learning to die. Theological humanism is learning to live in freedom. If this "yes" to life wells up through the complexity of one's existence, if one has – to put it differently – a sense for the integrity of life construed as the being of God, then theological humanism articulates that which one already knows and already loves and desires. There is a human capacity for a relation to the divine. Theological humanism thereby aims to provide a way to inhabit experiences of transcendence. One views existence from within the light of the world, not the abyss of death. One hears the call to respect and enhance the integrity of life as the freedom to endorse existence in one's own life and community and others as well.

The sensibility of a "yes" to life within the various tensions found in human beings as "things in between" is not the only reason for being a theological humanist. A theological humanist is also someone who has heard the call of conscience as the claim of the integrity of life on personal actions and social relations. The "yes" to life that characterizes the sensibilities of a theological humanism is rooted in a primary claim and permission and mandate for life. The cultivated conscience is the sense that one is claimed at the core of one's being to labor for the integrity of life and that, paradoxically enough, this claim is also freedom, a permission to live, and it entails a mandate for life, a mandate formulated in the imperative of responsibility. The dictate of conscience – its claim, permission, mandate – can be heard through the voice of another human being, in the realm of art, through the beauty or terror of natural events, in religious practice. We have charted the appearance of that dictate in part two of the book.

The dictate of conscience is not limited to other people, a work of art, a religious rite, or the beauty and sublimity of nature. Here too human beings are "things in between," for a theological humanist. We exist between those realities that bespeak the dictate of conscience within the depths of our lives and the awareness that this claim, permission, and mandate to respect and enhance the integrity of life transcends its messengers and means. It is as if a heavenly deity speaks a word of command and freedom. To violate conscience, to pit oneself against the integrity of life, is thereby to fall as a human being; to respond to the dictate of conscience is to rise to the height of human existence. Between the falling and the rising is the space and task of human existence, beings made good but changeable. Anyone who has been grasped by this experience thereby has reason to adopt theological humanism as a way to understand and orient life.

There is one more reason to note for being a theological humanist. If anything characterizes the present situation it is a terrible loss in our spiritual lexicon, that is, the symbols, stories, metaphors, practices, and images needed to make sense of and orient human life meaningfully and richly. One of the evils of overhumanization is the wholesale rejection of religious resources to make sense of life and thereby a kind of flattening of human existence. One of the evils of hypertheism is to reduce the symbolic treasures of a religious tradition to wooden dogmas and so nothing more than tests for obedience. On all sides, people are increasingly trying to live with impoverished symbolic and imaginary forms. Little wonder that there is so much despair and emptiness at the very moment when the global media system endlessly generates ever new pictures and images of our endangered age. Many are open but uncommitted to any orienting ideals and values. Some thinkers see the global era as "flat."[2] Theological humanism thinks otherwise. The world of global dynamics might indeed be flat, but human existence transpires within a sense of the complexity of goods that permeate life and also the dictate of conscience. How then to speak about the depth and scope of being human? What words ought we to use?

In our essay we have tried to answer those questions by excavating and using some of the images, metaphors, forms of thought and expressions developed within the long, long legacies of Western humanism and also the Christian tradition. As "third men," as believing Gentiles (to recall Paul Ricoeur's term), we have unabashedly sought critically to reclaim resources of the imagination in order to articulate the depth of conscience and the scope of human transcendence. This is why a theological humanist lives through a religious tradition. Religious communities enable people to cultivate their sensibilities for the divine or ultimate reality and other forms of life through participation in foundational myths, intellectual traditions, rituals, particular experiences, artistic forms and styles, and institutional structures.

They provide resources for the imagination which can combat the flattening of the world. True, human beings are in the presence of "God" at all moments and in all places. In principle one has access to transcendence in the integrity of life in (say) sport, or conversing in intimacy with one's spouse, or in listening to symphonies. None of these or other activities, however, *intend* to bring their participants into communion with the divine or the power of life in the same way that religious activities do and religious resources allow. The religions make contact with the divine and new life their central intention.

What is more, religious communities should be and are often communities of activism on behalf of important social causes. Frequently, the churches or other religious institutions are defenders of the poor or vulnerable; religious voices are often critics of unrestrained free-market capitalism and political tyranny. Religious communities oftentimes embody a passion for justice that has no other social outlet. They provide a setting where ethical discourse and education can flourish. In this regard, religious communities offer a bulwark against the proliferation of technical and purely rhetorical uses of language. They provide the means to articulate and orient the claims of conscience.

Religious communities frequently function as reflective spaces in which the meanings embedded in myth, ritual, and symbol are applied to the challenges and struggles to be human in the current moment. In this way, religious communities become interpretive workshops for the revitalizing of ancient traditions. They combat the despair and emptiness that comes with trying to live as a human being in a flat world. Carrying the past creatively into the future, religious interpretation practiced wisely and critically makes history a living reality, a past that is not past but that continues to open new possibilities for understanding what it means to be human. However, that is the case only if those resources are engaged critically with the freedom that is part of theological humanism and similar outlooks.

The reasons for being a theological humanist are then part and parcel of how we have tried to essay human and religious life in this book. They arise from within the goods of life, spring from the dictate of conscience that bespeaks the integrity of life, and are found in the religious resources within which a theological humanist freely and thankfully lives. Of course, these reasons do not somehow "prove" theological humanism or provide some kind of logical necessity to adopt this outlook and stance in life. They are, more simply, indications of the plausibility and truth of living as a theological humanist within particular traditions, religions, and cultures. And that means, we can now say, that one is always living between the extremes of doubt and certainty, always charged to essay, to put on trial, one's outlook and stance in life thereby better to respond to the human calling of responsible life.

Manifesto

Theological humanism means developing fundamental moods and attitudes that can ground habits of thinking and acting. Fundamental moods are ways of being open to truth, beauty, and goodness in the world, wherever they may appear. Moods of joy, dread, and courage; faith, hope, and love; awe, gratitude, and humility; compassion, generosity, and good will – these moods inform the heart of theological humanism. Fundamental moods are more than ways of being open to sources of meaning and worth; they are ways of actively seeking out the goodness in this world. To live as a theological humanist one vigilantly seeks the life of integrity in oneself and in others. A life so dedicated will become different through its call and commitment to see the truth of things and to serve goodness.

To inhabit a tradition self-critically means to apply the norm of the integrity of life to every aspect of the community's beliefs and practices. Theological humanists who are Christian (or Muslim or Jewish or Buddhist or ...) and wish to remain within their religion have a mandate to judge how that religious outlook is lived and expressed. It is to live religiously in a free and responsible way. It becomes incumbent upon religious people to work for the change they desire within their chosen communities. Appreciate whatever brings the integrity of life; criticize whatever demeans and destroys it. And in all things, seek a humane future for life in its many forms as the dedication in one's religious life.

We began this essay by noting conflicts among different attitudes towards the resources of Western culture and the religions: humanistic, religious, and open but skeptical attitudes. We took that as a signal about deep flaws in cultural and religious resources and the range of possible responses to those flaws. We have tried to articulate, analyze, and respond to those flaws that arise within the legacy of this civilization. Yet we have also provided a portrait, a sketch, of a way to inhabit religious and cultural resources that seeks to meet the future responsibly and hopefully.

This essay has sought, in other words, to meet an *interpretive and practical challenge* of our age in a way that thwarts the celebration of power that can and does lead to the clash among peoples and also the wanton destruction

174

of other forms of life. In this respect, an essay is a practical wager and not a proof. It is not a proof, because life is in the living and not in arguments. The wager is that by living theological humanism within religious traditions, it is possible to respect and enhance the integral relations of forms of life, natural, human, and divine. That is the challenge and possibility of religion and the human future.

Notes

Introduction

1 "The Power of Faith: How Religion Impacts Our World," in *Spiegel, Special International Edition* 9(2006): 8.
2 See Charles Taylor, *A Secular Age* (Cambridge, MA: Belknap, 2007).
3 See Samuel P. Huntington, *The Clash of Civilizations and the Remaking of World Order* (New York: Simon & Schuster, 1998). For different approaches, see William Schweiker, *Theological Ethics and Global Dynamics: In the Time of Many Worlds* (Oxford: Blackwell, 2004); Martin E. Marty, *When Faiths Collide* (Oxford: Blackwell, 2005); and Max L. Stackhouse et al. (eds.), *God and Globalization*, 4 vols. (Harrisburg, PA: Trinity Press International, 2000–6).
4 Gabriel Marcel, *Man Against Mass Society* (South Bend, IN: Gateway, 1962).

Chapter 1   Ideas and Challenges

1 See John Hick, *An Interpretation of Religion: Human Responses to the Transcendent* (New Haven, CT: Yale University Press, 1989).
2 On this shift see Louis Dupré, *Passage to Modernity: An Essay in the Hermeneutics of Nature and Culture* (New Haven, CT: Yale University Press, 1993).
3 See Margaret Mann Phillips, *Erasmus and the Northern Renaissance* (New York: Macmillan, 1950).
4 Tzvetan Todorov, *Imperfect Garden: The Legacy of Humanism*, trans. Carol Cosman (Princeton, NJ: Princeton University Press, 2002), p. 6.
5 Ibid., p. 30.
6 See Timothy G. McCarthy, *Christianity and Humanism* (Chicago: Loyola Press, 1996); Salvatore Puledaa, *On Being Human: Interpretation of Humanism from the*

Renaissance to the Present, trans. A. Hurley (San Diego, CA: Latitude Press, 1997); and Corliss Lamont, *The Philosophy of Humanism*, 5th edn. (New York: Frederick Ungar, 1967).

7 Tony Davies, *Humanism* (London: Routledge, 1996), p. 31. Emphasis ours.

8 Régis Debray, *Transmitting Culture*, trans. Eric Rauth (New York: Columbia University Press, 2000), p. 63.

9 Mircea Eliade, *The Quest: History and Meaning in Religion* (Chicago: University of Chicago Press, 1969), pp. 8–9.

10 Daily we read articles and see books on the upsurge of religion. For a popular example, see Andrew Higgins, "In Europe, God is (Not) Dead" in *The Wall Street Journal* CCI, no. 11, A1, A8.

11 Jonathan Sacks, *The Dignity of Difference: How to Avoid the Clash of Civilizations* (London: Continuum, 2003), p. 55.

12 Davies, *Humanism*, p. 125.

13 Paul Ricoeur, "What Does Humanism Mean?" in *Political and Social Essays*, ed. David Stewart and Joseph Bien (Athens, OH: Ohio University Press, 1975), pp. 86–7.

14 Laszlo Versényi, *Socratic Humanism* (New Haven, CT: Yale University Press, 1963), p. 131.

15 See Hannah Arendt, *The Human Condition* (Chicago: University of Chicago Press, 1998). For a theological rejoinder, see Reinhold Niebuhr, *The Nature and Destiny of Man* (Louisville, KY: Westminster John Knox Press, 1996).

16 Ernst Cassirer, *An Essay on Man* (New Haven, CT: Yale University Press, 1944), p. 68.

17 Other authors may use these terms differently, but we trust that our meanings are clear.

18 Thomas Merton, "Virginity and Humanism in the Western Fathers," in *Mystics and Zen Masters* (New York: Farrar, Straus & Giroux, 1967), p. 114. For a statement of this outlook in Protestant theology, see Karl Barth, *The Humanity of God*, trans. John Newton Thomas and Thomas Wieser (Richmond, VA: John Knox Press, 1960), and in Russian theology see Paul Valliere, *Modern Russian Theology: Bukharev, Soloviev, Bulgakov: Orthodox Theoogy in a New Key* (Grand Rapids, MI: William B. Eerdmans, 2000); and for a helpful general discussion of this point see R. William Franklin and Joseph Shaw, *The Case of Christian Humanism* (Grand Rapids, MI: William B. Eerdmans, 1991).

19 Interestingly, there are even post-theistic forms of humanism in organized religion. One thinks, for instance, of the Society for Humanistic Judaism. Sherwin Wine, its founder, formed a congregation which eliminated references to God in worship services and proclaimed "We revere the best in man." In certain Unitarian Universalist congregations there is also a denial of "God" and yet an assertion of humanism within the religion. Other examples could be cited.

20 Examples are as far-ranging as the philosophical deduction of "natural religion" by Jean-Jacques Rousseau, *Émile*, trans. Barbara Foxley (London: Everyman's Library, 1989), p. 259, and the set of universal "spiritual" qualities (especially

"concern for others' well-being" born of "love and compassion, patience, tolerance, forgiveness, contentment, a sense of responsibility, a sense of harmony") as articulated by the Dalai Lama in *Ethics for the New Millennium* (New York: Riverhead, 1999), pp. 22–3.

22   The religious phenomenology of Mircea Eliade interprets the meanings of myths and symbols to display the universal archetypes of *homo religiosus*, for whom "living as a human being is in itself a religious act ... to be – or, rather, to become – a man means to be 'religious'." Eliade, *The Quest*, preface. The point could be made by reference to any number of thinkers, such as Gerardus Van der Leeuw, Carl Jung, and others.

22   Hermann Hesse, *Die Einheit hinter den Gegensätzen* (Frankfurt am Main: Suhrkamp, 1986).

23   Kwame Anthony Appiah, *Cosmopolitanism: Ethics in a World of Strangers* (New York: W. W. Norton, 2006).

Chapter 2   The Humanist Imagination

1   See Immanuel Kant, *Fundamental Principle of the Metaphysics of Morals*, trans. Thomas K. Abbott, intro. Marvin Fox (New York: Liberal Arts Press, 1949); "The Westminster Shorter Catechism," in *The Creeds of Christendom*, ed. Philip Schaff, vol. 3 (Grand Rapids, MI: Baker Book House, 1983); Thomas Aquinas, *Summa Theologiae*, 5 vols. (Westminster: Christian Classics, 1981). Also see Emmanuel Levinas, *Entre nous* (Paris: Grasset, 1991).

2   John W. de Gruchy, *Confessions of a Christian Humanist* (Minneapolis: Fortress Press, 2006).

3   Jonathan Glover, *Humanity: A Moral History of the Twentieth Century* (New Haven, CT: Yale University Press, 2000) and Charles T. Mathewes, *Evil and the Augustinian Tradition* (Cambridge: Cambridge University Press, 2001).

4   For a brief study, see Kate Soper, *Humanism and Anti-Humanism* (La Salle, IL: Open Court, 1986).

5   See *Two Views of Man: Pope Innocent III, On Human Misery, Giannozzo Manetti, On the Dignity of Man*, trans. B. Murchland (New York: Frederick Ungar, 1966).

6   For the place of metaphor in humanism, see Ernesto Grassi, *Rhetoric as Philosophy: The Humanist Tradition* (University Park: Pennsylvania University Press, 1980).

7   Corliss Lamont, *The Philosophy of Humanism* (New York: Continuum, 1990), p. 3.

8   *Humanist Manifestos I and II* (Buffalo, NY: Prometheus Books, 1973), p. 16.

9   Lamont, *The Philosophy of Humanism*, pp. 50–1.

10   Todorov, *Imperfect Garden*, p. 5.

11   Edward W. Said, *Humanism and Democratic Criticism* (New York: Columbia University Press, 2004), p. 22.

12   Versényi, *Socratic Humanism*, p. 131.

13 Todorov, *Imperfect Garden*, p. 30.

14 See Charles Taylor, *Varieties of Religion Today: William James Revisited* (Cambridge, MA: Harvard University Press, 2002).

15 See, for instance, Epictetus, *The Handbook*, trans., N. P. White (New York: Hackett, 1983).

16 See Rebecca Goldstein, *Betraying Spinoza: The Renegade Jew Who Gave Us Modernity* (New York: Schocken, 2006), p. 246; also Benedict de Spinoza, *On the Improvement of the Understanding, The Ethics, and Correspondence*, trans. R. H. M. Elwes (New York: Dover, 1955).

17 B. A. G. Fuller and S. M. McMurrin, *A History of Philosophy*, 3rd edn., vol. 2 (New York: Holt, Rinehart & Winston, 1955), p. 353. See Arthur Schopenhauer, *The Basis of Morality*, trans. A. B. Bullock (Mineola, NY: Dover, 2005).

18 See Peter Singer, *Unsanctifying Human Life: Essays on Ethics* (Oxford: Blackwell), 2002.

19 For an example, see Leon R. Kass, *Life, Liberty and the Defense of Dignity: The Challenge for Bioethics* (New York: Encounter, 2004).

20 Those who used the theatre metaphor for the place of freedom in the world often had very different agendas and also different substantive moral and philosophical outlooks. The same is true of metaphors about the garden and the school.

21 Juan Luis Vives, "A Fable about Man," in *The Renaissance Philosophy of Man*, ed. Ernst Cassirer et al. (Chicago: Phoenix, University of Chicago Press, 1956), p. 388. One should also recall that the idea of "person" in Western thought had its origins in the theatre in terms of the masks worn by actors.

22 Giovanni Pico della Mirandola, *Oration on the Dignity of Man*, trans, A. R. Caponigri, intro. R. Kirk (Washington, DC: Regnery Publishing, 1999), p. 3.

23 Ibid., 7.

24 Ibid., xv–xvi.

25 Jean-Paul Sartre, "Existentialism is a Humanism" in *Basic Writings*, ed. Stephen Priest (New York: Routledge, 2001).

26 On this, see Heidegger's famous "Letter on Humanism" in *Basic Writings*, ed. David Farrell Krell (New York: Harper & Row, 1977), pp. 189–242.

27 See Mick Smith, *An Ethics of Place: Radical Ecology, Postmodernity, and Social Theory* (Albany: State University of New York Press, 2001).

28 Voltaire, *Candide and Other Stories*, trans. Roger Pearson (Oxford: Oxford University Press, 1990), pp. 99–100. Also see Terence J. Martin, *Living Words: Studies in Dialogues over Religion* (Atlanta: Scholars, 1998).

29 Michel de Montaigne, *The Complete Works: Essays, Travel Journal, Letters*, vol. 3, trans. Donald M. Frame (Stanford, CA: Stanford University Press, 1958), pp. 766–7.

30 Curtis W. Reese, *Humanism* (Chicago: Open Court, 1926), p. 49.

31 See Emmanuel Levinas, *Totality and Infinity: An Essay in Exteriority*, trans. Alphonso Lingus (Pittsburgh, PA: Dusquense University Press, 1969).

32 Emmanuel Levinas, *Humanism of the Other*, trans. N. Poller, intro. Richard A. Cohen (Urbana: University of Illinois Press, 2003).

33 For a helpful discussion, see Mary Midgley, *Ethical Primate: Humans, Freedom and Morality* (New York: Routledge, 1994).

34 Donna J. Haraway, *Simians, Cyborgs, and Women: The Reinvention of Nature* (New York: Routledge, 1991) and Bill McKibben, *The End of Nature* (New York: Anchor, 1990).

35 Todorov, *Imperfect Garden*, p. 137.

36 See Pierre Hadot, *Philosophy as a Way of Life: Spiritual Exercises from Socrates to Foucault*, ed. Arnold Davidson, trans. Michael Chase (Oxford: Blackwell, 1995); also Werner Jaeger, *Humanism and Theology*, The Aquinas Lecture 7 (Milwaukee: Marquette University Press, 1943).

37 Alasdair MacIntrye has been the most insistent on the idea of the school among virtue theorists. See his *Three Rival Versions of Moral Enquiry: Encyclopedia, Genealogy, Tradition* (Notre Dame: University of Notre Dame Press, 1990). For a Christian version, see Stanley Hauerwas, *A Community of Character: Toward a Constructive Christian Social Ethic* (Notre Dame: University of Notre Dame Press, 1981).

38 Florence M. Weinberg, *The Wine and the Will: Rabelais's Bacchic Christianity* (Detroit: Wayne State University Press, 1972).

39 John Dewey, *Democracy and Education* (New York: Free, 1944), p. 2.

40 Søren Kierkegaard, *Training in Christianity*, trans. Walter Lowrie (Princeton, NJ: Princeton University Press, 1944), p. 201.

41 For examples, see Michel Foucault, *Discipline and Punish: The Birth of the Clinic*, trans. Alan Sheridan (New York: Knopf, 1995); his *History of Sexuality: The Care of the Self*, vol. 3, trans. Robert Hurley (New York: Knopf, 1988); and also Richard Wolin, "Foucault the Neohumanist?" in *The Chronicle of Higher Education* 53(2006) no. 2: B12.

42 Midgley, *The Ethical Primate*, p. 168.

43 Of course, given the fallibility and folly of all things human, it is not possible to give an unquestionable "proof" for the necessity of a theological stance in ethics. All we can do is to attempt to show dialectically how this position isolates and answers a range of shared problems more adequately than other ethical outlooks.

44 See William Schweiker, *Power, Value and Conviction: Theological Ethics in the Postmodern Age* (Cleveland: Pilgrim, 1998).

45 On this see David Tracy, "Literary Theory and the Return of the Forms of Naming and Thinking God in Theology," *Journal of Religion* 74, no. 3 (1994): 302–19.

Chapter 3 Thinking of God

1 For examples of conservative religious grounds, see Stanley Hauerwas, *The Hauerwas Reader*, ed. John Berkman and Michael Cartwright (Durham:

University of North Carolina Press, 2001) and John Howard Yoder, *The Priestly Kingdom: Social Ethics as Gospel* (Notre Dame, IN: University of Notre Dame Press, 1984). For the use of postmodern theory to justify churchly theology, see John Milbank, Catherine Pickstock, and Graham Ward (eds.), *Radical Orthodoxy* (London: Routledge, 1999), and Graham Ward (ed.), *The Postmodern God: A Theological Reader* (Oxford: Blackwell, 1997).

2   Graham Ward, *True Religion* (Oxford: Blackwell, 2003), pp. 152–3.

3   John D. Caputo, *On Religion* (New York: Routledge, 2001); Thomas Carlson, *Indiscretion: Finitude and the Naming of God* (Chicago: University of Chicago Press, 1999); Mark C. Taylor, *Erring: A Postmodern A/theology* (Chicago: University of Chicago Press, 1984); Charles E. Winquist, *Epiphanies of Darkness: Deconstruction in Theology* (Philadelphia: Fortress, 1986).

4   Between churchly and post-theistic theologies is a dwindling group of liberal theologians, still trying to accommodate the claims of Christian faith with the rigors of modern thought.

5   Paul Ricoeur, *The Symbolism of Evil*, trans. Emerson Buchanan (Boston: Beacon, 1967), p. 349.

6   See David E. Klemm, *The Hermeneutical Theory of Paul Ricoeur* (Lewisburg, PA: Bucknell University Press, 1987), pp. 20, 69, 72–3, 120–1, 148, 160–1.

7   Interestingly, Max Weber thought that the difference between an immanent and transcendent deity separated the religions of India from biblical religion. Actually, one can find traces of both outlooks, and a third cluster, within Western thought, as we show. See Max Weber, *The Sociology of Religion*, trans. E. Fischoof, intro. T. Parsons (Boston: Beacon, 1963).

8   H. Denzinger (ed.), *Enchiridion Symbolorum*, 24–5 edn. (Barcelona: Herder, 1948), p. 6.

9   Paul Tillich, *The Courage to Be* (New Haven, CT: Yale University Press, 2000), p. 60.

10   Martin Luther, "The Freedom of a Christian" in *Luther: Selections from His Writings*, ed. John Dillenberger (Garden City, NY: Anchor, 1961), pp. 42–85.

11   See Heiko A. Oberman, *Luther: Man Between God and the Devil*, trans. Eileen Walliser-Schwarzbart (New Haven, CT: Yale University Press, 1989).

12   Gerhard Melanchthon, *Augsburg Confession*, trans. F. Bente and W. H. T. Dau, in *Triglot Concordia: The Symbolical Books of the Evangelical Lutheran Church* (St. Louis: Concordia, 1921), 25.11.

13   Johann S. Semler, *Abhandlung von freier Untersuchung des Canons* (1771), in *Texte zur Kirchen-und Theologiegeschichte*, Heft 5 (Gütersloh: Mohn, 1967), p. 60; Gottfried Hornig, *Anfänge der historisch-kritischen Theologie* (Göttingen: Vandenhoech und Ruprechr, 1961), pp. 65–73.

14   See Hans Frei, *The Eclipse of Biblical Narrative* (New Haven, CT: Yale University Press, 1974), pp. 61, 64, 111–12, 161–2, and 246–8.

15   Semler, *Abhandlung von freier Untersuchung des Canons*, p. 26; Hornig, *Anfänge der historisch-kritischen Theologie*, pp. 106–11.

16 Ludwig Feuerbach, *Lectures on the Essence of Religion*, trans. Ralph Manheim (New York: Harper & Row, 1967), p. 17.

17 Ibid, pp. xxxvii, 22.

18 Sigmund Freud, *The Future of an Illusion*, trans. and ed. James Strachey, intro. by Peter Gay (New York: W. W. Norton, 1989), p. 19.

19 Ibid, p. 38. See also Michael J. Buckley, SJ, *Denying and Disclosing God: The Ambiguous Progress of Modern Atheism* (New Haven, CT: Yale University Press, 2004), p. 108.

20 Hans-Georg Gadamer, "The Philosophical Foundations of the Twentieth Century," in *Philosophical Hermeneutics*, trans. and ed. David E. Linge (Berkeley: University of California Press, 1976), pp. 107–29.

21 Karl Barth, "The Word of God and the Task of Theology," in *The Word of God and the Word of Man*, trans. Douglas Horton (Gloucester, MA: Peter Smith, 1978), pp. 183–217.

22 The situation does not change with Barth's move from his dialectical theology in the 1920s into the *Church Dogmatics* by way of his 1931 study of Anselm's ontological argument. See Robert P. Scharlemann, "The No to Nothing and the Nothing to Know: Barth and Tillich and the Possibility of Theological Science," in *Inscriptions and Reflections* (Charlottesville: University Press of Virginia, 1989), pp. 109–24.

23 Plato, *The Republic*, trans. Desmond Lee (New York: Penguin Books, 1987), p. 238 (502c) and p. 243 (505e).

24 Ibid, p. 244 (506d).

25 Ibid, pp. 245–7 (507a–509c).

26 *Augustine: Earlier Writings*, ed. J. H. S. Burleigh (Philadelphia: Westminster, 1953), pp. 17–63.

27 Martin Heidegger, "The Onto-Logical Constitution of Metaphysics," in *Identity and Difference*, German and English, trans. Joan Stambaugh (New York: Harper & Row, 1969).

28 Thomas Aquinas, *Summa Theologiae*, Ia, q. 2, a. 12.

29 See David E. Klemm, "The Rhetoric of Theological Argument," in John S. Nelson, Allan Megill, and Donald N. McCloskey (eds.), *The Rhetoric of the Human Sciences: Language and Argument in Scholarship and Public Affairs* (Madison: University of Wisconsin Press, 1987), pp. 276–98.

30 *Summa Theologiae*, I, qu. 45, 7.

31 Immanuel Kant, *Critique of Pure Reason*, trans. and ed. Paul Guyer and Allen W. Wood (Cambridge: Cambridge University Press, 1998), B377, B76.

32 Ibid., A644/B672, A647/B675.

33 Ibid., A641/B669.

34 Defining God as the infinite in opposition to the finite constitutes what Hegel calls the "bad infinite." See Georg Wilhelm Friedrich Hegel, *Lectures on the Philosophy of Religion* (1827), ed. Peter C. Hodgson (Berkeley: University of

California Press, 1988), pp. 170–1. See also *Hegel's Science of Logic*, trans. A. V. Miller (Atlantic Highlands, NJ: Humanities Paperback Library, 1993), pp. 137–50 .

35 Friedrich Nietzsche, "History of European Nihilism," in *The Will to Power*, trans. Walter Kaufman (New York: Random House, 1967).

36 See Thomas J. J. Altizer, *Total Presence, The Self-Embodiment of God*, and his theological memoir *Living the Death of God* (Albany: State University of New York Press, 2006). Mark C. Taylor argues that the genuine endpoint of God's self-embodiment in the immanence of secular life and its forgetting of God is in the forgetting that we have forgotten God. For Taylor, "The death of God remains incomplete as long as theology continues." See "Betraying Altizer," in Lissa McCullough and Brian Schroeder (eds.), *Thinking Through the Death of God: A Critical Companion to Thomas J. J. Altizer* (Albany: State University of New York Press, 2004), pp. 11–28.

37 Paul Ricoeur, *The Symbolism of Evil*, p. 352.

38 See Robert P. Scharlemann, "The Being of God When God is Not Being God," *Inscriptions and Reflections* (Charlottesville: University of Virginia Press, 1989), 30–53.

39 Paul Tillich, *Systematic Theology*, vol. 1 (Chicago: University of Chicago Press, 1952), p. 174.

40 Ibid., p. 235.

41 Paul Tillich, *Dynamics of Faith* (New York: Harper & Row, 1957), p. 1.

42 The literature of these thinkers is extensive. For a brief account, see David Batstone et al. (eds.), *Liberation Theology, Postmodernity and the Americas* (New York: Taylor & Francis, 1977); and "Particularizing Theology," in David F. Ford (ed.), *The Modern Theologians* (Oxford: Blackwell, 2005), pp. 427–552.

43 The *Proslogion* is found in *The Prayers and Meditations of Saint Anselm*, trans. B. Ward (London: Penguin Books, 1973), pp. 238–67.

44 Martin Buber defined "God" as the "eternal You," the one Thou in all the many Thou's I encounter, noting that anything (e.g., a tree) can become a Thou for me. We are saying the same thing: in responding to anything, I respond to God, the ultimate subject-term.

45 On these debates, see Jean-Luc Marion, *God without Being*, trans. Thomas A. Carlson (Chicago: University of Chicago Press, 1995) and also Calvin Schrag, *God as Otherwise than Being: Towards a Semantics of the Gift* (Evanston, IL: Northwestern University Press, 2002).

46 See William Schweiker, *Responsibility and Christian Ethics* (Cambridge: Cambridge University Press, 1995).

47 On the idea of the sovereignty of good, see Iris Murdoch, *The Sovereignty of Good* (London: Routledge & Kegan Paul, 1970). Also see Maria Antonaccio, *Picturing the Human: The Moral Thought of Iris Murdoch* (Oxford: Oxford University Press, 2000).

Chapter 4   The Logic of Christian Humanism

1   Paul Ricoeur, "Faith and Culture," in *Political and Social Essays*, ed. David Stewart and Joseph Bien (Athens, OH: Ohio University Press, 1975), p. 126.

2   See John W. de Gruchy, *Confessions of a Christian Humanist* (Minneapolis: Fortress, 2006).

3   See James M. Gustafson, *Ethics from a Theocentric Perspective*, 2 Vol. (Chicago: University of Chicago Press, 1983). We address Gustafson's position later in this book and show that theological humanism, precisely as theological, does not fall to the charge of anthropocentrism.

4   Alasdair C. MacIntyre, *A Short History of Ethics: A History of Moral Philsophy from the Homeric Age to the Twentieth Century*, 2nd edn. (Notre Dame, IN: University of Notre Dame Press, 1998), p. 117.

5   John Calvin, *Institutes of the Christian* Religion, 2 vols., ed. John T. McNeill, trans. Ford Lewis Battles (Louisville, KY: Westminster John Knox Press, 1960), I, 3, 1.

6   John Wesley, "The Way to the Kingdom" in *Sermons on Several Occasions*, First Series (London: Epworth Press, 1944), p. 77.

7   See H. Richard Niebuhr, *Radical Monotheism and Western Culture* (Louisville, KY: Westminster John Knox, 1993).

8   See Martin Luther's *Lectures on Galatians* (1535) in *Luther's Works*, vols. 26–7 (St. Louis: Concordia Press, 1963).

9   See Athanasius, "On the Incarnation" in *Athanasius*, ed. Robert C. Gregg (New York: Paulist Press, 1980).

10 Paul Tillich, "Two Types of Philosophy of Religion" in *Theology of Culture*, ed. R. C. Kimball (Oxford: Oxford University Press, 1959), p. 10.

11 See David Tracy, *The Analogical Imagination: Christian Theology and the Culture of Pluralism* (New York: Crossroad, 1981).

12 For the use of Anselm's ontological argument as a theological criterion, see David E. Klemm and William Klink, "Constructing and Testing Theological Models" *Zygon: A Journal for Religion and Science*, 38, no. 3 (September, 2003): 495–528. Two very different twentieth-century thinkers, Karl Barth and Charles Hartshorne, each used this principle as well. See Karl Barth, *Anselm: Fides Quaerens Intellectum*, trans, Ian W. Robertson (Pittsburgh: Wipf & Stock, 1975) and Charles Hartshorne, *The Logic of Perfection* (LaSalle, IL: Open Court, 1962). Theological humanism represents a distinctive use of the Anselmic principle to test theological claims.

13 John Clayton, "The Otherness of Anselm" in *The Otherness of God*, ed. Orrin F. Summerell (Charlottesville: University of Virginia Press, 1998), p. 15.

14 By analyzing the concept of the highest good in terms of the mutual infusion of happiness and holiness this strand of thought not only draws on ancient themes in moral philosophy, but also anticipates modern forms of thought running from Immanuel Kant's ethics to recent discussions.

15 See William Schweiker, "And a Second is Like It: Christian Faith and the Claim of the Other" *Quarterly Review* 20, no. 3 (Fall 2000): 233–47; also Paul Mendes-Flohr, "A Postmodern Humanism from the Sources of Judaism," *Criterion* 41, no. 2 (Spring 2002): 18–23.

16 Martin Luther, "The Freedom of a Christian" in *Martin Luther: Selections From His Writings*, ed. John Dillenberger (Garden City, NY: Anchor 1961), p. 80.

17 See Margaret A. Farley, *Just Love: A Framework for Christian Sexual Ethics* (New York: Continuum, 2006); Darlene Fozard Weaver, *Self-Love and Christian Ethics* (Cambridge: Cambridge University Press, 2002).

18 See Gustavo Gutierrez, *On Job: God-Talk and the Suffering of the Innocent* (Maryknoll, NY: Orbis, 1987). Also see Susan Neiman, *Evil In Modern Thought: An Alternative History of Philosophy* (Princeton, NJ: Princeton University Press, 2002).

19 R. William Franklin and Joseph M. Shaw, *The Case for Christian Humanism* (Grand Rapids, MI: Eerdmans, 1991), p. 44.

20 Karl Barth, *The Humanity of God*, trans. J. N. Thomas and T. Wieser (Richmond, VA: John Knox Press, 196), p. 55. See also Paul Valliere, *Modern Russian Theology: Bukharev, Soloviev, Bulgakov: Orthodox Theology in a New Key* (Grand Rapids, MI: Eerdmans, 2000); Jacques Maritain, *Integral Humanism: Temporal and Spiritual Problems of a New Christendom*, trans. J. W. Evans (Notre Dame, IN: University of Notre Dame Press, 1973); Gustavo Gutierrez, *A Theology of Liberation: History, Politics, and Salvation*, trans. C. Inda and J. Eagleson (Maryknoll, NY: Orbis, 1973).

21 Augustine, *Enchiridion*, in *Nicene and Post-Nicene Fathers*, vol. 3, ed. Philip Schaff (New York: Charles Schribner's Sons, 1889), p. 245.

22 Martin Luther, "A Sermon on the Three Kinds of Good Life for the Instruction of Consciences" in *Luther's Works*, vol. 44 (Minneapolis: Fortress Press, 1966), p. 241.

Chapter 5 On the Integrity of Life

1 Martin Buber, *Good and Evil* (New York: Charles Scribner's Sons, 1953), pp. 129–30.

2 See William Schweiker, *Responsibility and Christian Ethics* (Cambridge: Cambridge University Press, 1995).

3 Augustine, *The City of God* (New York: Penguin Books, 1972), p. 860.

4 Our argument stands within a long tradition of thought that explores various sensibilities as the roots of awareness and action. These senses deliver the awareness – no matter how confused or ambiguous – of the moral texture of human reality and thus motivate behavior. As theorists of virtue have long known, our likings and dislikings, passions and appetites, motivate action and thereby must

be guided by careful reflection, what we will call the imperative of responsibility. There are even senses of moral reason, the force of conscience. It is not the purpose of this book to explore these matters in moral theory or the psychology of religion. We note our position and move on. We will engage current debates about basic goods and human capabilities, in thinkers like Martha Nussbaum, Amartya Sen and others, in Part II of this book.

5 There is of course considerable debate about which conditions might justify overriding claims to respect and enhancement as well as what would count as good reasons for doing so. Below, we note that the demand to "respect" forms of life before moving toward their enhancement is meant to place deontological constraints on sheer consequential reasons about such difficult cases.

6 Todorov, *Imperfect Garden*, p. 40.

7 For a similar argument, see Hans Jonas, *The Imperative of Responsibility: In Search for an Ethics of the Technological Age*, trans. H. Jonas and D. Herr (Chicago: University of Chicago Press, 1984).

8 See, for instance, Jeffrey Wattles, *The Golden Rule* (Oxford: Oxford University Press, 1996).

9 Emmanuel Levinas, *Totality and Infinity: An Essay on Exeriority*, trans. A. Lingis (Pittsburgh: Duquesne University Press, 1969).

10 See Hans Jonas, *Mortality and Morality: A Search for the Good After Auschwitz*, ed. L. Vogel (Evanston, IL: Northwestern University Press, 1996); Heidegger, "Letter on Humanism"; James M. Gustafson, *A Sense of the Divine: The Natural Environment from a Theocentric Perspective* (Cleveland: Pilgrim Press, 1994).

11 See Jonathan Lear, *Radical Hope: Ethics in the Face of Cultural Devastation* (Cambridge, MA: Harvard University Press, 2006).

12 On this, see Vaclav Havel, *Disturbing the Peace*, trans. P. Wilson (New York: Alfred A. Knopf, 1990).

13 Said, *Humanism and Democratic Criticism*, p. 142.

14 Our argument is that teleological concerns, the ends sought, must, in order to be moral, pass through a specific deontological test, and, conversely, those duties only make sense when ordered to proper ends. Our position, like many others, is then a mixed one.

15 We can easily imagine forms of *therapy* that would enhance life and still meet the demand of responsibility. The line between therapy and enhancement is of course difficult to draw, and would have to be decided in specific contexts.

16 Gustafson, *A Sense of the Divine*, p. 72.

17 We should note that these forms are analogous to Kant's forms of the categorical imperative (universalizability; respect for humanity; kingdom of ends) as the articulation of genuine autonomy or freedom.

18 The most extensive engagement with this challenge in Christian theology remains the work of Ernst Troeltsch. See, for example, Ernst Troeltsch, *The Absoluteness of Christianity and the History of Religions*, trans. D. Reid, intro. J. L. Adams (Richmond, VA: John Knox, 1971).

19 On this, see Iris Murdoch, *Metaphysics as a Guide to Morals* (London: Allen Lane/ Penguin, 1993); also Maria Antonaccio and William Schweiker (eds.), *Iris Murdoch and the Search for Human Goodness* (Chicago: University of Chicago Press, 1996).

20 William James, *Varieties of Religious Experience: A Study in Human Nature* (New York: Collier, 1961), p. 392. James is quoting Professor Leuba's essay, "The Contents of Religious Consciousness" in *The Monist* 11, no. 536 (July, 1901).

Chapter 6   Our Endangered Garden

1 William French, "Ecology" in *The Blackwell Companion to Religious Ethics*, ed. William Schweiker (Oxford: Blackwell, 2005), p. 469.

2 The most famous of these arguments is Lynne White, "The Historical Roots of Our Ecological Crisis," in *Science* 155 (March 10, 1967): 1203–7. For a discussion and response to these claims, see James A. Nash, *Loving Nature: Ecological Integrity and Christian Responsibility* (Nashville: Abingdon, 1991).

3 See George Ritzer, *The McDonaldization of Society: An Investigation into the Changing Character of Contemporary Social Life* (Thousand Oaks, CA: Pine Forge, 1993).

4 See Huntington, *Clash of Civilizations and the Remaking of World Order*; Benjamin R. Barber, *Jihad vs McWorld* (New York: Time, 1995); Arjun Appadurai, *Modernity at Large: Cultural Dimensions of Globalization* (Minneapolis: University of Minnesota Press, 1996); Anthony Giddens, *Modernity and Self-Identity: Self and Society in the Late Modern Age* (Stanford, CA: Stanford University Press, 1991); Anthony D. King (ed.), *Culture, Globalization and the World-System: Contemporary Conditions for the Representation of Identity* (Minneapolis: University of Minnesota Press, 1997).

5 On this, see Manfred B. Steger, *Globalization: A Very Short Introduction* (Oxford: Oxford University Press, 2003).

6 Roland Robertson, *Globalization: Social Theory and Global Culture* (London: Sage, 1992).

7 John Tomlinson, *Globalization and Culture* (Chicago: University of Chicago Press, 1999), p. 2. As the human rights theorist Richard Falk puts it, globalization "is creating a stronger sense of shared destiny among diverse peoples of the world, even while it is also generating a more stressful sense of ethnic, religious, and cultural difference." See Richard A. Falk, *Human Rights Horizon: The Pursuit of Justice in a Globalizing World* (New York: Routledge, 2000), p. 2.

8 See Saskia Sassen, *Globalization and Its Discontents: Essays on the New Mobility of People and Money* (New York: New Press, 1998), p. xx.

9 Ulrich Beck, Anthony Giddens, and Scott Lash, *Reflexive Modernization* (Cambridge: Polity, 1994).

187

10   See Lois Daly (ed.), *Feminist Theological Ethics: A Reader* (Lousiville, KY: Westminster John Knox, 1994); Claudia Card (ed.), *Feminist Ethics* (Lawrence: University of Kansas Press, 1991); Saba Mahmood, *Politics of Piety: The Islamic Revival and the Feminist Subject* (Princeton, NJ: Princeton University Press, 2004). Also see Paul Ricoeur, *The Course of Recognition*, trans. David Pellauer (Cambridge, MA: Harvard University Press, 2005) and Charles Taylor, *Multiculturalism*, ed. Amy Gutman (Princeton, NJ: Princeton University Press, 1994).

11   Steven R. Ratner and Jason S. Abrahms, *Accountability for Human Rights Atrocities in International Law: Beyond the Nuremberg Legacy*, 2nd edn. (Oxford: Oxford University Press, 2001).

12   See William Schweiker, *Power, Value and Conviction: Theological Ethics in the Postmodern Age* (Cleveland: Pilgrim, 1998).

13   On this, see Gerald P. McKenny, "Technology" in *The Blackwell Companion to Religious Ethics*, ed. William Schweiker (Oxford: Blackwell, 2005), pp. 459–68.

14   Brian Wicker, *Culture and Theology* (London: Sheed & Ward, 1966), p. 3.

15   "Whatever Next?" *The Economist* (March 1, 1997): 79.

16   See Paul Ramsey, *Fabricated Man: The Ethics of Genetic Control* (New Haven, CT: Yale University Press, 1970).

17   See, for example, Bill McKibben, *The End of Nature* (New York: Anchor, 1999).

18   See Jonas, *The Imperative of Responsibility*.

19   Martha Nussbaum, *Sex and Social Justice* (Oxford: Oxford University Press, 1999).

20   This was excerpted from Thich Nhat Hanh, *For A Future To Be Possible: Commentaries on the Five Wonderful Precepts* (Berkeley, CA: Parallax, 1993).

21   Peter Singer, *Writings on an Ethical Life* (New York: Ecco Press, 2000), p. 166.

22   For example, Richard Rorty, *Contingency, Irony and Solidarity* (Cambridge: Cambridge University Press, 1989).

23   For a fine study, see Erazim V. Kohak, *Green Halo: A Bird's-Eye View of Ecological Ethics* (LaSalle, IL: Open Court, 1999).

24   See Midgley, *Ethical Primates* and Alasdair MacIntyre, *Dependent Rational Animals* (LaSalle, IL: Open Court, 2000).

25   On this, see William Schweiker, Michael M. Johnson and Kevin Jung (eds.), *Humanity Before God: Contemporary Faces of Jewish, Christian and Islamic Ethics* (Minneapolis: Fortress, 2006).

Chapter 7   A School for Conscience

1   See Kwane Anthony Appiah, *The Ethics of Identity* (Princeton, NJ: Princeton University Press, 2004).

2   See Daniel C. Dennett, *Breaking the Spell: Religion as a Natural Phenomenon* (New York: Penguin, 2006). Also see Richard Dawkins, *The God Delusion* (New York: Houghton Mifflin, 2006). We return to these arguments in a later chapter.

3 Richard John Neuhaus *The Naked Public Square: Religion and Democracy in America*, 2nd edn. (Grand Rapids, MI: Eerdmans, 1986).

4 See Stanley Hauerwas, *A Community of Character: Toward a Constructive Christian Social Ethics* (Notre Dame, IN: University of Notre Dame Press, 1988).

5 Niccolo Machiavelli, *The Discourses* in *The Prince, with selections from the Discourses*, trans. and ed. Daniel Donno (New York: Bantam Classics, 1981), p. 113.

6 A profound statement of this worry remains Alexis de Tocqueville, *Democracy in America* (New York: Alfred A. Knopf, 1994).

7 See Charles Taylor, *The Ethics of Authenticity* (Cambridge, MA: Harvard University Press, 1992) and *Modern Social Imaginaries* (Durham, NC: Duke University Press, 2004).

8 See Jeffrey Stout, *Democracy and Tradition* (Princeton, NJ: Princeton University Press, 2004); Alasdair MacIntryre, *Whose Justice? Which Rationality?* (Notre Dame, IN: University of Notre Dame Press, 1989); and Stanley Hauerwas, *Dispatches from the Front: Theological Engagements with the Secular* (Durham, NC: Duke University Press, 1994).

9 Amartya Sen, *Identity and Violence: The Illusion of Destiny* (New York: W. W. Norton, 2006), p. 5.

10 The relation of freedom and rationality in the formation of the social contract is actually quite complex. For some thinkers, say, Hobbes, the State raises when it becomes rational for individuals to restrain their quest for power; reason imposes necessity on freedom. For other thinkers, the social contract embodies freedom insofar as it demarcates the domains of social liberties citizens can pursue, whatever their reasons. It is not possible or necessary in this chapter to enter into all of the nuances of social contract theory or, for that matter, communitarian arguments. Our concern is more general.

11 John Rawls, *Political Liberalism* (New York: Columbia University Press, 1993).

12 See *A Testament of Hope: The Essential Writings of Martin Luther King, Jr.*, ed. J. Washington (San Francisco: Harper Collins, 1990).

13 See Jean Bethke Elshtain, *Real Politics: At the Center of Everyday Life* (Baltimore, MD: Johns Hopkins University Press, 1997).

14 Franklin I. Gamwell, *Democracy on Purpose: Justice and the Reality of God* (Washington, DC: Georgetown University Press, 2000).

15 See Charles Spinosa, Fernando Flores, and Herbert L. Dreyfus, *Disclosing New Worlds: Entrepreneurship, Democractic Actions and the Cultivation of Solidarity* (Cambridge, MA: MIT Press, 1997).

16 See Pumla Gobodo-Madikizela, *A Human Being Died That Night: A South African Woman Confronts the Legacy of Apartheid* (New York: Houghton Mifflin, 2003).

17 Ernst Troelstch, *The Social Teachings of the Christian Churches*, 2 vols. (Lousiville, KY: Westminster/John Knox Press, 1992); H. Richard Niebuhr, *Christ and Culture* (New York: Harper, 1975); James M. Gustafson, *Treasure in Earthen Vessels* (Chicago: University of Chicago Press, 1985); Thomas W. Ogletree, *The World*

Calling: The Church's Witness in Politics and Society (Louisville, KY: Westminister/ John Knox, 2004); and Rita Nakashima Brock, Claudia Camp, and Serene Jones (eds.), *Setting the Table: Women in Theological Conversation* (St. Louis: Chalice, 1995), pp. 155–76.

18 One should note that the rule and stance enact our previous concern for universality, finality, locality, and autonomy, but now with respect to questions of identity in social life.

19 This argument is usually associated with communitarian and postliberal theologians like Stanley Hauerwas, Paul Griffiths, Sam Wells, Stephen Long, George Lindbeck, and others in the United States.

20 See Paul Ricoeur, *The Just*, trans. David Pellauer (Chicago: University of Chicago Press, 2000).

21 We are mindful that the debate about so-called just war theory is exceedingly complex. While we endorse some form of just war thinking, since one has an obligation to protect people from the desecration of their humanity by others, it is not possible in this book to enter into the details of just war theory. See Richard B. Miller, *The Interpretation of Conflict: Ethics, Pacificism and the Just-War Tradition* (Chicago: University of Chicago Press, 1991).

22 Hannah Arendt, *The Portable Hannah Arendt* (New York: Penguin, 2003).

23 BBC News, "Full Text: Kofi Annan's Final Speech," www.newsvote.bbc.co.uk/ mpapps/pagetools/print/news.bbc.co.uk/2/hi/americas/6170089.stm.

24 There are various types of current cosmopolitanism, the roots of which run back to ancient Stoic and Christian thought in the West. One can, for instance, stress human capabilities, as Amartya Sen and also Martha Nussbaum do; others, such as Appiah and also Todorov, extend ideas from liberal humanism; still others turn to human rights discourse, say, Richard Falk in his *Human Rights Horizons: The Pursuit of Justice in a Globalized World* (New York: Routledge, 2000). Our argument is built around responsibility, conscience, and the integrity of life.

Chapter 8 Masks of Mind

1 See Max Velmans and Susan Schneider (eds.), *The Blackwell Companion to Consciousness* (Oxford: Blackwell, 2007).

2 For a good summary, see Adam Zeman, *Consciousness: A User's Guide* (New Haven, CT: Yale University Press, 2002), pp. 303–42. Also see Malcolm Jeeves (ed.), *Human Nature* (Edinburgh: Royal Society of Edinburgh, 2006) and Marc. D. Hauser, *Moral Minds: How Nature Designed Our Universal Sense of Right and Wrong* (New York: Harper Collins, 2006).

3 John W. Searle, *Mind: A Brief Introduction* (Oxford: Oxford University Press, 2004), p. 34.

4 See David J. Chalmers, "Facing Up to the Problem of Consciousness," in *Explaining Consciousness – 'The Hard Problem,'* ed. Jonathan Shear (Cambridge, MA: MIT Press, 1997), pp. 9–32.

5 René Descartes, *Meditations on First Philosophy*, in *The Philosophical Writings of Descartes*, vol. 2, trans. John Cottingham, Robert Stoothoff, and Dugald Murdoch (Cambridge: Cambridge University Press, 1984), p. 18.

6 Plato, "Phaedo," in *The Last Days of Socrates*, trans. Hugh Tredennick (New York: Penguin, 1959).

7 David J. Chalmers, *The Conscious Mind: In Search of a Fundamental Theory* (Oxford: Oxford University Press, 1996), pp. 47, 234–5. Chalmers cites J. Levine's "Materialism and Qualia: The Explanatory Gap," *Pacific Philosophical Quarterly* 64 (1983): 354–61.

8 For problems with both materialism and dualism, see Searle, *Mind*, pp. 8–27.

9 Searle, *Mind*, pp. 79–80.

10 See David E. Klemm, "Religious Naturalism or Theological Humanism?" *Zygon: Journal of Religion and Science* 42, no. 2 (June 2007): 357–68.

11 One sees these trends in terms of interest in architecture, deconstructionism in literary theory, visual and New Media art, etc. – for example, see Mark C. Taylor, *Disfiguring: Art, Architecture, Religion* (Chicago: University of Chicago Press, 1992) – but also the fascination with the work of theologians like Hans Urs von Balthasar. Our purpose is not to engage these theological movements, but, rather, to go after the root issue, namely, consciousness.

12 "Religion and the Arts" comprises an interdisciplinary domain of reflection both in the academy and the wider public, fueled by David Jasper, *The Sacred Desert: Religion, Literature, Art, and Culture* (Oxford: Blackwell, 2004); George Steiner, *Real Presences* (Chicago: University of Chicago Press, 1989); S. Brent Plate (ed.), *Religion, Art, and Visual Culture* (New York: Palgrave, 2002), and others.

13 For a detailed examination of modeling in science and its application to theology, see David E. Klemm and William H. Klink, "Constructing and Testing Theological Models," *Zygon: A Journal for Religion and Science* 38, no. 3 (September, 2003): 495–528.

14 Thomas Kuhn, *The Structure of Scientific Revolutions* (Chicago: University of Chicago Press, 1970), pp. 174–91.

15 Max Black, *Models and Metaphors* (Ithaca, NY: Cornell University Press, 1962), pp. 219–43; Mary B. Hesse, *Models and Analogies in Science* (Notre Dame, IN: Notre Dame University Press, 1966), pp. 7–56; Paul Ricoeur, *The Rule of Metaphor: Multi-Disciplinary Studies of the Creation of Meaning in Language*, trans. Robert Czerny with Kathleen McLaughlin and John Costello, SJ (Toronto: University of Toronto Press, 1977), pp. 239–56.

16 Edmund Husserl, *Ideas: General Introduction to Pure Phenomenology*, trans. W. R. Boyce Gibson (New York: Humanities, 1976), p. 113.

17 Consider Caspar David Friedrich's painting, *Man and Woman Contemplating the Moon* (1820s), Metropolitan Museum of Art, New York City.

18 Jean-Paul Sartre, *The Transcendence of the Ego: An Existentialist Theory of Consciousness*, trans. F. Williams and R. Kirkpatrick (New York: Noonday, 1957), pp. 43–8.

19 Thomas Nagel, "What Is It Like To Be a Bat?" *Philosophical Review* 4: 81–108.

20 Husserl, *Ideas*, pp. 117, 122–3.

21 Individual events that are either simply random or wholly determined are *not* conscious events, in this view, because both cases necessarily fail to indicate the presence of embodied freedom. Random events are mindless occurrences. Determined events mechanically follow physical laws. Only the capacity to opt among alternatives, so that results are neither random nor determined, signals the presence of some forms of consciousness. For a detailed version of this argument, see David E. Klemm and William H. Klink, "Consciousness and Quantum Mechanics," forthcoming in *Zygon: Journal of Religion and Science*.

22 Clearly, even if one concedes that there is a proto-consciousness at the level of elementary particles, it is also clear that many macroscopic systems, such as rocks, tables, and buildings, show no elements of consciousness.

23 Arthur C. Danto, *After the End of Art: Contemporary Art and the Pale of History* (Princeton, NJ: Princeton University Press, 1997), p. 195.

24 See Jean-Paul Sartre, *The Imaginary: A Phenomenological Psychology of the Imagination*, trans. Jonathan Webber (London: Routledge, 2004), pp. 11–14.

25 Susanne K. Langer, *Problems of Art* (New York: Charles Scribner's Sons, 1957), pp. 13–26.

26 Paul Ricoeur, *The Rule of Metaphor*, trans. Robert Czerny (Toronto: University of Toronto Press, 1977).

27 For instance, see Paul Tillich, "Protestantism and Artistic Style," in *Theology of Culture* (Oxford: Oxford University Press, 1959), pp. 68–75. But one need not limit the analysis of culture just to so-called high culture, as Tillich did. On this, see Kelton Cobb, *The Blackwell Guide to Theology of Popular Culture* (Oxford: Blackwell, 2004).

28 Danto, *After the End of Art*.

29 Hans Belting, *Likeness and Presence: A History of the Image Before the Era of Art*, trans. Edmund Jephcott (Chicago: University of Chicago Press, 1994).

30 Danto, *After the End of Art*, p. 73.

31 *The Letters of Vincent Van Gogh*, ed. Ronald de Leeuw, trans. Arnold Pomerans (New York: Penguin, 1997), pp. 394–5, 451–2.

32 Wassily Kandinsky, *Concerning the Spiritual in Art* (New York: Dover, 1977).

33 For example, one could say art "deconstructs visual experience to show us what is really going on" (cubist Picasso), or "reveals the hidden yet intrusive world of the unconscious" (Miro), or "judges our historical crises as the results of a mythical past" (Kiefer).

34 See Arthur C. Danto, *The Abuse of Beauty: Aesthetics and the Concept of Art* (Chicago: Open Court, 2003), pp. 1–38.

35 Danto, *After the End of Art*, p. 34.
36 These terms are systematic terms, to describe formal possibilities for producing art. They are not art historical terms and should not be taken to refer to any actual movements in the art world.
37 Donald Kuspit, *The End of Art* (Cambridge: Cambridge University Press, 2005), pp. 82–3.
38 Ibid., pp. 96–7.
39 Ibid., p. 85.
40 Ibid., p. 74.
41 For a retrospective, see Donald Kuspit, *Hans Breder: Works/Arbeiten 1964–2004* (Münster: Hachmeister, 2002). See also David E. Klemm, "Intermedial Being," pp. 67–78 in Klaus-Peter Busse (ed.), *Intermedia: Enacting the Liminal* (Dortmund: Schriften zur Kunst, 2005), a collection of essays on Breder's work.
42 See David E. Klemm, "Material Grace," in William Schweiker and Charles Mathewes (eds.), *Having: Property and Possession in Religious and Social Life* (Grand Rapids, MI: Eerdmans, 2004), pp. 222–45.

Chapter 9   Religion and Spiritual Integrity

1 Daniel Dennett writes, "According to the ARIS (American Religious Identification Survey) in 2001, the three categories with the largest gain in membership since the previous survey of 1990 were evangelical/born-again (42 percent), non-denominational (37 percent), and no religion (23 percent). These data support the view that evangelicalism is growing in the USA, but they also support the view that secularism is on the rise. We are apparently becoming polarized, as many informal observers have recently maintained." Dennett, *Breaking the Spell*, p. 206. To his credit, Dennett questions the reliability of polling data.
2 See Richard Dawkins, *The God Delusion* (Boston: Houghton Mifflin, 2006), p. 1.
3 Tzvetan Todorov, *The New World Disorder: Reflections of a European*, trans. Andrew Brown (Cambridge: Polity Press, 2005), p. 70.
4 Friedrich Schleiermacher, *On Religion: Speeches to Its Cultured Despisers*, trans. and ed. Richard Crouter (Cambridge: Cambridge University Press, 1988), pp. 28–9.
5 Mircea Eliade, *The Sacred and the Profane: The Nature of Religion*, trans. Willard R. Trask (New York: Harper & Row, 1961), p. 11.
6 Tillich, *Dynamics of Faith* 1. These are just some of the important modern definitions of religion. Missing are scholars like Joachim Wach, Gerardus Van der Leeuw, and others.

7   For the importance of Clifford Geertz on particularism, see Daniel Pals, *Eight Theories of Religion* (New York: Oxford University Press, 2006). See also Gavin Flood, *Beyond Phenomenology: Rethinking the Study of Religion* (London: Cassell, 1999), pp. 143–50.

8   Loyal Rue writes, "It is true that religion in general does not exist, but the same is true of language in general, and this has not precluded the construction of insightful general theories about the nature, origins, and the functions of language." Loyal Rue, *Religion Is Not About God* (Brunswick, NJ: Rutgers University Press, 2005), p. 8.

9   Diana L. Eck, *A New Religious America: How a "Christian Country" Has Now Become the World's Most Religiously Diverse Nation* (New York: Harper San Francisco, 2001), p. 3.

10   Eck quoting Governor Kirk Fordice of Arkansas in 1992, *A New Religious America*, p. 41. According to the American Religious Identity Survey, conducted in 2001 and extrapolated to population levels in 2004, Christians comprise 76.5 percent of the American population, non-religious or secular individuals comprise 13.2 percent, Jews comprise 1.3 percent, and Muslims, Buddhists, agnostics, atheists, and Hindus, each comprise about 0.5 percent of the population, or slightly less. Other religions are represented in smaller percentages.

11   "It is no insult to Fundamentalism to see them as militant … Fundamentalists see themselves as militant." M. E. Marty and R. S. Appleby, "The Fundamentalism Project: A User's Guide," in M. E. Marty and R. S. Appleby (eds.), *The Fundamentalism Project: Fundamentalisms Observed* (Chicago: University of Chicago Press, 1991), pp. ix–x.

12   Nancy Ammerman, "North American Protestant Fundamentalism," in Marty and Appleby, *The Fundamentalist Project*, p. 14.

13   Nancy Ammerman, *Bible Believers: Fundamentalists in the Modern World* (Brunswick, NJ: Rutgers University Press, 1987), p. 5.

14   Again, this is true not just of Christian hypertheists. In radical Islam, the Qur'an functions in a similar way.

15   See Verna Ehret, "Gobalization and the Future of a Theology of Redemption: Beyond Fundamentalism and Postmodernism" (PhD thesis: University of Iowa, 2007).

16   See such studies as Kevin Phillips, *American Theocracy* (New York: Viking Books, 2006); Jim Wallis and Mel White, *Religion Gone Bad: The Hidden Danger of the Christian Right* (New York: Penguin, 2006); and Ray Suarez, *The Holy Vote: The Politics of Faith in America* (New York: Harper Collins, 2006).

17   Quoted from Rob Boston, "Weekend Warriors" in *Church and State* 55, no. 6 (2002): 6.

18   Dawkins, *The God Delusion*, p. 100.

19 Quotation from the homepage of the Council for Secular Humanism at www. secularhumanism.org. The full statement is: "Secular Humanism is a way of thinking and living that aims to bring out the best in people so that all people can have the best in life. Secular humanists reject supernatural and authoritarian beliefs. They affirm that we must take responsibility for our own lives and the communities and world in which we live. Secular humanism emphasizes reason and scientific inquiry, individual freedom and responsibility, human values and compassion, and the need for tolerance and cooperation."

20 Sam Harris, *The End of Faith* (New York: W. W. Norton, 2004), p. 26. Harris cites conflicts in Palestine (Jews v. Muslims), the Balkans (Orthodox Serbians v. Catholic Croatians; Orthodox Serbians v. Bosnian and Albanian Muslims), Northern Ireland (Protestants v. Catholics), Kashmir (Muslims v. Hindus), Sudan (Muslims v. Christians and animists), Nigeria (Muslims v. Christians), Ethiopia and Eritrea (Muslims v. Christians), Sri Lanka (Sinhalese Buddhists v. Tamil Hindus), Indonesia (Muslims v. Timorese Christians), and the Caucasus (Orthodox Russians v. Chechen Muslims; Muslim Azerbaijanis v. Catholic and Orthodox Armenians).

21 Ibid, p. 12. See also Dennett's more indirect claim in *Breaking the Spell*, p. 285, that religions perpetrate "moral certainties" and "absolutes" on which zealotry depends. See also Dawkins, *The God Delusion*, pp. 286–8.

22 Dennett, *Breaking the Spell*, p. 9.

23 Harris, *The End of Faith*, p. 23. Religion, for Harris, is "unjustified belief in matters of ultimate concern."

24 Ibid, p. 45.

25 Rue, *Religion Is Not About God*, pp. 21–164. Rue stands outside the new atheists because he remains neutral on the question of God and claims not to be hostile to religion. For an assessment of Rue's book, see Klemm, "Religious Naturalism or Theological Humanism?"

26 Rue, *Religion Is Not About God*, p. 9. According to Rue, religions as we know them will die when the global environmental crisis produces a cataclysm. Following this apocalyptic event, a new religion will emerge – an earth-centered "religious naturalism."

27 He maintains a more complete list on his website: www.richarddawkins.net.

28 Rousseau, *Émile*, 220–78.

29 "Revealed religion" means religion received from a cumulative historical tradition.

30 One very good example is Sam Harris, who has deeply spiritual inclinations. See *The End of Faith*, pp. 204–21.

31 Leon Wieseltier, "The God Genome," *New York Times Book Review*, February 19, 2006, 12.

32 Rousseau, *Émile*, p. 261.

Chapter 10   Living Theological Humanism

1   For a related conception of a form of transcendence around the fullness of life that exceeds what he calls "exclusive humanism" see Charles Taylor, *A Secular Age* (Cambridge, MA: Harvard University Press, 2007). While similar to the proposal of theological humanism, we trust that out account of transcendence offers a gain in thought and life through the argument made for the integrity of life and how to construe what is of ultimate importance and reality with respect to human actions and relations.

2   Thomas L. Friedman, *The Worlds is Flat: A Brief History of the Twentieth Century*, revd. edn. (New York: Picador, 2007). Also see Zygmunt Bauman, *Liquid Life* (Cambridge: Polity, 2005).

Index